DATE DUE

MY 6 '95			
NO 27 '95			
AP 19 '96			
MY 28 '98			
MY 6 '99			

DEMCO 38-296

BIP+
10-22-93

The universe is vast, and men are but tiny specks on an insignificant planet.

But the more we realize our minuteness and our impotence in the face of cosmic forces, the more astonishing becomes what human beings have achieved.

It is to the possible achievements of Man that our ultimate loyalty is due, and in that thought the brief troubles of our unquiet epoch become endurable.

Much wisdom remains to be learned, and if it is only to be learned through adversity, we must endeavor to endure adversity with what fortitude we can command.

But if we can acquire wisdom soon enough, adversity may not be necessary, and the future of Man may be happier than any part of his past.

Bertrand Russell
Australian Radio Talk, July 9, 1950

The Quotable Bertrand Russell

Edited by Lee Eisler

Prometheus Books • Buffalo, New York

Dedicated to the memory of Bertrand Russell,
who let light into dark corners
of the past and present
and
saw a happy future for Man,
despite current troubles,
with Intelligence showing the way

Published 1993 by Prometheus Books

97 96 95 94 93   5 4 3 2 1

Library of Congress Cataloging-in-Publication Data

Russell, Bertrand, 1872–1970.
    [Selections. 1993]
    The quotable Bertrand Russell / edited by Lee Eisler.
        p.   cm.
    ISBN 0-87975-728-0 (pbk.)
    1. Philosophy—Miscellanea. I. Eisler, Lee.
B1649.R91   1993
192—dc20   93-20291
                                                                CIP

Printed in the United States of America on acid-free paper.

I would like to thank some friends
in The Bertrand Russell Society
for their helpful suggestions:
Ken Blackwell, Bob Davis, Don Jackanicz, Marvin Kohl,
Michael Rockler, Harry Ruja, Tom Stanley;
and last but not least, my wife, Jan.

Contents

Preface

The aim of this book is to present Russell's thinking on a number of topics of continuing interest . . . and to do it in a concise and convenient way.

The record he left behind is very large. He thought a great deal, and wrote a great deal, and lived a long time. He died in 1970, at age 98. The record consists of 89 books, numerous articles, countless newspaper and magazine stories, and many, many interviews.

Because the record is so large, it is not always easy to locate Russell's views on a particular subject.

This book makes it possible to do so—and quickly—for the many topics listed in the "Questions" section.

• • •

Russell wrote for two wholly different audiences. Philosopher Russell wrote for philosophers. Citizen Russell wrote for the ordinary citizen. His contributions to both areas were notable, in both quantity and quality.

With his collaborator, Alfred North Whitehead, he wrote—for philosophers and mathematicians—the landmark *Principia Mathematica,* which profoundly changed logic, and dethroned Aristotle's logic. It also helped make computers possible.

For the general public, he wrote about nearly everything . . . and not without effect. He is probably the most widely read—and arguably the most influential—philosopher/social critic/political activist of the twentieth century. As an instance of his influence: the SALT talks and the Limited Test Ban Treaty are descendants of the Pugwash Conferences, which Russell initiated in 1957.

He was the first person of eminence to speak out against The Bomb, against rigid sexual constraints, against the U.S. in Vietnam, and against the game of chicken played by the two superpowers with nuclear weapons—views which were not popular at the time.

Today these views have come to be accepted: the superpowers now realize that nuclear weapons are suicide weapons that cannot ever be used; the Vietnam War is now regarded as a tragic American mistake; and the hypocritical Victorian sexual morals that prevailed when Russell was a young man can hardly be said to apply today. Russell did his part—perhaps more than any other single individual—to bring about these changes for the better.

His Nobel Prize could have been awarded for his philosophical writings, but in fact was not. It was awarded for his other writings, those for "ordinary citizens." Here is an excerpt from the Presentation Speech that accompanied his Nobel Prize in Literature in 1950:

> His works in the sciences concerned with human knowledge and mathematical logic are epoch-making and have been compared to Newton's fundamental results in mechanics. Yet it is not these achievements in special branches of science that the Nobel Prize is primarily meant to recognize. What is important, from our point of view, is that Russell has so extensively addressed his books to a public of laymen, and, in doing so, has been so eminently successful in keeping alive an interest in general philosophy. His whole life's work is a stimulating defense of the reality of common sense.

This book deals with topics that Russell addressed to "a public of laymen."

●   ●   ●

Russell's views are presented here as if they were answers to questions. They are not really answers to questions (except a few); they are excerpts from his writings. The question-and-answer format focuses attention on a particular point.

Some questions appear more than once among the questions. For instance, the question—*What's wrong with Christian ethics?*—appears under the topics ETHICS and CHRISTIANITY.

But why read this book, when one can read the originals—great books by Russell himself? Few people have time to read the large Russell record, or have access to it. Besides, how would one know where to look to locate Russell's views on a particular question?

Nevertheless, we hope that this book—which can be thought of as a Russell sampler—may induce some readers to venture forth and read some of Russell's books from cover to cover. Most are still in print today. They can be found in libraries and bookstores.

• • •

HOW TO USE THIS BOOK

Choose questions from the "Questions" section. Questions are sorted by topic.

If, for example, you wish to see the questions that are listed under the topic, DEMOCRACY, you can quickly locate DEMOCRACY because topics are listed in alphabetical order.

Then choose a question.

Suppose you choose the question, *What are two great merits of democracy?*

The question provides the page number of the answer.

The answer repeats the question and gives the answer.

The answer to the above question on democracy appears on page 89.

All answers are in Russell's own words. Some offer advice. Some answer puzzling questions. Some provide glimpses into the past that affect our lives today.

• • •

People have said that Russell's writings changed their lives. The following pages may indicate why.

Questions

To find the answer to a question, turn to the page indicated. There the question is repeated, and the answer given.

DEATH

DEMOCRACY

DESIRE

DEVOLUTION

DICTATORSHIPS

DISCIPLINE

DOGMATISM

ECONOMICS

EDUCATION

EMOTIONS

FREETHOUGHT

FUTURE

GENTLEMAN

GOD

GOOD LIFE

GOVERNMENT

HUMAN NATURE

HYSTERIA

IDEAL

IDEOLOGY

IMPERMANENCE

IMPULSE

INCEST

INCONSISTENCY

INDIVIDUALS

INNOVATION

INTELLECTUALS

INTELLIGENCE

ISLAM

JEWS

JUSTICE

PLATO

PLUTARCH

POLICE

POLITICS

PRIDE

PROBLEMS

PROGRESS

PROOF

PROPAGANDA

PROVERBS

PSYCHOLOGY

PYTHAGORAS

RACISM

RATIONALITY

REASON

RELIGION

REVOLTS

ROMANTICISM

ROME

ROUSSEAU

WAR

WEST

WISDOM

Answers

AGGRESSION

What happens when our aggressive impulses are ignored?

People who live a life which is unnatural beyond a point are likely to be filled with envy, malice and all uncharitableness. They may develop strains of cruelty, or, on the other hand, they may so completely lose all joy in life that they have no longer any capacity for effort.

This latter result has been observed among savages brought suddenly in contact with modern civilization.

Anthropologists have described how Papuan head hunters, deprived by white authority of their habitual sport, lose all zest, and are no longer able to be interested in anything.

I do not wish to infer that they should have been allowed to go on hunting heads, but I do mean that it would have been worthwhile if psychologists had taken some trouble to find some innocent substitute activity.

Civilized man everywhere is, to some degree, in the position of the Papuan victims of virtue.

We have all kinds of aggressive impulses, and also creative impulses, which society forbids us to indulge, and the alternatives that it supplies in the shape of football matches and all-in wrestling are hardly adequate.

Anyone who hopes that in time it may be possible to abolish war should give serious thought to the problem of satisfying harmlessly the instincts that we inherit from long generations of savages.

For my part I find sufficient outlet in detective stories, where I

51

alternately identify myself with the murderer and the huntsman-detective, but I know that there are those for whom this vicarious outlet is too mild, and for them something stronger should be provided. (AI 8)

AMERICA

In what way was America important during the nineteenth century?

America remained a land of promise for lovers of freedom.

Even Byron, at a moment when he was disgusted with Napoleon for not committing suicide, wrote an eloquent stanza in praise of Washington.

Admiration of America as the land of democracy survived through the greater part of the nineteenth century.

Richard Cobden, who was in most respects the opposite of a romantic, cherished illusions about the United States, when admirers presented him with a large sum of money: he invested it in the Illinois Central Railroad and lost every penny.

When my parents visited America in 1867, it still had for them a halo of romance.

This survived even for me through Walt Whitman, whose house was the first place I visited when I went to America. (FF 17)

How did Andrew Jackson change the American presidency?

American democracy underwent a great transformation when Andrew Jackson became president.

Until his time, presidents had been cultivated gentlemen, mostly with a settled position as landowners.

Andrew Jackson represented a rebellion against these men on the part of pioneers and immigrants.

He did not like culture and was suspicious of educated men since they understood things that puzzled him.

This element of hostility to culture has persisted in American democracy ever since, and has made it difficult for America to make the best use of its experts. (FF 83)

What was the result in America of electing state judges?

In America, when people in Jackson's time became conscious of this danger [of judges who thwarted the popular will], they decided that state judges, though not federal judges, should be elected.

This remedy, however, proved worse than the disease.

It increased the power of the political boss who had secured the election of his favorites to judgeships and could be tolerably certain that his favorites would decide cases as he wished, and not in accordance with the law.

In fact, the political boss acquired a position not wholly unlike that of the Greek tyrant.

There was, however, an important difference.

It was possible to remedy the evil by wholly constitutional methods without the need of revolution or assassination. (FF 84)

ANARCHY

When a state of anarchy occurs, what is likely to follow?

After anarchy, the natural first step is despotism, because this is facilitated by the instinctive mechanism of dominion and submission; this has been illustrated in the family, in the state, and in business.

Equal cooperation is much more difficult than despotism, and much less in line with instinct.

When men attempt equal cooperation, it is natural for each to strive for complete mastery, since the submissive impulses are not brought into play. (P 23)

ANTI-SEMITISM

What brought on anti-Semitism?

Though I know it is not considered the right thing to say—anti-Semitism came in with Christianity; before that there was very, very much less.

The moment the Roman government became Christian, it became

anti-Semitic. [That was] because they said that the Jews killed Christ, and so it became a justification for hating the Jews.

I have no doubt that there really were economic motives, but that was the justification. (SHM 118)

ARISTOTLE

What were Aristotle's innovations? His merits and demerits?

In reading any important philosopher, but most of all in reading Aristotle, it is necessary to study him in two ways: with reference to his predecessors, and with reference to his successors.

In the former aspect, Aristotle's merits are enormous; in the latter, his demerits are equally enormous. For his demerits, however, his successors are more responsible than he is.

He came at the end of the creative period in Greek thought, and after his death it was two thousand years before the world produced any philosopher who could be regarded as approximately his equal.

Toward the end of this long period his authority had become almost as unquestioned as that of the Church, and in science, as well as in philosophy, had become a serious obstacle to progress.

Ever since the beginning of the seventeenth century, almost every serious intellectual advance has had to begin with an attack on some Aristotelian doctrine; in logic, this is still true at the present day.

But it would have been at least as disastrous if any of his predecessors (except perhaps Democritus) had acquired equal authority.

To do him justice, we must, to begin with, forget his excessive posthumous fame, and the equally excessive posthumous condemnation to which it led.

At about the age of eighteen, Aristotle came to Athens and became a pupil of Plato; he remained in the Academy for nearly twenty years, until the death of Plato in 348-47 B.C.

Aristotle, as a philosopher, is in many ways very different from all his predecessors.

He is the first to write like a professor: his treatises are systematic, his discussions are divided into heads, he is a professional teacher, not an inspired prophet.

His work is critical, careful, pedestrian, without any trace of Bacchic enthusiasm.

The Orphic elements in Plato are watered down in Aristotle, and mixed with a strong dose of common sense; where he is Platonic, one feels that his natural temperament has been overpowered by the teaching to which he has been subjected.

He is not passionate, or in any sense religious.

The errors of his predecessors were the glorious errors of youth attempting the impossible; his errors are those of age which cannot free itself from habitual prejudices. He is best in detail and in criticism; he fails in large construction, for lack of fundamental clarity and Titanic fire. (HWP 159)

What is Russell's advice to students studying logic?

Logic was practically invented by Aristotle.

For nearly two thousand years, his authority in logic was unquestioned.

To this day teachers in Catholic educational institutions are not allowed to admit that his logic has defects, and any non-Catholic who criticizes it incurs the bitter hostility of the Roman Church.

I once ventured to do so on the radio, and the organizers who had invited me were inundated with protests against the broadcasting of such heretical doctrines.

Undue respect for Aristotle, however, is not confined to Catholic institutions.

In most universities, the beginner in logic is still taught the doctrine of the syllogism, which is useless and complicated, and an obstacle to a sound understanding of logic.

If you wish to become a logician, there is one piece of advice that I cannot urge too strongly, and that is, DO NOT learn the traditional formal logic.

In Aristotle's day, it was a creditable effort, but so was Ptolemaic astronomy. To teach either in the present day is a ridiculous piece of antiquarianism. (AP 37)

How should Aristotelian logic be viewed today?

Aristotle's influence, which was very great in many different fields, was greatest of all in logic.

In late antiquity, when Plato was still supreme in metaphysics, Aristotle was the recognized authority in logic, and he retained this position throughout the Middle Ages.

Even at the present day, all Catholic teachers of philosophy and many others still obstinately reject the discoveries of modern logic, and adhere with strange tenacity to a system which is as definitely antiquated as Ptolemaic astronomy.

This makes it difficult to do historical justice to Aristotle. His present-day influence is so inimical to clear thinking that it is hard to remember how great an advance he made upon all his predecessors (including Plato), or how admirable his logical work would still seem if it had been a stage in a continual progress, instead of being (as in fact it was) a dead end, followed by over two thousand years of stagnation.

Aristotle is still, especially in logic, a battleground, and cannot be treated in a purely historical spirit.

[We will not go into Russell's analysis of Aristotle's logic (on pp. 196–202); it is quite technical. Here is his conclusion (on p. 202):]

I conclude that the Aristotelian doctrines with which we have been concerned are wholly false, with the exception of the formal theory of the syllogism, which is unimportant.

Any person in the present day who wishes to learn logic will be wasting his time if he reads Aristotle or any of his disciples.

Nonetheless, Aristotle's logical writings show great ability, and would have been useful to mankind if they had appeared at a time when intellectual originality was still active.

Unfortunately they appeared at the very end of the creative period of Greek thought, and therefore came to be accepted as authoritative.

By the time that logical originality revived, a reign of two thousand years made Aristotle very difficult to dethrone. Throughout modern times, practically every advance in science, in logic, or in philosophy has had to be made in the teeth of the opposition from Aristotle's disciples. (HWP 195, 202)

How much was Alexander influenced by his tutor, Aristotle?

A great deal of nonsense has been written about Aristotle and Alexander, because, as both were great men, and Aristotle was Alexander's tutor, it is supposed that the tutor must have greatly influenced the pupil.

Hegel goes so far as to say that Alexander's career shows the value of philosophy, since his practical wisdom may be attributed to his teacher.

In fact there is not the faintest evidence that Aristotle had any effect at all on Alexander, who hated his father, and was rebellious against everyone whom his father set in authority over him.

There are certain letters professing to be from Alexander to Aristotle, but they are generally considered spurious.

In fact the two men ignored each other.

While Alexander was conquering the East, Aristotle continued to write treatises on politics which never mentioned what was taking place, but discussed minutely the constitutions of various cities which were no longer important.

It is a mistake to suppose that great men who are contemporaries are likely to be quick to recognize each other's greatness; the opposite happens much more frequently. (UH 24)

Why did Aristotle call man a rational animal?

His reason for this view was one which does not now seem very impressive; it was that some people can do sums.

It is in virtue of the intellect that man is a rational animal.

The intellect is shown in various ways, but most emphatically by mastery of arithmetic.

The Greek system of numerals was very bad, so that the multiplication table was quite difficult, and complicated calculations could be made only by very clever people.

Nowadays, however, calculating machines do sums better than even the cleverest people.

As arithmetic has grown easier, it has come to be less respected. (UE 72)

Why did Russell call Aristotle one of philosophy's misfortunes?

He came at the end of the creative period in Greek thought, and after his death it was two thousand years before the world produced any philosopher who could be regarded as approximately his equal.

Toward the end of this long period his authority had become almost as unquestioned as that of the Church, and in science, as well as in philosophy, had become a serious obstacle to progress.

Ever since the beginning of the seventeenth century, almost every serious intellectual advance has had to begin with an attack on some Aristotelian doctrine; in logic, this is still true at the present day. (HWP 159–60)

ARMY

How may the army be a threat to democracy?

States need armies, and armies can take control of governments if individual soldiers are willing to obey their officers when their officers give orders that are illegal.

This danger was so present to the minds of British politicians in the time of William III that they only consented to the creation of a standing army on condition that the penalties for mutiny should be enacted afresh by Parliament every year.

This provision continues down to the present day, and, if at any moment Parliament should become suspicious of the armed forces, it might refuse to pass the Mutiny Act, and every soldier would be absolved from obedience to the orders of his officers.

In the time of William III, it was the experience of Cromwell that inspired caution, but in many countries at many times, this caution has been absent. (FF 85)

ASIA

Why is it difficult to decide on a wise policy toward Asia?

Western men of liberal outlook cannot but sympathize with the wish of Asia to be independent, but it would be a pity if this sympathy were to blind Western thought to certain matters of the gravest import.

The Western world has achieved, not completely but to a considerable extent, a way of life having certain merits that are new in human history.

It has nearly eliminated poverty.

It has cut down illness and death to a degree that a hundred years ago would have seemed fantastic.

It has spread education throughout the population, and it has achieved a quite new degree of harmony between freedom and order.

These are not things which Asia, if it becomes quickly independent, can hope to achieve.

We in the West, aware of the appalling poverty of Southeast Asia, and convinced that this poverty is a propaganda weapon in the hands of the Russians, have begun to think for the first time that something ought to be done to raise the standard of life in these regions.

But their habits and our beliefs, between them, make the task, for the present, a hopeless one.

Every increase in production, instead of raising their standard of life, is quickly swallowed up by an increase in population.

Eastern populations do not know how to prevent this, and Western bigots prevent those who understand the problem from spreading the necessary information.

What is bad in the West is easily spread: our restlessness, our militarism, our fanaticism, and our ruthless belief in mechanism.

But what is best in the West—the spirit of free inquiry, the understanding of the conditions of general prosperity, and emancipation from superstition—these things powerful forces in the West prevent the East from acquiring.

So long as this continues, Eastern populations will remain on the verge of destitution, and in proportion as they become powerful, they will become destructive through envy.

In this they will, of course, have the help of Russia, unless and until Russia is either defeated or liberalized.

For these reasons, a wise policy toward Asia is still to seek. (NHCW 6)

BELIEF

What are the causes of belief?

Belief, when it is not simply traditional, is a product of several factors: desire, evidence, and iteration.

When either the desire or the evidence is nil, there will be no belief; when there is no outside assertion, belief will only arise in exceptional characters, such as founders of religions, scientific discoverers, and lunatics.

To produce a mass belief, of the sort that is socially important, all three elements must exist in some degree; but if one element is increased while another is diminished, the resulting amount of belief may be unchanged.

More propaganda is necessary to cause acceptance of a belief for which there is little evidence than of one for which the evidence is strong, if both are equally satisfactory to desire; and so on. (P 144)

Why is it only half-true that beliefs are all-important?

It is easy to make out a case for the view that opinion is omnipotent, and that all other forms of power are derived from it.

Armies are useless unless the soldiers believe in the cause for which they are fighting, or, in the case of mercenaries, have confidence in the ability of their commander to lead them to victory.

Law is impotent unless it is generally respected.

Economic institutions depend on respect for the law; consider, for example, what would happen to banking if the average citizen had no objection to forgery.

Religious opinion has often proved itself more powerful than the State.

If, in any country, a large majority were in favor of Socialism, Capitalism would become unworkable.

On such grounds it might be said that opinion is the ultimate power in social affairs.

But this would only be a half-truth, since it ignores the forces which cause opinion.

While it is true that opinion is an essential element in military force, it is equally true that military force may generate opinion.

Almost every European country has, at this moment, the religion which was that of its government in the late sixteenth century, and this must be attributed mainly to the control of persecution and propaganda by means of the armed forces in the several countries. (P 140)

How do creeds get started? What are the stages in their evolution?

A creed never has force at its command to begin with, and the first steps in the production of a widespread opinion must be taken by means of persuasion alone.

We have thus a kind of seesaw: first, pure persuasion leading to the conversion of a minority; then force exerted to secure that the rest of the community shall be exposed to the right propaganda; and finally a genuine belief on the part of the great majority, which makes the use of force again unnecessary.

Some bodies of opinion never get beyond the first stage, some reach the second and then fail, others are successful in all three.

The Society of Friends has never got beyond persuasion.

The other nonconformists acquired the forces of the State in the time of Cromwell, but failed in their propaganda after they had seized power.

The Catholic Church, after three centuries of persuasion, captured the State in the time of Constantine, and then, by force, established a system of propaganda which converted almost all the pagans and enabled Christianity to survive the Barbarian invasion.

The Marxist creed has reached the second stage, if not the third, in Russia, but elsewhere it is still in the first stage [1938]. (P 141)

Beliefs instilled during childhood tend to be firmly held; but are they valid?

It is clear that the whole system of Christian ethics, both in the Catholic and the Protestant form, requires to be reexamined, as far as possible without the preconceptions to which a Christian education predisposes us.

Emphatic and reiterated assertion, especially during childhood, produces in most people a belief so firm as to have a hold even over the unconscious, and many of us who imagine that our attitude toward orthodoxy is quite emancipated are still, in fact, subconsciously controlled by its teachings.

We must ask ourselves quite frankly what led the Church to condemn all fornication. Do we think it had valid grounds for the condemnation? Or, if we do not, are there grounds, other than that adduced by the Church, which ought to lead us to the same conclusion?

The attitude of the early Church was that there is something essentially impure in the sexual act, although this act must be excused when it is performed after fulfilling certain preliminary conditions.

This attitude in itself must be regarded as purely superstitious. Those who first inculcated such a view must have suffered from a diseased condition of body or mind, or both.

The fact that an opinion has been widely held is no evidence whatever that it is not utterly absurd; indeed in view of the silliness of the majority of mankind, a widespread belief is more likely to be foolish than sensible.

The Pelew Islanders believe that the perforation of the nose is necessary for winning eternal bliss. Europeans think that this end is better attained by wetting the head while pronouncing certain words. The belief of the Pelew Islanders is a superstition; the belief of the Europeans one of the truths of our holy religion. (MM 38)

BERGSON

What is Bergson's place in twentieth-century philosophy?

It is a curious thing that Bergson should have been hailed as an ally by the pragmatists, since, on the face of it, his philosophy is the exact antithesis to theirs.

While pragmatists teach that utility is the test of truth, Bergson teaches, on the contrary, that our intellect, having been fashioned by practical needs, ignores all the aspects of the world which it does not pay to notice, and is in fact an obstacle to the apprehension of truth.

We have, he thinks, a faculty called "intuition" which we can use if we take the trouble, and which will enable us to know, in theory at least, everything past and present, though apparently not the future.

But since it would be inconvenient to be troubled with so much knowledge, we have developed a brain, the function of which is to forget.

But for the brain we should remember everything; owing to its sieve-like operations, we usually remember only what is useful, and that is all wrong.

Utility, for Bergson, is the source of error, while truth is arrived at by a mystic contemplation from which all thought of practical advantage is absent.

Nevertheless, Bergson, like the pragmatists, prefers action to reason, Othello to Hamlet.

It is this that makes pragmatists regard him as an ally.

His great reputation began with *L'Évolution créatrice,* published in 1907—not that this book was better than the others, but that it contained less argument and more rhetoric, so that it had a more persuasive effect.

This book contains, from beginning to end, no argument, and therefore no bad argument; it contains merely a poetical picture appealing to the fancy.

There is nothing in it to help us to a conclusion as to whether the philosophy which it advocates is true or false; this question, which might be thought not unimportant, Bergson has left to others.

But according to his own theories, he is right in this, since truth is to be attained by intuition, not by intellect, and is therefore not a matter of argument. (SE 65)

BOOKS

How important have books been in your life, Lord Russell?

Books that influenced me when I was young—that is to say, broadly speaking, from the age of fifteen to the age of twenty-one.

I have not found in later years that books were as important to me as they were when I was first exploring the world and trying to determine my attitude toward it.

In those days a book might be a great adventure, expressing ideas or emotions which one could absorb and assimilate.

In later life, one has more or less decided upon a fundamental outlook that seems congenial and only something very rare can effect an important change.

But when the great books of the world were new to me, when I first learnt what had been thought and felt and said by men who had thought and felt profoundly, there was a great liberation in the discovery that hopes and dreams and systems of thought which had remained vague and unexpressed for lack of sympathy in my environment had been set forth in clear and shining words by men whom the world acknowledged to be great.

From books I derived courage and hope and freedom in arduous endeavor. (FF 9)

CATHOLICISM

What are the sources of Catholic doctrine?

One of the most fascinating studies in the history of culture is the gradual building up of the Catholic synthesis, which was completed in the thirteenth century.

In the Church as it existed at the time of the fall of the Western Empire [in the fifth century], there were elements derived from three sources, Jewish, Greek, and Roman.

The Church took over from the Jews their sacred books and sacred history, their belief in a Messiah (whom the Christians, but not the Jews, believed to have already appeared), their somewhat fierce morality, and their intolerance of all religions but one.

The Hellenic element appeared especially in the realm of dogma.

St. John, St. Paul, and the Fathers gradually developed, by adaptations of Greek philosophy, an elaborate theology, wholly foreign to the Jewish spirit.

St. John's gospel, unlike Matthew, Mark, and Luke, shows the early stages of Christian Hellenistic philosophy. The Fathers, especially Origen and St. Augustine, make Platonism an integral part of Christian thought; it is astonishing how much of essential Christian doctrine St. Augustine confesses to having found in Plato.

As soon as the [Roman] Empire became Christian, the bishops acquired administrative and judicial functions; the ecumenical councils promoted by the Emperors supplied the beginnings of a central authority, though at first only in matters of doctrine.

Without the strength derived from Roman governmental methods, it is doubtful whether the Church could have survived the shock of the barbarian invasion. (UH 43)

What caused the rise and fall of the (Catholic) Renaissance Church?

The rise and decline of papal power are worthy of study by anyone who wishes to understand the winning of power by propaganda.

It is not enough to say that men were superstitious and believed in the power of the keys.

Throughout the Middle Ages there were heresies, which would have spread, as Protestantism spread, if the Popes had not, on the whole, deserved respect.

And without heresy secular rulers made vigorous attempts to keep the Church in subordination to the state, which failed in the West though they succeeded in the East.

For this there were various reasons.

First, the Papacy was not hereditary, and was therefore not troubled with long minorities, as secular kingdoms were.

A man could not easily rise to eminence in the Church except by piety, learning, or statesmanship; consequently most Popes were men considerably above average in one or more respects.

Secular sovereigns might be able, but were often quite the reverse; moreover, they had not the training in controlling their passions that ecclesiastics had.

Repeatedly, kings got into difficulties from desire for divorce, which, being a matter for the Church, placed them at the mercy of the Pope.

Another great strength of the Papacy was its impersonal continuity.

In the contest with Frederick II, it is astonishing how little difference is made by the death of a Pope.

There was a body of doctrine, and a tradition of statecraft, to which kings could oppose nothing equally solid.

It was only with the rise of nationalism that secular governments acquired any comparable continuity or tenacity of purpose.

In the eleventh, twelfth, and thirteenth centuries, kings, as a rule, were ignorant, while most Popes were both learned and well-informed.

Moreover, kings were bound up with the feudal system, which was cumbrous, in constant danger of anarchy, and hostile to the newer economic forces.

On the whole, during these centuries, the Church represented a higher civilization than that represented by the State.

But by far the greatest strength of the Church was the moral respect which it inspired.

It inherited, as a kind of moral capital, the glory of the persecutions in ancient times.

Its victories, as we have seen, were associated with the enforcement of celibacy, and the medieval mind found celibacy very impressive.

Very many ecclesiastics, including not a few Popes, suffered great hardships rather than yield on a point of principle.

It was clear to ordinary men that, in a world of uncontrolled rapacity, licentiousness, and self-seeking, eminent dignitaries of the Church not infrequently lived for impersonal aims, to which they willingly subordinated their private fortunes.

In successive centuries, men of impressive holiness—Hildebrand, St. Bernard, St. Francis—dazzled public opinion, and prevented the moral discredit that would otherwise have come from the misdeeds of others.

But to an organization which has ideal ends, and therefore an excuse for love of power, a reputation for superior virtue is dangerous, and is sure, in the long run, to produce a superiority only in unscrupulous ruthlessness.

The Church preached contempt for the things of this world, and in doing so acquired domination over monarchs.

The Friars took a vow of poverty, which so impressed the world that it increased the already enormous wealth of the Church.

St. Francis, by preaching brotherly love, generated the enthusiasm required for the victorious prosecution of a long and atrocious war.

In the end, the Renaissance Church lost all the moral purpose to which it owed its wealth and power, and the shock of the Reformation was necessary to produce regeneration.

All this is inevitable whenever superior virtue is used as a means of winning tyrannical power for an organization.

Except when due to foreign conquest, the collapse of traditional power is always the result of its abuse by men who believe, as Machiavelli believed, that its hold on men's minds is too firm to be shaken by even the grossest crimes. (italics added) (P 74)

How did the Church become strong, and then falter?

In the centuries that followed [the fall of the Roman Empire], the Church, though imperfectly, represented the Mediterranean culture, while the lay aristocracy represented Northern barbarism.

The Church, at times, nearly lost its distinctive character, and almost became part and parcel of the feudal system.

But this was prevented by the gradually increasing power of the Pope, and by Papal insistence on clerical celibacy, which prevented Church lands from descending from father to son.

From the beginning of the eleventh century to the end of the thirteenth century, the Church gained rapidly in power, discipline, and learning; in the latter respect, Catholics still bow to the authority of St. Thomas Aquinas, whose word, on all philosophical questions, is law in all Catholic educational institutions.

Yet Aquinas, in his day, was a bold innovator.

Arabic influences caused him to prefer Aristotle to Plato, and on this account he was condemned by the universities of Paris and Oxford.

This opposition to Aquinas and Aristotle (who was also condemned) has now been forgotten, and Aristotle is now regarded by Catholics almost as if he were one of the Fathers.

It is perhaps permissible, though in dubious taste, to question the efficacy of his cure for insomnia in elephants, but his mistakes in the doctrine of the syllogism must not be acknowledged.

For this reason, modern logic is forbidden territory to Catholics.

The misfortunes of the Church in the fourteenth, fifteenth, and sixteenth centuries were so great that its survival might almost be claimed as a miracle.

First came the Great Schism, during which there were two men who claimed to be Pope. No one knew which was the true Pope; each claimant excommunicated the other.

One of the excommunications was valid, but which?

Whichever was the true Pope must of course be right in proclaiming his rival to be a wicked man, but no one knew which was the Holy Father and which was the impudent imposter.

This was awkward, and a potent cause of scandal.

When at last the Schism was healed, the Renaissance began, and the Popes lost sight of the interests of the Church to play the game of Italian power politics and fight to enlarge their secular dominions.

A series of free-thinking, worldy, and licentious Popes, who taxed the faithful throughout the Catholic world to keep up their own pomp, so shocked Northern piety as in the end to produce the Reformation. (UH 44)

How did the Catholic Church survive the Reformation?

At first the Reformation carried everything before it in most countries north of the Alps.

But the Catholic cause was rescued by Loyola, Charles V, and the Fuggers.

Loyola founded the Jesuit Order, which secured power by zeal, cunning and education.

Charles V happened to combine under his sway the Empire, Spain, and the Netherlands.

The rich banking house of the Fuggers had already lent him so much money that his success became vital to them; they therefore backed him with all their resources, and made him financially superior to his opponents.

In the end they went bankrupt through lending to Hapsburgs, but by that time the Church was saved. (UH 45)

Why was the Catholic Church so hard on Galileo?

For my part, I think the belief [in God] lost whatever rationality it once possessed when it was discovered that the earth is not the center of the universe.

So long as it was thought that the sun and the planets and the stars revolved about the earth, it was natural to suppose that the universe had a purpose connected with the earth, and, since man was what man most admired on earth, this purpose was supposed to be embodied in man.

But astronomy and geology have changed all this.

The earth is a minor planet of a minor star which is one of many millions of stars in a galaxy which is one of many millions of galaxies.

Even within the life of our own planet, man is only a brief interlude.

Nonhuman life existed for countless ages before man evolved.

Man, even if he does not commit scientific suicide, will perish ultimately through failure of water or air or warmth.

It is difficult to believe that omnipotence needed so vast a setting for so small and transitory a result. (RGR 89)

What is the Catholic Church's future? Will it survive?

Does the past history of the Church give any basis for prophesy as to its future?

The wars of the eighteenth century, and the subsequent expansion of the United States, gave dominion to Protestants throughout all of the American Continent north of the Mexican border.

France was vehemently anticlerical during the Revolution, and again at the time of the rehabilitation of Dreyfus.

The Russian Revolution was anti-Christian, and the Nazis have done all in their power to destroy the influence of the Church in Germany.

Nevertheless, Catholics have considerable grounds for confidence in the future.

Napoleon found it expedient to make peace with the Pope, and Napoleon III, until his downfall, preserved the temporal power by a French garrison in Rome.

What France will be like after the war, it is impossible to know; but at present the leaders of all parties are pious Catholics.

In Germany when the Nazis fall, there will be danger of chaos, and the Catholic Church will be one of the few forces making for stability.

In the United States, Catholics are already sufficiently powerful to control education in New York and Boston, and they were able to compel the State Department to be friendly to Franco during the Spanish Civil War.

They make many converts, and breed much faster than Protestants.

Statistics show that, unless some new factor enters in, they will have a majority in the United States in about fifty years.

There is therefore every reason to expect that their power at the end of the present century will be greater than at any time since the French Revolution.

For my part, I view this prospect with alarm [1943]. (UH 45)

What has been the Catholic Church's attitude toward science?

Whoever wishes to become a philosopher will do well to pay attention to the history of science, and particularly to its warfare with theology.

With the exception of pure mathematics, every science has had to begin by fighting to establish its right to exist.

Astronomy was condemned in the person of Galileo, geology in the person of Buffon.

Scientific medicine was, for a long time, made almost impossible by the opposition of the Church to the dissection of dead bodies.

Darwin came too late to suffer penalties, but Catholics and the Legislature of Tennessee still regard evolution with abhorrence.

Each step has been won with difficulty and each new step is still opposed, as if nothing were to be learnt from past defeats.

In our day, it is the newest science, psychology, that encounters opposition, particularly when it seems in danger of interfering with the doctrine of "sin."

The conception of "sin" was the Church's way of preventing anti-social behavior.

If the police failed, the sinner could not congratulate himself on his escape, for God would punish him.

In ethics, equally, the old obscurantism continues.

No one is injured when a man marries his deceased wife's sister, yet the Church is still shocked by such wicked behavior, since it defines "sin" not as what does harm, but as what the Bible or the Church condemns. (AP 17)

CENSORSHIP

How widespread is censorship throughout the world?

Take practically any school in the world; you will find that a certain kind of belief is taught.

It's one sort in Christian countries and another in Communist countries.

But in both, something is taught, and the evidence for what is taught is not impartially examined, and the children are not encouraged to find out what there is to say on the other side. (SHM 21)

What's wrong with censoring pornography?

There ought to be no rules whatever prohibiting improper publications.

I think that partly because stupid magistrates will condemn really valuable work because it happens to shock them.

Another reason is that prohibitions immensely increase people's interest in pornography, as in anything else.

I used often to go to America during Prohibition and there was far more drunkenness there than before; the prohibition of pornography has much the same effect.

Suppose, for instance, filthy postcards were permitted. I think for the first year or two, there would be a great demand for them, and then people would get bored and nobody would look at them again. (SHM 56)

CHARACTER

What traits are to be found in the ideal character?

Four characteristics seem to me jointly to form the basis of an ideal character: vitality, courage, sensitiveness, and intelligence.

I do not suggest that this list is complete, but I think it carries us a good way.

Moreover, I firmly believe that by proper physical, emotional, and intellectual care of the young, these qualities could all be made very common. (EGL 60)

CHILDREN

How can a child be taught to love its parents?

Love cannot exist as a duty; to tell a child that it *ought* to love its parents and its brothers and sisters is utterly useless, if not worse.

Parents who wish to be loved must behave so as to elicit love, and must try to give to their children those physical and mental characteristics which produce expansive affections. (EGL 188)

Should small children be left with each other, without adult supervision?

In a community of children which is left without adult interference, there is a tyranny of the stronger, which is likely to be far more brutal than most adult tyranny.

Consideration for others does not, with most children, arise spontaneously, but has to be taught, and can hardly be taught except by the exercise of authority.

This is perhaps the most important argument against the abdication of the adults. (IPI 129)

CHINA

What's the main difference between the Chinese and ourselves?

I should say that they, in the main, aim at enjoyment, while we, in the main, aim at power.

We like power over our fellow men, and we like power over Nature.

For the sake of the former, we have built up strong states, and for the sake of the latter, we have built up Science.

The Chinese are too lazy and good-natured for such pursuits.

To say that they are lazy is only true in a certain sense. They will work hard for their living.

Employers of labor find them extraordinarily industrious.

But they will not work as Americans and Western Europeans do, simply because they would be bored if they did not work, nor do they love hustle for its own sake.

When they have enough to live on, they live on it, instead of trying to augment it by hard work.

They have an infinite capacity for leisurely amusements—going to the theater, talking while they drink tea, admiring the Chinese art of earlier times, or walking in beautiful scenery.

To our way of thinking, there is something unduly mild about such a way of spending one's life; we respect more a man who goes to his office every day, even if all that he does in his office is harmful. (SE 107)

What can China teach—and learn from—the West?

I think the tolerance of the Chinese is in excess of anything that Europeans can imagine from their experience at home.

We imagine ourselves tolerant, because we are more so than our ancestors, but we still practice political and social persecution, and what is more, we are firmly persuaded that our civilization and our way of life are immeasurably better than any other, so that when we come across a nation like the Chinese, we are convinced that the kindest thing we can do to them is to make them like ourselves.

I believe this to be a profound mistake.

It seemed to me that the average Chinaman, even if he is miserably poor, is happier than the average Englishman, and is happier because the nation is built upon a more humane and civilized outlook than our own.

Restlessness and pugnacity not only cause obvious evils, but fill our lives with discontent, incapacitate us for the enjoyment of beauty, and make us almost incapable of the contemplative virtues.

In this respect we have grown rapidly worse during the past hundred years.

I do not deny that the Chinese go too far in the other direction; but for that very reason I think contact between East and West is likely to be fruitful to both parties.

They may learn from us the indispensable minimum of practical efficiency, and we may learn from them something of that contemplative wisdom which has enabled them to persist while all the other nations of antiquity have perished. (SPBR 222)

What are the benefits of laziness?

Living in the East has, perhaps, a corrupting influence upon a white man, but I must confess that, since I came to know China, I have regarded laziness as one of the best qualities of which men in the mass are capable.

We achieve certain things by being energetic, but it may be questioned whether, on balance, the things that we achieve are of any value.

We develop wonderful skill in manufacture, part of which we devote to making ships, automobiles, telephones, and other means of living luxuriously at high pressure, while another part is devoted to making guns, poison gases, and aeroplanes for the purpose of killing each other wholesale.

We have a first class system of administration and taxation, part of which is devoted to education, sanitation, and such useful objects, while the rest is devoted to war.

In England at the present day most of the national revenue is spent on past and future wars and only the residue on useful objects.

On the Continent, in most countries, the proportion is even worse.

In China, until recently, they had none of these things. The result was that in China, as compared to white man's country, there was freedom for all, and a degree of diffused happiness which was amazing in view of the poverty of all but a tiny minority [1928]. (SE 107)

CITY VERSUS COUNTRY

Has there always been antagonism between city and country?

Economic history, in one of its aspects, represents a perennial conflict between city and country.

Culture has at all times been mainly urban, and piety mainly rural.

In antiquity, almost everything of importance to posterity was urban.

Greek philosophy and science began in the rich commercial cities of Asia Minor and Sicily; thence they passed to Athens, and thence, finally, to Alexandria.

The Romans who fought in the Punic Wars were largely agriculturists, and had very little culture; but after victory had made the Romans rich, they left agriculture to slaves and subject nations, while they themselves took to Greek culture and Oriental luxury.

Commerce between the different parts of the Roman Empire rapidly increased, and reached a maximum in the second century. Great cities flourished, even in regions which are now desert; their ruins astonish the traveller in the parched wastes of North Africa.

Throughout the long period from 600 B.C. to 299 A.D., the city was dominant over the country, which was not the case before and after those dates.

The changes are reflected in religious conceptions: Paradise, in Genesis, is rural, and so is Dante's Earthly Paradise; in the intervening period, men's aspirations are embodied in Plato's Republic, the New Jerusalem, and the City of God, all of which are urban.

The barbarian invasion destroyed the Roman roads and made travel unsafe; they therefore put an almost complete end to commerce, and compelled each small area to raise its own food.

At the same time they established a rural aristocracy of conquerors, who gradually developed the feudal system.

The lay culture of the Middle Ages, except in Italy, was rural and aristocratic, not urban and commercial.

This rural character survived in England, Germany, and Russia until quite recent times.

The tone of English poetry was set by Shakespeare's "native wood-notes wild"; Bismark was militantly bucolic; and Tolstoy held that all virtue is connected with the land.

But the industrial revolution made this point of view a mere survival; though John Bull is a farmer, the typical Englishman of the present day is urban.

In America the conflict of town and country begins with the opposition between Hamilton and Jefferson; it continues with Andrew Jackson, who secured a temporary victory for the rural population; passing through the Populists and W. J. Bryan, it persists in our day in the struggle between the Farm Bloc and the anti-inflationists.

These conflicts are illuminated by being seen in their historical perspective. (UH 32)

CIVILIZATION

Civilization: What is it? How can we define it?

The first essential character [of civilization], I should say, is *forethought.*

This, indeed, is what mainly distinguishes men from brutes and adults from children.

But forethought being a matter of degree, we can distinguish more or less civilized nations and epochs according to the amount of it that they display.

And forethought is capable of precise measurement.

I will not say that the average forethought of a community is inversely proportional to the rate of interest, though this is a view which might be upheld.

But we can say that the degree of forethought involved in any act is measured by three factors: present pain, future pleasure, and the length of the interval between them.

That is to say, the forethought is obtained by dividing the present pain by the future pleasure and then multiplying by the interval of time between them.

All the characteristic works of industrialism exhibit a high degree of collective forethought in this sense, those who make railways, or harbors, or ships, are doing something of which the benefit is only reaped years later.

It is true that no one in the modern world shows as much forethought as the ancient Egyptians showed in embalming their dead, for this was done with a view to their resurrection after some 10,000 years.

This brings me to another element which is essential to civilization, namely *knowledge.* Forethought based upon superstition cannot count as fully civilized, although it may bring habits of mind essential to the growth of true civilization.

For instance, the Puritan habit of postponing pleasures to the next life undoubtedly facilitated the accumulation of capital required for industrialism.

We may then define civilization as: *A manner of life due to the combination of knowledge and forethought.* (IPI 98)

How was civilization spread?

History shows that the spread of civilization to new areas, as opposed to its intensification in a given region, has usually been due to military conquest.

When a more civilized group conquers one which is less civilized, the conquered, if they are not too far beneath their conquerors, learn before long whatever their masters have to teach.

But the converse also happens, when the conquerors are less civilized, if the war of conquest has not been too long or too destructive, they are apt to learn from their subjects.

Greek civilization was diffused throughout the East by Alexander's victories, but throughout the West by the defeats inflicted on the Greeks by the Romans. Gaul and Spain were civilized by becoming subject to Rome; the Arabs, conversely, were civilized by conquering the Eastern portions of the Roman Empire.

But although conquest has had a great effect in increasing the *area* of civilization, it has usually damaged its quality.

Greece was less civilized after Alexander than before, and Rome was never as civilized as Greece had been. (UH 14)

What distinguishes the civilized man from the savage?

The civilized man is distinguished from the savage by *prudence,* or, to use a slightly wider term, *forethought.*

He is willing to endure present pains for the sake of future pleasures, even if the future pleasures are rather distant.

This habit began to be important with the rise of agriculture; no animal and no savage would work in the spring in order to have food next winter, except for a few purely instinctive forms of action, such as bees making honey or squirrels burying nuts. In these cases there is no forethought; there is direct impulse to act, which, to the human spectator, is obviously going to prove useful later on.

True forethought only arises when a man does something toward which no impulse urges him, because his reason tells him that he will profit by it at some future date.

Hunting requires no forethought, because it is pleasurable; but tilling the soil is labor, and cannot be done from spontaneous impulse.

Civilization checks impulse not only through forethought, which is a self-administered check, but also through law, custom, and religion.

This check it inherits from barbarism, but it makes it less instinctive and more systematic.

Certain acts are labeled criminal, and are punished; certain others, though not punished by law, are labeled wicked, and expose those who are guilty of them to social disapproval.

The institution of private property brings with it the subjection of women, and usually the creation of a slave class.

On the one hand, the purposes of the community are enforced upon the individual, and, on the other hand, the individual, having acquired the habit of viewing his life as a whole, increasingly sacrifices his present to his future.

It is evident that this process can be carried too far, as it is, for instance, by the miser.

But without going to such extremes, prudence may easily involve the loss of some of the best things in life.

The worshiper of Bacchus reacts against prudence.

In intoxication, physical or spiritual, he recovers an intensity of feeling which prudence had destroyed; he finds the world full of delight and beauty, and his imagination is suddenly liberated from the prison of everyday preoccupations.

The Bacchic ritual produced what was called "enthusiasm," which means etymologically, having the god enter into the worshiper, who believed he became one with the god.

Much of what is greatest in human achievement involves some element of [mental] intoxication, some sweeping away of prudence by passion.

Without the Bacchic element, life would be uninteresting; with it, it is dangerous.

Prudence versus passion is a conflict that runs through history.

It is not a conflict in which we ought to side wholly with either party. (Italics added) (HWP 15)

How can one view one's own civilization properly?

To see one's own civilization in a true perspective is by no means easy.

There are three obvious means to this end, namely, travel, history, and anthropology . . . but no one of the three is as great a help to objectivity as it appears to be.

The traveler sees only what interests him; for example, Marco Polo never noticed Chinese women's small feet.

The historian arranges events in a pattern derived from his preoccupations, the decay of Rome has been variously ascribed to imperialism, Christianity, malaria, divorce, and immigration—the last two being the favorites in America with parsons and politicians respectively.

The anthropologist selects and interprets facts according to the prevailing prejudices of his day.

What do we, who stay at home, know about the savage? Rousseauites say he is noble, imperialists say he is cruel; ecclesiastically minded anthropologists say he is a virtuous family man, while advocates of divorce law reform say he practices free love; Sir James Frazer says he is always killing his god, while others say he is always engaged in initiation ceremonies.

In short, the savage is an obliging fellow who does whatever is necessary for the anthropologist's theories.

In spite of these drawbacks, travel, history, and anthropology are the best means, and we must make the most of them. (IPI 98)

COMMUNISM

Some say they would rather be dead than Red. How to respond, Lord Russell?

I'd ask them if they think they're the only people in the world.

I myself would certainly rather die than live under a communist tyranny . . . or indeed any other tyranny, but I don't think that on that ground, I have a right to say that every inhabitant of (say) India should die.

I have no right to say that they should die for my convictions.

And of course you must remember that exactly the same feelings exist among earnest communists. The earnest communist will feel that he would rather die than live in a capitalist world.

Well, those sentiments are foolish.

When you extend them beyond yourself . . . you have a perfect right to sacrifice your own life . . . you do not have a right to sacrifice the life of the whole of mankind. (CBC)

What's wrong with the "Dictatorship of the Proletariat"?

I think the most important thing that is wrong in communist doctrine is the belief in benevolent despotism, a belief which is really ancient and existed in all sorts of communities, but has always proved itself wrong, because when you take a benevolent man and make him a despot, his despotism survives but his benevolence rather fades away.

The whole theory of communism is that you give an enormous amount of power to people who are adherents of a certain creed, and you hope that they will exercise that power benevolently.

Whereas it seems to me that everybody—with very few exceptions—misuses power, and therefore the important thing is to spread power as evenly as you can, and not give immense power to some small clique. (P 45)

COMPETITION

Why did Russell disapprove of competition in 1926?

It is amazing how deeply the competitive motive has eaten into all our activities.

If you wish to persuade a borough to improve the public provision for the care of children you have to point out that some neighboring borough has a lower infant mortality.

If you wish to persuade a manufacturer to adopt a new process which is clearly an improvement, you have to emphasize the danger of competition. Nothing is done to promote constructiveness for its own sake, or to make people take an interest in doing their job efficiently, even if no one is to be injured thereby.

Our economic system has more to do with this than school games.

But school games, as they now exist, embody the spirit of competition.

If the spirit of cooperation is to take its place, a change in school games will be necessary. (EGL 134)

Why did Russell approve of competition in 1949?

I do not think that ordinary human beings can be happy without competition, for competition has been, ever since the origin of Man, the spur to most serious activities.

We should not, therefore, attempt to abolish competition, but only to see that it takes forms which are not too injurious.

Primitive competition was a conflict as to which should murder the other man and his wife and children; modern competition in the shape of war still takes this form.

But in sport, in literary and artistic rivalry, and in constitutional politics it takes forms which do very little harm and yet offer a fairly adequate outlet for our combative instincts.

What is wrong in this respect is not that such forms of competition are bad, but that they form too small a part of the lives of ordinary men and women.

Apart from war, modern civilization has aimed increasingly at security, but I am not at all sure that the elimination of all danger makes for happiness. (AI 8)

CONFUCIUS

What are Confucius's merits and inadequacies?

I must confess that I am unable to appreciate the merits of Confucius.

His writings are largely occupied with trivial points of etiquette, and his main concern is to teach people how to behave correctly on various occasions.

When one compares him, however, with the traditional religious teachers of some other ages, one must admit that he has great merits, even if they are mainly negative.

His system, as developed by his followers, is one of pure ethics, without religious dogma; it has not given rise to a powerful priesthood, and has not led to persecution.

It certainly has succeeded in producing a whole nation possessed of exquisite manners and perfect courtesy.

Nor is Chinese courtesy merely conventional; it is quite as reliable in situations for which no precedent has been provided. And it is not confined to one class; it exists even in the humblest coolie.

It is humiliating to watch the brutal insolence of white men received by the Chinese with a quiet dignity which cannot demean itself to answer rudeness with rudeness.

Europeans often regard this as weakness, but it is really strength, the strength by which the Chinese have hitherto conquered all their conquerors. (SPBR 213)

CONSCIENCE

Can we rely on conscience as a guide?

In the orthodox Christian conception, the good life is the virtuous life, and virtue consists in obedience to the will of God, and the will of God is revealed to each individual through the voice of conscience.

Conscience is a most fallacious guide, since it consists of vague reminiscences of precepts heard in early youth, so that it is never wiser than its possessor's nurse or mother. (WIB 60)

COURAGE

What other forms of courage are there besides physical courage?

Courage in fighting is by no means the only form, nor perhaps even the most important.

There is courage in facing poverty, courage in facing derision, courage in facing the hostility of one's own herd.

In these, the bravest soldiers are often lamentably deficient.

And above all, there is the courage to think calmly and rationally in the face of danger, and to control the impulse of panic fear or panic rage. (WIB 74)

When is courage especially important?

Courage is needed to retain a rational outlook when reason can offer no certainty of a happy outcome.

Many people, under the influence of fear, are inclined to relapse into some form of superstition, or to advocate on our side the very same detestable regimentation which leads us to condemn totalitarian regimes, not perceiving that this is to suffer moral defeat before the contest has begun.

Meanwhile we must retain sanity, which is difficult if we brood too much over what is dark and tragic.

Whatever may be in store for us and for the world, it is well that our leisure should be spent in enjoying whatever can be enjoyed without injury to others.

There are still dewy mornings and summer evenings and the sea and the stars; there are still love and friendship and music and poetry.

And when we need some consolation nearer to the stuff of our anxieties, it is always to be found by removing our gaze from the immediate foreground.

There have been earlier cataclysms, but the spirit of man has survived.

In spite of some alarmists, it is hardly likely that our species will completely exterminate itself.

And so long as man continues to exist we may be pretty sure that, whatever he may suffer for a time, and whatever brightness may be eclipsed, he will emerge sooner or later, perhaps strengthened and reinvigorated by a period of mental sleep.

The universe is vast, and men are but tiny specks on an insignificant planet.

But the more we realize our minuteness and our impotence in the face of cosmic forces, the more astonishing becomes what human beings have achieved.

It is to the possible achievements of Man that our ultimate loyalty is due, and in that thought the brief troubles of our unquiet epoch become endurable.

Much wisdom remains to be learnt, and if it is only to be learnt through adversity, we must endeavor to endure adversity with what fortitude we can command. But if we can acquire wisdom soon enough, adversity may not be necessary, and the future of Man may be happier than any part of his past. (Italics added) (RSN52 5)

CROWDS

What brings timid people together?

Among the timid, organization is promoted, not only by submission to a leader, but by the reassurance which is felt in being one of a crowd who all feel alike.

In an enthusiastic public meeting with whose purpose one is in sympathy, there is a sense of exaltation, combined with warmth and safety: the emotion which is shared grows more and more intense until it crowds out all other feelings except an exultant sense of power produced by the multiplication of the *ego*.

Collective excitement is a delicious intoxication, in which sanity, humanity, and even self-preservation are easily forgotten, and in which atrocious massacres and heroic martyrdom are equally possible.

This kind of intoxication, like others, is hard to resist when its delights have once been experienced, but leads in the end to apathy and weariness, and for the need for a stronger and stronger stimulus if the former fervor is to be reproduced. (P 27)

Why do leaders like to talk to large crowds?

Although a leader is not essential to this emotion [the emotion of an excited crowd], which can be produced by music, and by some exciting event which is seen by the crowd, the words of an orator are the easiest and most usual method of inducing it.

The pleasure of collective excitement is, therefore, an important element in the power of leaders. (P 28)

Is mob hysteria on the increase?

I think that education, which leads people to be able to read, has through the press immensely increased mob hysteria.

But there's a contrary tendency coming in now, mainly I think through television, because people get their news of the world now sitting at home and not sitting in large halls of excited crowds of people who begin to shout.

And I think it's large assemblies such as you get in big public meetings that are the main cause of mob hysteria.

Insofar as meetings count for less, I think mob hysteria will grow less. (SHM 36)

CULTURE

Why is culture worth studying?

The history of culture, conceived in its widest sense, includes religion, art, philosophy, and science. (UH 38)

The material is vast, and selection is necessary.

Selection must be guided at least in part by a sense of values: we must have some touchstone by which to decide who deserves to be remembered.

This cannot, it is true, be our sole principle of selection; some men must be studied because of their influence.

Even if we have no very high opinion of Mahomet (say), we cannot ignore him, because a large section of mankind believes in him.

But even then, standards are necessary if the history of culture is to be studied with any profit; we must not indiscriminately admire whoever has been influential, for if we do we may find ourselves worshiping Satan.

The ultimate value of culture is to suggest standards of good and evil which science alone cannot supply. (Italics added) (UH 41)

What are the sources of the Western mentality?

Western Europe and America have a practically homogeneous mental life, which I should trace to three sources: (1) Greek culture; (2) Jewish religion and ethics; (3) modern industrialism, which itself is an outcome of modern science.

We may take Plato, the Old Testament, and Galileo as representing these three elements, which have remained singularly separable down to the present day.

From the Greeks we derive literature and the arts, philosophy and pure mathematics; also the more urbane portions of our social outlook.

From the Jews we derive fanatical belief, which its friends call "faith";

moral fervor, with the conception of sin; religious intolerance; and some part of our nationalism.

From science, as applied in industrialism, we derive power and the sense of power, the belief that we are as gods, and may justly be the arbiters of life and death for unscientific races.

We derive also the empirical method by which almost all real knowledge has been acquired.

These three elements, I think, account for most of our mentality. (SPBR 219)

What should the government leave strictly alone?

In cultural matters, diversity is a condition of progress.

Bodies that have a certain independence of the State, such as universities and learned societies, have great value in this respect.

It is deplorable to see, as in present-day Russia [1949], men of science compelled to subscribe to obscurantist nonsense [by Lysenko*] at the behest of scientifically ignorant politicians [Stalin] who are able and willing to enforce their ridiculous decisions by the use of economic and police power.

Such pitiful spectacles can only be prevented be limiting the activities of politicians to the sphere in which they may be supposed competent.

They should not presume to decide what is good music, or good biology, or good philosophy.

I should not wish such matters to be decided in this country by the personal taste of any Prime Minister, past, present, or future, even if, by good luck, his taste was impeccable. (AI 68)

How do economic facts influence culture?

Modern views as to the relation of economic facts to general culture have been profoundly affected by the theory, first explicitly stated by Marx, that the mode of production of an age (and to a lesser degree

---

*TROFIM DENISOVICH LYSENKO (1898–1976). Soviet biologist who believed acquired characteristics could be inherited. Stalin supported him. He wanted to wet and freeze spring wheat so it would behave like winter wheat.

the mode of exchange) is the ultimate cause of the character of its politics, laws, literature, philosophy, and religion.

Like all sweeping theories, this doctrine is misleading if accepted as dogma, but it is valuable if used a means of suggesting hypotheses.

It has indubitably a large measure of truth, though not so much as Marx believed.

R. H. Tawney's *Religion and the Rise of Capitalism,* a most valuable and interesting book, illustrates with a wealth of illuminating detail a theory which is in some sense the converse of Marx's doctrine.

Tawney is concerned to trace a connection between Protestantism and capitalism, in which, largely by way of individualism, Protestantism is the cause and capitalism the effect, laissez faire in theology may be regarded as the source of laissez faire in business.

It is undeniable that modern capitalism began in Protestant countries, but I doubt whether the connection is quite what Tawney represents it as being.

In the seventeenth century, England and Holland were the leading commercial countries. Both were Protestant, and both had abundant political reasons for their Protestantism. The Pope had bestowed the East Indies and Brazil on Portugal, and the rest of the Western hemisphere on Spain.

This did not suit Northern nations that wished to trade with India and establish colonies in America.

Moreover Spain was a danger to both; Holland owed its existence to a successful revolt against Spain, and England owed its survival to the defeat of the Spanish Armada.

Protestantism went naturally with hostility to Spain, which was the leading Catholic Power.

There were therefore ample secular reasons for the Protestantism of England and Holland.

Their commerical success, however, was due to their excellence as seamen and to their geographical position.

Perhaps success colored their religion, which was in some ways different in temper from German Lutheranism.

But I doubt whether Protestantism was actually in any important degree a *cause* of the capitalist doctrines which were naturally engendered by commerce and manufactures.

In an earlier age, North Italy had led the world in economic development, but had not quarreled with the Pope, and had not acquired what Tawney regards as the Protestant mentality.

I do not deny an element of truth in his thesis, but I think it is less than he supposes. (UH 33)

Why should eccentricity be tolerated?

A few societies have perished from excess of individualism and skepticism; of these Greece and Renaissance Italy are the chief examples.

These, before perishing, produced a great outburst of genius, from which the world has profited ever since; they did far more for mankind than if they had survived in humdrum respectability.

And their way of perishing is not the usual way.

The usual way is to become sunk in conservatism, awed by precedent, terrified of novelty, completely stereotyped in word and deed.

Many more nations have been brought to destruction by fear of change than by love of it.

No nation can long flourish unless it tolerates exceptional individuals, whose behavior is not exactly like that of their neighbors.

Everyone knows the men who achieve great things in art or literature or science are apt in youth, to be eccentric; when eccentricity in youth is not tolerated, there will be little of great achievement among adult men and women.

But although these things are known, it is difficult to cause them to be embodied in the practice of education.

It is right that men should live with some reference to the community, and with some hope of being useful to it, but this does not mean that all men should be alike, for exceptional services require exceptional characters. (UH 53)

DEATH

Can fear of death be overcome without religion?

Religion, since it has its source in terror, has dignified certain kinds of fear, and made people think them not disgraceful.

In this it has done mankind a great disservice; *all* fear is bad, and ought to be overcome not by fairy tales, but by courage and rational reflection.

I believe that when I die, I shall rot, and nothing of my ego will survive.

I am not young, and I love life. But I should scorn to shiver with terror at the thought of annihilation.

Happiness is nonetheless true happiness because it must come to an end, nor do thought and love lose their value because they are not everlasting.

Many a man has borne himself proudly on the scaffold; surely the same pride should teach us to think truly about man's place in the world.

Even if the open windows of science at first make us shiver after the cosy indoor warmth of traditional humanizing myths, in the end the fresh air brings vigor, and the great spaces have a splendor of their own. (WIB 13)

DEMOCRACY

What are two great merits of democracy?

Democracy was invented as a device for reconciling government with liberty.

It is clear that government is necessary if anything worthy to be called civilization is to exist, but all history shows that any set of men entrusted with power over another set will abuse their power if they can do so with impunity.

Democracy is intended to make men's tenure of power temporary and dependent upon popular approval.

Insofar as it achieves this it prevents the worst abuses of power. (UE 141)

We are right to be horrified by Stalin's ruthlessness, but we are wholly mistaken if we think that, given opportunity, we should be any better.

It is only democracy that makes us better.

While the English upper class had a monopoly of political power, it was just as bad as Stalin.

Democracy is to be valued because it prevents such large-scale atrocities.

This is its first and greatest merit.

It has, however, others only slightly less important.

It makes possible a degree of intellectual freedom which is not at all likely to exist under a despotic regime.

In Russia at the present day, no literature is permitted which might instill a doubt as to the wisdom and virtue of the Masters.

Despotic monarchs have always suppressed, as far as they were able, every suggestion that their power was excessive. Churches have been equally to blame in this respect [1953]. (FF 88)

The first and strongest argument for democracy is human selfishness.

When a group of men has power over another group, it will almost always ill-treat the subject group. White men have ill-treated Negroes, aristocrats have ill-treated peasants, men have ill-treated women.

It is hardly possible to find, except for brief periods in rare circumstances, cases where a dominant group has behaved with tolerable humanity toward one over which it had control.

This was not only true in the past.

It is true at least as much in the present.

Stalin's government kept millions of workers in slave conditions, and punished the faintest whisper of opposition in the most savage manner.

Hitler's atrocities are too notorious to need recapitulating.

I value democracy, first of all, because where it exists, such horrors are scarcely possible.

The second great merit of democracy is that it affords a possible method of settling disagreements.

Where there is no democracy, if any large section is discontented, it has no remedy except rebellion.

Democracy gives a legal method of redressing grievances, and makes possible a respect for law which can hardly exist in an autocracy.

Consider, for example, the plot to murder Hitler in 1944. The men involved in this plot were some of the best men in Germany, and their motives were wholly laudable.

One cannot imagine, at the same time, an English plot to murder Churchill.

It is mainly the existence of democracy in England that makes this unimaginable.

Although as we saw, there can be democracy without liberty, there can never be secure liberty without democracy.

Such liberty as has existed under autocracies has depended upon the whim of the momentary despot, and has been liable to disappear overnight.

It is only where there is a recognized orderly process of changing the government, or altering the laws, that liberty can be secure.

If I had to choose between liberty and democracy, I should be hard put to it to know which to prefer, since it is only by means of liberty that progress, whether intellectual or moral, is possible.

Fortunately, no such choice is forced upon us. (FF 107–108)

Democracy is desirable, not because the ordinary voter has any political wisdom, but because any section of mankind which has a monopoly of power is sure to invent theories designed to prove that the rest of mankind had better do without the good things of life.

This is one of the least amiable traits of human nature, but history shows there is no adequate protection against it except the just distribution of political power throughout all classes and both sexes. (MAO 111)

Does democracy guarantee individual freedom?

The connection of democracy with individual liberty is not as close as is sometimes thought.

Theoretically, and as a matter of definition, democracy is compatible with a complete absence of liberty for minorities.

In New England colonial communities, there was at first theological uniformity enforced by persecution, and it would not be verbally correct to regard this as an infringement of democracy.

The most difficult kind of liberty to preserve in a democracy is the kind which derives its importance from services to the community that are not very obvious to ignorant people. New intellectual work is always unpopular because it is subversive of deep-seated prejudices, and appears to the uneducated as wanton wickedness.

Luther thought Copernicus a mere paradox monger who wished to be known for his eccentricity.

Calvin took the same view, and so did the Catholic Church in the time of Galileo.

Democracy would not have saved Galileo from persecution.

In present-day America, while a teacher is not likely to suffer legal penalties for his views, he will probably suffer very severe economic penalties if he teaches history or economics or social science and does not agree with intolerant and ignorant men. (FF 101)

In what ways has democracy diminished freedom in America?

A sentiment in favor of liberty is somewhat more often found where there is democracy than where there is autocracy. Although I believe this to be true, I think, nonetheless, that individual liberty is insufficiently valued in many modern democratic countries.

This is a matter in which there has been retrogression since the nineteenth century.

The retrogression is caused by fear, and I cannot say that the fear is irrational, but I do not think that a diminution of liberty is a method of escaping from the dangers that are feared.

In America, for example, the question as to what foreigners shall be admitted is left in the hands of uneducated policemen, who have a general belief that all European physicists are spies who will sell to the stupid Russians the atomic secrets discovered by the clever Americans.

The result is that international congresses of scientists have become difficult in America, and that American scientists who are not free to travel get out of touch with valuable work done in Europe.

An American will not be encouraged to work at nuclear physics unless his politics are reactionary, and this is almost sure to diminish the technical efficiency of America in the next war if it comes.

This suggests a wider problem connected with democracy. Democracy is based historically upon the maxim that all men are equal.

But if this maxim is to be true, it must be carefully interpreted.

It is not the case that all men are the equals of Newton in mathematical ability, or of Beethoven in musical genius.

To say that all men are equal is only true if it means that justice requires an absence of discrimination between one man and another in political matters.

It is not true if it is held to imply that, even in the most complex matters, one man's judgment is as good as another's.

Yet it is only in this latter untrue form that it can justify the ordinary voter in deciding what shall be taught in universities.

In American state universities the taxes pay the teachers, and the ordinary taxpayer infers that he has a right to object to the teaching of anything that he does not agree with.

It does not occur to him that perhaps a man who has devoted his life to a difficult subject knows more about it than a man who has never studied it at all.

When democracy is thought to justify such conclusions, it becomes absurd. (FF 105–106)

Is democracy dictator-proof? Does it prevent dictatorship?

Lenin, Mussolini, and Hitler owed their rise to democracy.

It requires only a high degree of the same qualities as are required by democratic politicians in general, at any rate, in excited times. (P 47)

What is the great virtue of representative government?

The institution of representative government: to us this seems an essential part of democracy, but the Ancients never thought of it, and, in its earlier forms in the Middle Ages, it was not very democratic.

Its immense merit was that it enabled a large constituency to exert indirect power, and thus made possible the distribution of political responsibility throughout the great states of modern times, whereas formerly such distribution had only been possible in single cities. (FF 81)

Why is tolerance essential in a democracy?

Tolerance is, in many ways, absolutely essential to the success of democracy.

If people hold their principles so strongly that they feel they ought to die or kill for them, every difference of opinion will lead to war or to a *coup d'état.*

Democracy requires, in fact, a rather difficult combination of individual initiative with submission to the majority.

It requires that a man who has strong political convictions should argue for them and do what he can to make them the convictions of the majority, but that if the majority proves adverse, he should submit with a good grace.

There was, some twenty years ago, a small country—I will not say which—in which opposing parties were very nearly balanced.

The Members of Parliament of the minority party, in the middle of the session, shot a sufficient number of their opponents to become the majority.

This expedient was not adopted by the Conservative Party in England in 1959, nor by the Labour Party in 1951.

Any really fanatical belief tends to be incompatible with democracy.

When in 1918 the Russian Constituent Assembly proved to have an anti-Bolshevik majority, the Bolsheviks dissolved it by military force, and ever since then have ruled Russia without regard to popular feeling.

In the sixteenth and seventeenth centuries, the Protestant and Catholic governments acted similarly.

Fascist governments in Germany, Italy, and Spain have been indifferent to majority opinion.

Whenever any large and important section of any nation has this kind of fanaticism, democracy is hardly likely to survive.

On this ground, believers in democracy ought to do everything in their power to cause a tolerant spirit to be inculcated in education.

This is not at all adequately done at present.

There are everywhere beliefs favored by the State, and it is thought proper that the young should be caused to accept these beliefs unquestioningly and dogmatically.

The most destructive of these at the present time is nationalism.

The world is divided into a number of areas, and in each area the young are taught that the inhabitants of that area are virtuous, while the inhabitants of other areas are degraded and wicked.

This does not make for the peace of the world. (FF 94)

How did democracy fare in ancient Greece?

Democracy, both the word and the thing, was invented by the Greeks.

So far as is known, nobody conceived of it before their time.

There had been monarchies, theocracies, and aristocracies, but nobody had imagined a system in which all the citizens should have a voice in government.

Even the most extreme forms of democracy developed by the Greeks were limited in certain respects; women and slaves had no part in government.

As far as women were concerned, Plato thought this limitation unjust, but he had few followers in this matter.

Where democracy prevailed in ancient Greece, the individual had, in many ways, more power than he has in a modern democratic state.

He could vote on every proposed law, judges were chosen by lot from among the citizens, and there was no powerful bureaucracy to place obstacles in the way of the popular will. Such a system was only technically possible in a city-state, since it presupposed that the citizens could assemble and vote directly on each measure, a thing which, in a large modern state, is not possible.

It cannot be said that the system was very successful.

It arose in opposition to aristocracy, which itself had arisen in opposition to monarchy.

Aristocracy, in most Greek city-states, was defeated by democracy, but democracy itself, as a rule, gave way to tyranny. A tyrant, as the Greeks understood the word, was not necessarily a bad ruler; he was merely a man who had acquired the powers of monarchy by force or the popular favor, and not by heredity.

He generally made himself the champion of the people against aristocrats and plutocrats, and when he had acquired sufficient popularity, he represented that his enemies were plotting to assassinate him and that he needed a bodyguard if his life was to be preserved.

When once he had got the bodyguard, he only had to favor the men who composed it, and the people were forgotten.

The Greeks never discovered any method of making democracy secure against this sort of thing. (FF 79)

How did democracy fare in ancient Rome?

Rome, on a larger scale, repeated the Greek experience.

There was a long period of strife between the aristocracy and the populace.

Julius Caesar won favor as the champion of democracy, which he abolished as soon as he was securely established.

After his day, democracy disappeared from the world for a long time. (FF 80)

Where did modern democratic theory get its start?

Democratic theory, in the modern sense, was not invented by Rousseau but by the progressive element in Cromwell's army. These men failed at home but carried their doctrines across the Atlantic where, after a period of incubation, they at last gave birth to American democracy.

The success of America was largely influential in spreading democratic ideas in France and also, though less directly, in England. (FF 82)

What circumstance affects the character of a democracy?

The character of a democracy is very largely determined by the forces which it regards as its enemies.

American democracy at first was directed mainly against England.

French democracy was directed in 1789 mainly against the large land owners.

English democracy in the first half of the nineteenth century was engaged in acquiring power for the middle class, but, after that, was seeking power for wage earners and was regarding large employers as the enemy. (FF 83)

What is the proper role of experts in a democracy?

One of the problems which every modern democracy has to face is that of the utilization of experts.

There are many matters of the utmost importance which are too difficult for ordinary citizens to understand.

Of these, perhaps finance is the most obvious.

Jackson abolished the Bank of America, chiefly because he could not understand banking.

The problem is to secure that, when expert opinion is necessary, it shall be in accordance with a popularly chosen policy and not covertly such as to favor some minority policy.

A good example of this has been trade union legislation in England. Urban working men acquired the vote in 1867.

Repeatedly acts have been passed which were thought to have secured the objects of trade unionists, but the House of Lords, in its judicial capacity, has discovered that the acts did not mean what they seemed to mean.

This has only somewhat delayed matters, since the working-class vote was sufficient to secure the passage of new amending acts, but it shows what legal experts can do to defeat the popular will. (FF 83)

Why are citizens of a democracy more easily deceived?

One of the advantages of democracy, from a governmental point of view, is that it makes the average citizen easier to deceive, since he regards the government as *his* government. Opposition to a war which is not swiftly successful arises much less readily in a democracy than under any other form of constitution.

In a democracy, a majority can only turn against the government by first admitting to themselves that they were mistaken in formerly thinking well of their chosen leaders, which is difficult and unpleasant. (P 146)

Why are democracies less warlike than autocracies?

Another advantage of democracy is that it is less likely to be warlike than an autocratic government.

The advantages of war, such as they are, fall only to the eminent in victor nations.

The disadvantages fall upon the common people.

I have little doubt that if the will of the Russian people could prevail at the present moment, the danger of war between East and West would be at an end.

Consider the motives which make the Russian government such a source of danger to Western countries, and vice versa.

These are of various sorts.

There is first, on both sides, a fanatical creed which it is thought desirable to spread.

There is next a possibility of glory.

And, perhaps more powerful than either of these, there is the sheer lust for power.

These are not motives which have anything like the same potency in the lives of ordinary men and women as they have in the thoughts of eminent statesmen.

For this reason, where ordinary men and women have power, there is much less likelihood of a warlike policy than there is under a despotic regime.

Although it cannot be said in any absolute way that democracies are against war, I do think it can be said that they are less apt to be warlike than autocracies are [1953]. (FF 90)

How can democracies be made less belligerent?

To make democracies peaceable rather than warlike is mainly a matter for the schools.

History should be taught as the history of the rise of civilization, and not as the history of this nation or that.

It should be taught from the point of view of mankind as a whole, and not with undue emphasis upon one's own country. Children should learn that every country has committed crimes, and that most crimes were blunders.

They should learn how mass hysteria can drive a whole nation into folly and into persecution of the few who are not swept away by the prevailing madness.

They should be shown movies of foreign countries in which the children, though aliens, would be enjoying much the same pleasures, and suffering much the same sorrows, as those enjoyed and suffered by children at home.

All this could be done by UNESCO if the national governments permitted.

All this, if it were done throughout the world, would immensely diminish the warlike proclivities of democracies. (FF 97)

Why have democracies failed to curb their own nationalism?

Nationalism is one of the matters in which democracies, so far, have proved least satisfactory.

In the old days, when wars were dynastic and were conducted for the glory of individual rulers, the bulk of the population often regarded them with indifference or hostility.

Throughout the Napoleonic wars, English people of the lower classes took no interest in English victories and were quite ready to believe that the French were as good as the English.

This belief did not exist in the upper class.

Nelson, for instance, taught his midshipmen that they should hate a Frenchman as they would the Devil.

But the upper class had the government.

In France, equally, there was no enthusiam for that war except upon the part of those who were encouraged by Napoleon's victories.

Napoleon acquired power on the 18th Brumaire [1799] by promising peace, just as Lenin acquired power in 1917 by the same promise.

The unpopularity of wars in the past set a limit to their intensity.

When they became too serious, there was discontent—even mutiny.

But in a democratic country, the ordinary voter feels that the war is *his* war.

His ego is involved in it in a way that does not occur under an autocracy.

This has the good point that it makes a democracy more likely to win, but it has the bad point that it makes it possible for a democratic government to wage war to the bitter end, and, before the war has taken place, to be threatening and bellicose in its policy.

But within the compass of democratic government, there is only one cure for this evil, which is that by agreement among the nations, education should dwell more upon the common tasks of mankind than upon rivalries between different states.

In the eighteenth century, war could be a profitable business.

With the exception of the War of American Independence, England emerged from the wars of that century with a balance of profit, from a merely financial point of view.

Nowadays, things are different.

We have been brought to the verge of ruin by complete and absolute victory in two successive wars, and it is no longer difficult to persuade

English people that war is not good business, though in America this lesson has still to be learned. (FF 95)

Does democracy guarantee intellectual freedom?

It has frequently happened in the past that important men have been protected from popular fury by undemocratic rulers.

Aristotle was safe in Athens so long as Alexander was alive to protect him, but when Alexander died, Aristotle had to flee.

Averroës was protected by Mohammedan rulers from the fury of the mob until near the end of his life, when popular pressure became too great for the government to resist.

Hobbes was befriended by Charles II when Parliament decided that Divine anger was the cause of the Plague.

When Tennessee decided against evolution, the decision was not undemocratic.

As these examples show, intellectual liberty is not rendered secure by democracy alone.

But it would be quite unhistorical to conclude that intellectual liberty is, in general, safer under an undemocratic regime.

There have been a few examples of enlightened autocrats, but the immense majority of autocrats have been completely unenlightened and completely willing to restrain intellectual liberty even more completely than the worst democracies.

At the present day, Russia is, of course, the supreme example.

Stalin thought he knew more about genetics than any geneticist, and those who ventured to disagree suffered very extreme penalties.

In eighteenth-century France, the government was completely obscurantist.

It compelled Buffon,* for example, to recant publicly the opinion that not all existing mountains had existed since the beginning of the world [1953]. (FF 192)

---

*GEORGES-LOUIS LECLERC DE BUFFON (1707–1788). French naturalist. (Ed.)

How does the two-party system protect against worship of the state?

Worship of government is the modern form of idolatry and is exceedingly dangerous.

Far the most effective antidote to it is the two-party system.

I lived in America under [F. D.] Roosevelt, and most of the people that I met considered him a dangerous lunatic.

I did not agree with them in this, but I thought it thoroughly wholesome that people should have this opinion of the Head of State.

Liberty will only exist where there is an effective division of opinion with influential men of both sides.

It began in the West with the conflict between Church and State in the time of St. Ambrose.

It exists at the present day owing to the conflict between Conservatives and Socialists in England and between Democrats and Republicans in America.

Where democracy prevails, it is hardly possible to have that worship of the State as the Garment of God which Hegel sycophantically inculcated as he drew his pay from the Prussian Exchequer. (FF 104)

Do some circumstances not favor the introduction of democracy?

I do not think it can be said that democracy, always and everywhere, is the best form of government.

I do not think that it can be successfully practiced among totally uncivilized people.

I do not think it is workable where there is a population of mixed groups which fundamentally hate each other.

I do not think it can be introduced quite suddenly in countries that have no experience of the give and take that goes with freedom in government.

If every compromise is viewed as a surrender of principle, it is impossible for rival groups to make a bargain representing the middle point between their respective interests.

For such reasons I do not think one ought to advocate the introduction of democracy immediately in every part of the world.

But having conceded so much to the opponents of democracy, I should wish to state with the utmost emphasis the arguments in its favor wherever it is practicable. (FF 106)

What are some dangers to modern democracy?

Modern democracies are exposed to certain dangers which did not exist in former times.

The most important of these dangers comes from the police.

When the Communists were acquiring control of satellite countries, they were willing to enter into coalitions provided they had control of the police. Given control of the police, they could arrest almost anybody they disliked and concoct fantastic stories of plots.

It was largely by this method that they passed from participation in coalition governments to exclusive control.

The same sort of thing, though on a lesser scale, can easily happen elsewhere.

Who, in America, would wish to fall foul of the F.B.I.?

And who, not in America, can deny that the F.B.I. has a corporate interest and a corporate bias which may be quite out of harmony with the interests of the American people?

Apart from police, important pressure groups can cause individuals and even whole sections of opinion to be unjustly condemned.

Accusations often repeated are in the end believed by all but an exceptionally skeptical minority.

The evil is one which is not very easy to deal with.

In England the libel laws are so strict that even perfectly just accusations can only be made with great risk. It is not altogether easy to draw the line between preventing unjust accusations and permitting just ones.

What is perhaps even more important is that where public opinion is intolerant, a man may be gravely damaged by the publication of something which is in no way to his real discredit.

If you have lived in Russia and studied Russian opinion, your mere knowledge makes you suspect, and you will have to walk very warily if you are not to be regarded as a fellow traveler.

There cannot long be liberty without tolerance, for liberty without tolerance leads to civil war.

The ultimate basis of liberty, therefore, lies not merely in political institutions, but in the general diffusion of a conviction that all opinions have their rights, and that however convinced you may be, it is nevertheless possible that you may be mistaken. (FF 69)

Why is democracy more important than ever in this age of technology?

It is possible to establish a technological power over men which is based upon power over matter.

Those who have the habit of controlling powerful mechanisms, and through this control have acquired power over human beings, may be expected to have an imaginative outlook toward their subjects which will be completely different from that of men who depend upon persuasion, however dishonest.

Is it likely that such a government will have any profound concern for the happiness of its subjects?

Is it not, on the contrary, practically certain that it will view them, when all goes well, in the impersonal manner in which it views its machines, but that, when anything happens to suggest that after all they are not machines, it will feel the cold rage of men whose axioms are questioned by underlings, and will exterminate resistance in whatever manner involves least trouble?

All this, the reader may think, is mere unnecessary nightmare.

I wish I could share this view.

Mechanical power, I am convinced, tends to generate a new mentality, which makes it more important than in any former age to find ways of controlling governments.

Democracy may have become more difficult owing to technical developments, but it has also become more important.

The man who has vast mechanical power at his command is likely, if uncontrolled, to feel himself a god—not a Christian God of Love, but a pagan Thor or Vulcan. (P 31)

What is a powerful reason for expecting democracy to survive?

Democracy, as a form of government, has the advantage of making everybody a participant in war.

I think it may be doubted whether a country under an undemocratic regime would be as unmoved in disaster as England was in 1940.

This is one of the strongest reasons for expecting democracy to survive. (UH 28)

DEVOLUTION

How to combine maximum freedom with needed state authority?

National governments must leave as much scope as possible to local authorities. (AI 67)

Can there be nongeographical devolution?

Devolution presents difficulties where a group is geographically distributed and not concentrated in one area.

I think, however, that it should be possible, and is certainly desirable, to have for certain purposes constituencies which are not geographical but occupational or ideological.

Consider, for example, some country in which practically every geographical constituency contains five percent of Jews.

As things stand, these Jews will be everywhere out-voted, and their interests may be quite inadequately represented in Parliament.

It might be better if they voted separately, and had in Parliament, a number of representatives proportional to their number in the general population.

I should not advocate this particular measure except where anti-Semitism is strong.

What I think more important is an industrial application of the same sort of principle.

Socialists have always advocated nationalization of railways and mines.

The late Labour Government carried out this program, but the difference to the employees was not quite so great as Socialists had hoped.

The place of the capitalist was taken by State officials, and there was always the same possibility as before of a clash between employees and management.

I should like to see the internal affairs of any great industry, such as railways or mining, determined democratically not by the State, but by the employees of that industry, leaving only the external affairs in the hands of the State.

The modern State is so vast, and even in a democracy, officials are so remote from voters, that very little sense of personal initiative remains to the employees of large nationalized industry.

I think lack of opportunity for personal initiative is one of the great dangers of the modern world.

It leads to apathy, to a sense of impotence, and thence to pessimism.

There should be, for everyone who is energetic and who has strong convictions, some sphere, great or small, where he may hope to be effective, and this is only possible by means of much more devolution than exists at present. (Italics added) (FF 97)

DICTATORSHIPS

What happens when dictatorships are ideological?

History has known many dogmatic dictatorships, and their record is not encouraging.

The medieval Church which, though nominally founded upon a religion of love, endeavored to enforce its tenets by means of the Inquisition.

Cromwell's rule of the Saints was in many ways similar to Lenin's system, beginning with advocacy of democracy and freedom, it ended by establishing a hated military tyranny.

The French Revolution, starting from the Rights of Man, produced first Robespierre and then Napoleon, neither of whom had any noticeable respect for human rights.

In all these cases, the trouble came from dogmatic belief in a panacea so splendid that any cruelty was thought permissible in bringing about the desired end. (Italics added) (DMMM 50)

Is the successor to a founding dictator the same kind of man?

When once a dictatorship has been established, the qualities by which a man succeeds a dead dictator are totaly different from those by which the dictatorship was originally created.

Wire-pulling, intrigue, and Court favor are the most important methods when heredity is discarded.

For this reason, a dictatorship is sure to change its character very considerably after the death of its founder.

And since the qualities by which a man succeeds to a dictatorship are less generally impressive than those by which the regime was created, there is a likelihood of instability, palace revolutions, and ultimate reversion to some different system.

It is hoped, however, [by the successor] that modern methods of propaganda may successfully counteract this tendency, by creating popularity for the Head of the State without the need for any display of popular qualities on his part.

How far such methods can succeed it is as yet impossible to say. (P 48)

DOGMATISM

How is dogmatism a threat to social liberty?

Social liberty is intimately bound up with certain intellectual virtues.

It can hardly exist in a world where large groups of people feel dogmatic certainty about matters which are theoretically doubtful.

It is the nature of the human animal to believe not only things for which there is evidence, but also very many things for which there is no evidence whatever.

And it is the things for which there is no evidence that are believed with passion.

Nobody feels any passion about the multiplication table or about the existence of Cape Horn, because these matters are not doubtful.

But in matters of theology or political theory, where a rational man will hold that at best there is a slight balance of probability on one side or the other, people argue with passion and support their opinions by physical slavery imposed by armies and mental slavery imposed by schools.

So accustomed do people become to feeling certain where they ought to feel doubtful that they become incapable of acting on a probability.

If you come to a fork in the road at a point where there is no signpost and no passer-by of whom to inquire, and if you have no map to tell you which is the right road, you will, if you are rational, choose one of the two roads at haphazard, but inquire as you come upon anybody likely to know.

If, on the other hand, you have lived always in a dogmatic atmosphere, you will either stay still in hopeless bewilderment, or, if you choose at haphazard, you will become dogmatically convinced that you have chosen rightly and will never stop to inquire when opportunity occurs. (FF 75)

ECONOMICS

Can economic history throw light on earlier times?

Economic history was studied hardly at all in ancient or medieval times so that the facts are often hard to ascertain.

It has, however, as compared to older kinds of history, the merit of concentrating on the common man as opposed to the exceptional individual.

Did the Egyptian peasant at the time when the pyramids were being built get enough to eat?

How intolerable was the lot of slaves in Roman times?

Who was exploited to supply the income that enabled Plato to be bland?

What went wrong with the economic structure of the Roman Empire at the end of the second century?

How well off was the average inhabitant of a prosperous commercial city in the Middle Ages?

Was the lot of the agricultural laborer under a pre-industrial aristocratic regime better or worse than that of a factory worker in the early stages of industrialism?

Such questions are interesting, and economic history supplies at least hints as to the answers. (UH 30)

What are the stereotypes in economic history?

The economic historians, it must be said, are somewhat addicted to stereotypes.

Almost any book of economic history, no matter what the region and the period dealt with, will contain some pages of lamentation to the following effect:

> At this period the ancient yeomanry was sinking into decay; the land was mortgaged to rapacious urban money lenders, to whom the cultivators of the soil became actually or virtually enslaved. The old aristocracy, which, for all its faults, had had some sense of public responsibility, was being replaced by a new plutocracy, ignorant of agricultural needs, and anxious only to extract the maximum of revenue in the shortest possible time. Ruined and dispossessed yeomen flocked into the cities, where they became an element of proletarian unrest, and apt material for the machinations of demagogues. The old simple pieties decayed, to be replaced by skepticism and violence.

You will find this, or something like it, in accounts of Greece at any time from that of Hesiod onwards; again in descriptions of Italy after the Punic Wars; again in accounts of England under the Tudors.

In our day writers are more diffuse; the corresponding account of California fills two long books, *Grapes of Wrath* and Norris' *Octopus.*

What the historians say is no doubt true in the main as regards the evils of their own period, but it is often mistaken in supposing other periods to have been better.

This point of view is in part a product of specialization. A man who knows much about a certain period, and little about the immediately preceding period, imagines—partly because of a well established literary convention—that the evils he observes in the period with which he is familiar were new.

In fact, agriculturists have at all times been liable to fall into debt, as a result of optimism and bad harvests.

The men who can lend money during a famine are likely to be urban, since otherwise they also would be poor.

Aristocracies have at all times been addicted to certain vices, such as gambling, fighting, and overbuilding, which have compelled them to part with their land to new men.

The old simple pieties were never so simple or so pious as historians pretend.

Throughout the Middle Ages, barons and eminent ecclesiastics borrowed from Jews, and when they could no longer pay the interest, they instituted a pogrom.

At the beginning of the modern age, capital became largely Christian, and therefore pogroms of capitalists were no longer tolerated.

To describe this change as a decay of the "old simple pieties" is somewhat misleading.

It had, however, the important effect of causing abandonment of the condemnation of "usury" (i.e., interest), a condemnation which, though supported by the authority of Aristotle, ceased to be effective as soon as creditors were no longer mainly Jews. (UH 31)

EDUCATION

"To know how to command, first learn to obey." Is this good advice?

We believe a boy ought to show spirit and should on occasion have the pluck to defy the authorities and take the consequences.

At any rate, this is the belief where the sons of the well-to-do are concerned; courage in wage earners is less admired by the authorities.

The adult world is growing less and less suitable to the qualities of the "bad" boy.

Nelson was a bad boy to the end of his days; so was Julius Caesar.

But nowadays almost every young man has to begin with a very subordinate post in some vast organization.

His superiors seldom have the tolerance of the experienced schoolmaster and are likely to give promotion to the "good" boy.

Unfortunately docility is not a quality which is often found in the man capable of initiative or leadership.

Some fool, long ago—probably a Roman—said that to know how to command, a man must first learn how to obey. This is the opposite of the truth.

The man who has learned to obey will either have lost all personal initiative or will have become so filled with rage against the authorities that his initiative will have become destructive and cruel. (MAO 41)

What attitude toward the teacher should students avoid?

Passive acceptance of the teacher's wisdom is easy to most boys and girls.

It involves no effort of independent thought, and seems rational because the teacher knows more than his pupils; it is moreover the way to win favor with the teacher unless he is a very exceptional man.

Yet the habit of passive acceptance is a disastrous one in later life.

It causes men to seek a leader, and to accept as a leader whoever is established in that position.

It makes the power of Churches, Governments, party caucuses, and all the other organizations by which plain men are misled into supporting old systems which are harmful to the nation and to themselves. (PSR 113)

What are possible goals of education?

Before considering how to educate, it is well to be clear as to the sort of result which we wish to achieve.

Dr. Arnold wanted "humbleness of mind," a quality not possessed by Aristotle's "magnanimous man."

Nietzsche's ideal is not that of Christianity.

No more is Kant's, for while Christ enjoins love, Kant teaches that no action of which love is the motive can be truly virtuous.

And even people who agree as to the ingredients of a good character may differ as to their relative importance.

One man will emphasize courage, another learning, another kindliness, and another rectitude.

One man, like the elder Brutus, will put duty to the State above family affection; another, like Confucius, will put family affection first.

All these divergences will produce differences as to education.

We must have some conception of the kind of person we wish to produce, before we can have any definite opinion as to the education which we consider best. (EGL 47)

What should a liberal education instill?

This is the task of a liberal education: to give a sense of the value of things other than domination, to help to create wise citizens of a free community, and through the combination of citizenship with liberty in individual creativeness, to enable men to give to human life that splendor which some few have shown that it can achieve. (P 319)

How could education work to lessen prejudices?

It ought to be the aim of education to produce open-mindedness and a willingness to listen to arguments without growing angry because they tend to conclusions that we dislike.

Wherever there are mass prejudices, whether of nationalism or of race or of religious bigotry, the schools ought to set themselves consciously to the softening of such prejudices.

I would have the schools in India teach the virtues of Mohammedans, and the schools in Pakistan teach the virtues of Hindus.

I would have Zionists taught the merits of Arabs, and Arabs taught the merits of Jews.

I would have the West taught that even Russians are human beings, and the Russians taught that not all Westerners are lackeys of capitalism.

All such large collective prejudices are harmful.

It is they that make war seem not a destructive madness.

It is they that cause comparatively decent people to acquiesce in persecution.

It is they that inhibit the impulses of humanity.

It is they that make it seem practical and reasonable to organize vast communities for purposes of mutual homicide rather than for cooperation in the common tasks of mankind.

All this would be different if the schools were different, but the schools will not be different until the governments are different, and the governments, I fear, will not be different until by touching the very depths of misery, mankind have learnt the folly of their present divisions. (FF 71)

What should schools not teach?

Education is not at present designed with a view to eliminating prejudice.

Large-scale education is conducted, as a rule, by either a state or a church.

In the former case, it teaches nationalism; in the latter case, bigotry.

In the present state of the world, nationalism is the greater danger.

Schoolchildren are taught to reverence the national flag, and by the time they leave school, they have become incapable of realizing what worship of the national flag means.

The national flag symbolizes belief in the superior excellence of one geographical group.

If the geographical group is large enough, the schoolchildren will be expected to consider that it is justified in putting members of other groups to death whenever they interfere with its desires.

The justification is derived from the preeminent merit of the group to which the schoolchild belongs.

And this preeminent merit is taught so persuasively and hypnotically that at the end of the school years hardly any child is able to question it.

You may reply, "But at any rate, so far as my country is concerned, the belief is true. My country is immeasurably better than any other. It has always stood for . . ." And then will follow a long list of virtues.

Let it be granted, dear reader, that in the case of your country, there is not a word to be said against the claims of nationalism.

It then follows logically that in all other countries the doctrines of nationalism are unjustified, and even if you belong to the largest country in the world, other countries comprise the immense majority of mankind.

The teaching of nationalism in schools is therefore far more frequently a teaching of lies than a teaching of truth.

You know, of course, that in your own country, it is a teaching of truth, and therefore, if it is the purpose of education to teach truth, schoolchildren in all other countries should be taught to salute *your* flag. (FF 73)

Should schoolchildren be exposed to Shakespeare's plays?

To study things either because you must or because you wish to be cultured makes it almost impossible to acquire what they have to offer.

Shakespeare wrote with a view to causing delight, and if you have any feeling for poetry, he will delight you.

But if he doesn't, you had better leave him alone.

It is a dismal thing to inflict him on schoolchildren until they hate the sound of his name; it is an insult to him and an injury to them.

The *opportunity* to enjoy him should be offered to them, and will frequently be successful if it takes the shape of performing a play; but those to whom he is merely a bore should be allowed to occupy their time in some other way. (UH 10)

What harm is done by doctrinaire teaching?

The habit of teaching some one orthodoxy, political, religious or moral, has all kinds of bad effects.

To begin with, it excludes from the teaching profession men who combine honesty with intellectual vigor, who are just the men likely to have the best moral and mental effect upon their pupils.

I will give three illustrations.

First, as to politics, a teacher of economics in America is expected to teach such doctrines as will add to the wealth and power of the very rich; if he does not, he finds it advisable to go elsewhere, like Mr. Laski, formerly of Harvard, now one of the most valuable teachers in the London School of Economics.

Second, as to religion, the immense majority of intellectually eminent men disbelieve in Christian religion, but they conceal the fact in public, because they are afraid of losing their incomes.

Thus on the most important of all subjects most of the men whose opinion and arguments would be best worth having are condemned to silence.

Third, as to morals, practically all men are unchaste at some time of their lives; clearly those who conceal this fact are worse than those who do not, since they add the guilt of hypocrisy.

But it is only to the hypocrites that teaching posts are open.

So much for the effect of orthodoxy upon the choice and character of teachers. (SE 202)

How should history be taught?

In the teaching of history as opposed to literature, a smattering can be of great utility.

For those who are not going to be professional historians, the sort of thing that in America is called a survey course can, if it is rightly done, give a valuable sense of the larger process within which things that are near and familiar take place.

Such a course should deal with the history of man, not with the history of this or that country, least of all one's own.

It should begin with the oldest facts known through anthropology and archeology, and should give a sense of the gradual emergence of those things in human life which give man such a place in our respect as he may deserve.

It should not present as the world's heroes those who have slaughtered the greatest number of "enemies," but rather those who have been most notable in adding to the world's capital of knowledge and beauty and wisdom.

It should show the strange resurgent power of what is valuable in human life, defeated time and again by savagery and hate and destruction, but nevertheless, at the very first possible opportunity, emerging again like grass in the desert after rain.

It should, while youth leaves hopes and desires still plastic, fix those hopes and desires not upon victory over other human beings, but upon victory over those forces which have hitherto filled the life of man with suffering and sorrow—I mean the forces of nature reluctant to yield her fruits, the forces of militant ignorance, the forces of hate, and the deep slavery to fear which is our heritage from the original helplessness of mankind.

All this a survey of history should give and can give.

All this, if it enters into the daily texture of men's thoughts, will make them less harsh and less mad. (FF 163)

Does discipline belong in progressive education?

I am not a believer in complete freedom during childhood.

I think children need a fixed routine, though there should be days when it is not carried out.

I think also that, if a person when adult is to be able to fit into a society, he must learn while still young that he is not the center of the universe and that his wishes are not often the most important factor in a situation.

I think also that the encouragement of originality without technical skill, which is practised in many progressive schools, is a mistake.

There are some things that I like very much in progressive education, especially freedom of speech, and freedom to explore the facts of life, and the absence of a silly kind of morality which is more shocked by the utterance of a swear-word than by an unkind action.

But I think that those who have rebelled against an unwise discipline have often gone too far in forgetting that some discipline is necessary.

This applies more especially to the acquisition of knowledge. (PFM 14)

What attitude toward new knowledge should be fostered?

Neither acquiescence in skepticism nor acquiescence in dogma is what education should produce.

It should produce a belief that knowledge is attainable in a measure, though with difficulty; that much of what passes for knowledge at any given time is likely to be more or less mistaken, but that the mistakes can be rectified by care and industry. (WW 24)

What should good university teachers convey to their students?

They should exemplify the value of intellect and of the search for knowledge.

They should make it clear that what at any time passes for knowledge may, in fact, be erroneous.

They should inculcate an undogmatic temper, a temper of continual search and not of comfortable certainty.

They should try to create an awareness of the world as a whole, and not only of what is near in space and time.

Through the recognition of the likelihood of error, they should make clear the importance of tolerance.

They should remind the student that those whom posterity honors have very often been unpopular in their own day and that, on this ground, social courage is a virtue of supreme importance.

Above all, every educator who is engaged in an attempt to make the best of the students to whom he speaks must regard himself as the servant of truth and not of this or that political or sectarian interest.

Truth is a shining goddess, always veiled, always distant, never wholly approachable, but worthy of all the devotion of which the human spirit is capable. (FF 173)

What's wrong with authoritative education?

"The greatest disadvantage of an authoritarian education," says Adler,* "lies in the fact that it gives the child an ideal of power, and shows him the pleasures which are connected with the possession of power."

Authoritative education, we may add, produces the slave type as well as the despotic type, since it leads to the feeling that the only possible relation between two human beings is that in which one issues orders and the other obeys them. (P 17)

What should be taught along with science?

A dictatorship of men of science would very soon become horrible.

Skill without wisdom may be purely destructive, and would be very likely to prove so.

For this reason, if for no other, it is of great importance that those who receive a scientific education should not be *merely* scientific, but should have some understanding of that kind of wisdom which, if it can be imparted at all, can only be imparted by the cultural side of education.

Science enables us to know the means to any chosen end, but it does not help us to decide what ends we shall pursue.

---

*ALFRED ADLER (1870–1937). Viennese psychologist, psychiatrist, and author of several books. Disagreed with Freud on role of sex, substituting his own theory of inferiority complex. (Ed.)

If you wish to exterminate the human race, it will show you how to do it.

If you wish to make the human race so numerous that all are on the very verge of starvation, it will show you how to do that.

If you wish to secure adequate prosperity for the whole human race, science will tell you what you must do.

But it will not tell you whether one of these ends is more desirable than another.

Nor will it give you that instinctive understanding of human beings that is necessary if your measures are not to arouse fierce opposition which only ferocious tyranny can quell.

It cannot teach you patience, it cannot teach you sympathy, it cannot teach you a sense of human destiny.

These things, in so far as they can be taught in formal education, are most likely to emerge from the learning of history and great literature. (FF 162)

What's the difference between truth and truthfulness?

Truth is for the gods; from our human point of view it is an ideal toward which we can approximate, but which we cannot hope to reach.

Education should fit us for the nearest possible approach to truth, and to do this it must teach truthfulness.

Truthfulness, as I mean it, is the habit of forming our opinions on the evidence, and holding them with that degree of conviction which the evidence warrants.

The degree will always fall short of complete certainty, and therefore we must always be ready to admit new evidence against previous beliefs.

Moreover, when we act on a belief, we must, if possible, only take such action as will be useful even if our belief is more or less inaccurate; we should avoid actions which are disastrous unless our belief is *exactly* true.

In science, an observer states his result along with the "probable error"; but who ever heard of a theologian or a politician stating the probable error of his dogmas, or even admitting that any error is conceivable?

That is because in science, where we approach nearest to real knowledge, a man can safely rely on the strength of his case, whereas, where nothing is known, blatant assertion and hypnotism are the usual ways of causing others to share our beliefs.

If the fundamentalists thought they had a good case against evolution, they would not make the teaching of it illegal [1928]. (SE 201)

What's the connection between education and war?

The reasons which have induced civilized countries to adopt universal education are various.

There were enthusiasts for enlightenment who saw no limits to the good that could be done by instruction.

Then there were practical men who realized that a modern state and modern processes of production and distribution cannot easily be managed if a large proportion of the population cannot read.

A third group were those who advocated education as a democratic right.

There was a fourth group, more silent and less open, which saw the possibilities of education from the point of view of official propaganda.

The importance of education in this regard is very great.

In the eighteenth century, most wars were unpopular; but since men have been able to read the newspapers, almost all wars have been popular.

This is only one instance of the hold on public opinion which authority has acquired through education. (Italics added) (FF 168)

ETHICS

What's wrong with Christian ethics?

The fundamental defect of Christian ethics consists in the fact that it labels certain classes of acts "sins" and others "virtue" on grounds that have nothing to do with their social consequences.

An ethic not derived from superstition must decide first upon the kind of social effects which it desires to achieve and the kind which it desires to avoid.

It must then decide, as far as our knowledge permits, what acts will promote the desired consequences; these acts it will praise, while those having a contrary tendency it will condemn. (EMW 110)

How may politics be related to ethics?

It's very difficult to separate ethics altogether from politics.

Ethics, it seems to me, arise in this way: a man is inclined to do something that benefits him and harms his neighbors.

If it harms a good many of his neighbors, they will combine together and say, "Look here, we don't like this sort of thing, and we'll see to it that it doesn't benefit the man," and that leads to the criminal law, which is perfectly rational. (SHM 53)

Does might make right? What does history say?

The power conferred by military conquest often ceases, after a longer or shorter period of time, to be merely military.

All the provinces conquered by the Romans, except Judea, soon became loyal subjects of the Empire, and ceased to feel any desire for independence.

In Asia and Africa the Christian countries conquered by the Mohammedans submitted with little reluctance to their new rulers.

Wales gradually acquiesced in English rule, though Ireland did not.

After the Albigensian heretics had been overcome by military force, their descendents submitted inwardly as well as outwardly to the authority of the Church.

The Norman Conquest produced, in England, a royal family which, after a time, was thought to possess a Divine Right to the throne.

Military conquest is stable only when it is followed by psychological conquest, *but the cases in which this has occurred are very numerous.* (Italics added) (P 84)

Can science contribute to ethics?

It is not the province of science to decide on the ends of life.

Science can show that an ethic is unscientific, in the sense that it does not minister to any desired end.

Science can also show how to bring the interest of the individual into harmony with that of society.

We make laws against theft, in order that theft may become contrary to self-interest.

We might, on the same ground, make laws to diminish the number of imbecile children born into the world.

There is no evidence that existing marriage laws, particularly where they are very strict, serve any social purpose; in this sense we may say that they are unscientific.

But to proclaim the ends of life, and make men conscious of their value, is not the business of science; it is the business of the mystic, the artist, and the poet. (BW 349)

What was the effect of Christianity on the status of women?

The Christian ethics inevitably, through the emphasis laid upon sexual virtue, did a great deal to degrade the position of women.

Since the moralists were men, woman appeared as the temptress; if they had been women, man would have had this role.

Since woman was the temptress, it was desirable to curtail her opportunities for leading men into temptation; consequently respectable women were more and more hedged about with restrictions, while the women who were not respectable, being regarded as sinful, were treated with the utmost contumely.

It is only in quite modern times that women have regained the degree of freedom which they enjoyed in the Roman Empire.

The patriarchal system, as we saw, did much to enslave women, but a great deal of this was undone just before the rise of Christianity. After Constantine [who made Christianity the official religion of the Roman Empire], women's freedom was again curtailed under the pretense of protecting them from sin.

It is only with the decay of the notion of sin in modern times that women have begun to regain their freedom.

The writings of the Fathers are full of invectives against Woman.

Woman was represented as the door of Hell, as the mother of all human ills. She should be ashamed at the very thought that she is a woman. (Lecky, *History of European Morals,* vol. II, p. 357)

The laws of property and inheritance were altered in the same sense against women, and it was only through the freethinkers of the French Revolution that daughters recovered their rights of inheritance. (MM 41)

Is Life influenced by Ethics? Do our ethical beliefs affect our actions?

It is difficult to agree with Dr. Schweitzer in the importance which he attaches to ethical opinions as a cause.

If all the professors of ethics in all the universities of the world had taught his ethical system throughout the last one hundred years, I doubt whether one line of the Versailles Treaty would have been different from what it is.

It is true that the ethical opinions of the average man have altered during the last century, but they have altered as a result of machinery, not of academic theory, and they have altered so as to justify what the average man was going to do in any case.

Speaking causally, our ethics are an effect of our actions, not vice versa; instead of practicing what we preach, we find it more conveninent to preach what we practice.

When our practice leads us to disaster we tend to alter it, and at the same time to alter our ethics; but the alteration of our ethics is not the cause of our alteration of our practice.

Experience of pain affects the behavior of infants and animals, although they have no morals; it affects the behavior of adult human beings in the same way, but the change is accompanied by ethical reflections which we falsely imagine to be its cause.

Dr. Schweitzer's book [*The Philosophy of Civilizations, Part II,* translated by John Naish] is an example of such reflections, but neither it nor its academic predecessors seem to the present reviewer to have that importance in molding events which the author attributes to them. (*The Dial,* April 1924, pp. 353–56)

EVILS

What kinds of evils are there, and how may they be classed?

When we consider the evils in the lives we know of, we find that they may be roughly divided into three classes.

There are, first, those due to physical nature: among these are death, pain, and the difficulty of making the soil yield a subsistence.

These we will call "physical evils."

Second, we may put those that spring from defects in the character or aptitudes of the sufferer: among these are ignorance, lack of will, and violent passions.

These we will call "evils of character."

Third come those that depend upon the power of one individual or group over another: these comprise not only obvious tyranny, but all interference with free development, whether by force or by excessive mental influence such as may occur in education.

These we will call "evils of power."

A social system may be judged by its bearing upon these three kinds of evils.

The three sorts of evils are intertwined.

Nevertheless, broadly speaking, we may distinguish among our misfortunes those which have their proximate cause in the material world, those which are mainly due to defects in ourselves, and those which spring from our being subject to the control of others. (SPBR 134)

EXCELLENCE

How can human excellence be made universal?

When I examine my own conception of human excellence, I find that, doubtless owing to early environment, it contains many elements which have hitherto been associated with aristocracy, such as fearlessness, independence of judgment, emancipation from the herd, and leisurely culture.

Is it possible to preserve these qualities, and even make them widespread, in an industrial community?

And is it possible to dissociate them from the typical aristocratic vices: limitation of sympathy, haughtiness, and cruelty to those outside a charmed circle?

These bad qualities could not exist in a community in which the aristocratic virtues were universal.

But that could only be achieved through economic security and leisure, which are the two sources of what is good in aristocracies.

It has at last become technically possible, through the progress of machinery and the consequent increased productivity of labor, to create a society in which every man and woman has economic security and sufficient leisure—for complete leisure is neither necessary nor desirable.

But although the technical possibility exists, there are formidable political and psychological obstacles.

It would be necessary to the creation of such a society to secure three conditions: first, a more even distribution of the produce of labor; second, security against large-scale wars; and third, a population which is stationary or very nearly so.

Until these conditions are secured, industrialism will continue to be used feverishly, to increase the wealth of the richest individuals, the territory of the greatest empires, and the population of the most populous nations, no one of which is of the slightest benefit to mankind.

These three considerations have inspired what I have written and said on political and social questions since the outbreak of the war [World War I], and more particularly since my visits to Russia and China. (SPBR xv)

FAITH

What is faith?

We may define "faith" as a firm belief in something for which there is no evidence.

We do not speak of faith that two and two are four or that the earth is round. We only speak of faith when we wish to substitute emotion [feelings] for evidence.

The substitution of emotion for evidence is apt to lead to strife, since different groups substitute different emotions.

Christians have faith in the resurrection, Communists have faith in Marx's theory of value.

Neither faith can be defended rationally, and each is therefore defended by propaganda and, if necessary, by war.

The two are equal in this respect.

If you think it immensely important that people should believe something which cannot be rationally defended, it makes no difference what the something is.

Where you control the government, you teach the something to the immature minds of young children and you burn or prohibit books which teach the contrary.

When you do not control the government, you will, if you are strong enough, build up armed forces with a view to conquest.

All this is an inevitable consequence of any strongly held faith unless, like the Quakers, you are content to remain forever a tiny minority. (RGR 283)

What's the harm in having faith?

There is a very widespread belief that people can be induced to believe in what is contrary to fact in one domain while remaining scientific in another.

This is not the case.

It is by no means easy to keep one's mind open to fresh evidence, and it is almost impossible to achieve this in one direction if, in another, one has a carefully fostered blindness. (RGR 286)

Aren't people entitled to feel proud of their faith, as many do?

There is something feeble, and a little contemptible, about a man who cannot face the perils of life without the help of comfortable myths. (RGR 286)

FAME

Who deserves fame, and who gets it?

In Locke's theory of government, there is little that is original.

In this Locke resembles most of the men who have won fame for their ideas.

As a rule, the man who first thinks of a new idea is so much ahead of his time that everyone thinks him silly, so that he remains obscure and is soon forgotten.

Then, gradually, the world becomes ready for the idea, and the man who proclaims it at the fortunate moment gets all the credit.

So it was, for example, with Darwin; poor Lord Monboddo* was a laughingstock. (HWP 624)

FANATICISM ✓

How to define fanaticism?

A man is a fanatic if he thinks one matter is so overwhelmingly important that it outweighs anything else at all.

To take an example, I suppose all decent people dislike cruelty to dogs; but if you thought that cruelty to dogs was so atrocious that no other cruelty should be objected to in comparison, then you would be a fanatic. (SHM 117)

✓*Why is the problem of fanaticism so very important?*

Because a very great part of the evils that the world is suffering is due to fanaticism. (SHM 120)

When will the waves of fanaticism die down?

They only die down when the world is in a fairly stable condition.

As long as it is in a very unstable condition you have conditions which foster fanaticism, so I think you have got to try to establish some sort of stability in the world.

I think it depends on politics.

I think that if we had a system where the danger of world war was not very great, there would be a very rapid growth of toleration and reasonableness both in the East and in the West.

But I think as long as this tension exists, it is very difficult. (SHM 123)

Is East-versus-West fanaticism more deadly than medieval religious fanaticism?

The difference is one of scope.

The Roman Catholic Church was not worldwide.

There were many people it couldn't catch: but the H-Bomb could catch everybody.

I think that the East-West tension which is threatening us all in the most terrible fashion is mainly due to fanatical belief in Communism or anti-Communism, as the case may be.

Both sides believe their creed too strongly; the prevention of what they regard as wicked on the other side is more important even than the continued existence of the human race—and that is fanatical. (SHM 121)

FOOD

What does a higher output of food make possible?

The specially human activities which distinguish man from other animals all depend upon the lessening of his bondage to physical nature.

So long as he had to spend all his time in food-gathering, he could not devote much of his energy to war or politics or theology or science.

These things are offshoots of the productivity of labor; they depend upon the excess of one man's production over one man's consumption of food.

The greater this excess becomes, the more possible it becomes for a man to devote himself to politics and war and culture and such luxuries. (NHCW 21)

FORCE

Can anything good be said about the rule of force?

Although the rule of force is not a thing to be admired, and although one must be glad when it is replaced by something gentler and less unjust, it has nevertheless had a useful part to play in the development of social institutions.

Government is a difficult art, and submission to government is difficult except as submission to force.

In the formation of communities, governments imposed by force have played a part which seems to have been essential.

Most English people at the present day submit to their government because they realize that the alternative would be disastrous anarchy and chaos.

But there were long ages during which people preferred anarchy and chaos, if they could get it.

There were long wars beween kings and barons in which, fortunately, the barons extirpated each other.

In the end the king emerged victorious; people obeyed him because he could compel obedience.

And so the kingdom acquired unity and the habit of obeying the law.

When in the course of time the kingly power was curbed, it was curbed not by a revival of anarchy, but by new forms of government.

It may be doubted, however, whether a single stable government of the whole realm could ever have been achieved, except by passing through the stage of royal power. (NHCW 70)

FREE SPEECH

Why is the free expression of opinion desirable?

The fundamental argument for freedom of opinion is the doubtfulness of all our beliefs.

If we certainly knew the truth, there would be something to be said for teaching it.

But in that case it could be taught without invoking authority, by means of its inherent reasonableness.

It is not necessary to make a law that no one should be allowed to teach arithmetic if he holds heretical opinions on the multiplication table, because here the truth is clear, and does not require to be enforced by penalties.

When the State intervenes to ensure the teaching of some doctrine, it does so *because* there is no conclusive evidence in favor of that doctrine.

The result is that the teaching is not truthful, even if it should happen to be true.

In the State of New York, it was till lately illegal to teach that Communism is good; in Soviet Russia, it is illegal to teach that Communism is bad.

No doubt one of these opinions is true and one is false, but no one knows which.

Either New York or Soviet Russia was teaching truth and proscribing falsehood, but neither was teaching truthfully, because each was representing a doubtful proposition as certain. (SE 200)

What becomes of communities that suppress free speech?

Mental freedom, although primarily important only to the minority, is in the long run immensely valuable to the whole community.

Mental freedom from a public point of view has two branches: on the one hand, a man should not suffer for holding or proclaiming opinions other than those of the government; on the other hand, education should not be such as to make its victim incapable of ever thinking an original thought.

Any state that despises freedom of thought can secure results if it so desires.

There will be no limit whatever to the possibilities in the way of exploitation of the majority by the governing minority.

There will be no need to punish new ideas, because there will be no new ideas to punish.

A nation so enslaved may show for a time a monolithic strength, but will inevitably before very long be outstripped by the nations that have retained intellectual initiative and a capacity for scientific progress —if, that is, any such nations remain. (FF 60)

The modern revolt against democracy on the part of certain sections of Left opinion is necessarily, whether by intention or not, antiscientific.

Marx laid it down that the interests of wage earners were in some mysterious way bound up with materialism.

As a philosophy, modern physics makes materialism very unplausible; therefore, modern physics is a bourgeois invention.

But modern physics had led to the atomic bomb, which cannot be ignored, therefore, some theological subtlety has to be invented to reconcile quantum theory with dialectical materialism.

In the long run, however, this sort of thing produces a time lag, just as the condemnation of Galileo by the Inquisition caused astronomy to flourish mainly in Protestant countries.

Any despotic and dictatorial system, though it may at first be abreast of scientific opinion, is sure to fall increasingly behind as time goes on; and as it falls behind, the result will be disastrous, not only in theory, but in technique.

It is only in an atmosphere of freedom that progress can long be maintained, even in such matters as military technique which governments are most anxious to promote.

New opinions are almost always distasteful to the authorities, but where they are suppressed, communities ossify.

I should, therefore, confidently expect that the countries which preserve scientific and intellectual freedom will be more efficient in war than those which submit to dictatorship. (FF 117)

What has been the history of free inquiry over the years?

The love of free inquiry and free speculation has never been common.

When it has existed, it has existed in only a tiny minority and has always roused furious hatred and opposition in the majority.

There have been times when it has seemed wholly extinct, but over and over again it has revived.

Although the life that it inspires is arduous and dangerous, the impulse which leads some men to adopt it has been so overwhelming that they have braved all the obloquy to which they were exposed by devoting themselves to the greatest service that man can do to man.

It is this indominable quality of the human mind at its best that gives hope for mankind, and that causes me in spite of the unprecedented dangers of our age to believe that the human race will emerge as it has emerged from other dark times, with renewed vigor and with a more confident and triumphant hope of overcoming not only the hostile forces of nature but also the black nightmares inspired by atavistic fears which have caused men, and still cause them, to create and endure great worlds of sorrow and suffering for which there is no longer any reason except in human folly.

We know as never before the road to a happy world.

We have only to choose this road to lead our tortured species into a land of light and joy. (FF 41)

How did Milton state the case for free speech?

Above all, I admired *Areopagitica*. I treasured such sentences as, "As good almost kill a man as kill a good book, who kills a man kills a reasonable creature, God's image; but he who destroys a good book, kills reason itself."

This was an inspiring sentiment for an intending writer who devoutly hoped that his books would be "good books."

And more especially, encouraging to a budding philosopher was the statement, "Where there is much desire to learn, there of necessity will be much arguing, much writing, many opinions; for opinion in good men is but knowledge in the making."

This might almost be taken as the sacred text for free speech and free discussion.

"Opinion in good men is but knowledge in the making," says in a few words what is essential for the condemnation of censorship.

Alas, I did not know in those days that to cure Milton of opposing censorship, they made him a censor.

This is the almost invariable logic of revolutions, while in the making, they praise liberty; but when successful, they establish tyranny. (FF 34)

In what way, at present, is freedom of the press inadequate?

It is an essential element in democracy that any member of the public should be able, without too much trouble, to find out the truth when there is a dispute as to facts.

It is generally recognized in the West that this demands freedom of the press.

The authorities must not be at liberty to suppress information merely because they do not like it.

But freedom of the press, though necessary, is not sufficient.

There must be quick methods of correcting gross misstatements.

For this purpose the machinery of libel actions is quite inadequate, partly because it is slow, partly because it is expensive, and partly because there are cases where it is inapplicable.

Suppose, for example, that a Right Wing Republican in the United States were to say that many prominent Democratic statesmen are in the pay of the Kremlin.

No action would lie so long as he named no names.

There ought to be a judicial body with the right and duty to pronounce on any statement injurious to a man or organization; and, in the event of there being no *prima facie* case for the statement, the journal making the statement should be under legal obligation to print this fact with the same prominence as the original statement.

This is important, for, while freedom of information is essential, freedom to correct misinformation is equally essential. (FF 104)

Why is free speech important not only to intellectuals?

It has been customary in recent decades, among certain persons who profess to have the interests of the wage earners at heart, to sneer at intellectual freedom as a matter concerning a small minority of highbrows, who can be liquidated without serious loss to anybody but themselves.

This point of view shows an equal ignorance of history and of human nature: where free discussion is prohibited, it is not only intellectuals who suffer, but all except those who regulate official propaganda.

Consider, for example, the rise of women to equality with men.

The movement for women's equality had its origin, it is true, among a few intellectuals, mostly male, but at first the majority of women were as shocked by it as men were.

If free discussion and free speech had been prohibited, the movement could never have made any progress; women's earnings would still belong to their husbands, and men would still have the right to beat their wives with a stick no thicker than their thumb.

The change in these respects is not one by which only intellectuals profit.

Or take again the rise of trade unionism: this would have been quite impossible but for the liberal atmosphere of free discussion which hampered the activities of those who wished unions to remain illegal.

Free publicity is by far the best safeguard against arbitrary injustice, as well as against ancient and traditional folly. (FF 116)

FREEDOM

What is freedom? How to describe it?

In its most elementary sense, freedom means the absence ot external control over the acts of individuals or groups.

It is thus a negative conception, and freedom alone will not confer any high value upon a community.

The Eskimos, for example, can dispense with government, with compulsory education, with traffic regulations, and with the incredible complications of company law.

Their life, therefore, has a very high degree of freedom, but nevertheless few civilized men would prefer it to life in a more organized community.

Freedom is a requisite for many kinds of good things, but the good things have to come from the impulses, desires, and beliefs of those who enjoy the freedom.

Great poets confer luster upon a community, but one cannot be sure that a community will produce great poetry merely because there is no law against it.

We think it right to compel the young to learn reading and writing, though most of them would much rather not.

This is because we believe in positive goods which only literacy makes possible.

But although liberty does not constitute the total of social goods, it is so necessary for most of them and so liable to be unwisely curtailed that it is scarcely possible to exaggerate its importance. (FF 51)

What kinds of freedom are there?

There are various kinds of freedom, and at least two different forms of classification of these kinds.

First, freedoms may be classified according as they are enjoyed by a nation, a group within a nation, or an individual.

And secondly, they may be classified according as they are economic, political, or mental, though this latter division can never be made very sharp.

In the eighteenth and early nineteenth centuries, it was especially national freedom that was emphasized.

When it was said that "Britons never shall be slaves," what was meant was that they should not be under the orders of foreigners.

It was not thought that the press gang, for example, interfered with freedom, or that there was any inconsistency in speaking of England as a free country at a time when men were liable to be transported for radical opinions. It may even be freedom from freedoms which is especially desirable.

When Eire acquired freedom, one of the advantages sought and obtained was extinction of the freedom to read books disliked by the Roman Catholic Church—a kind of freedom which the brutal English had insisted upon inflicting upon Ireland.

National freedom will always be energetically sought wherever it does not exist.

It is, at present, a dominant aim in North Africa and in those parts of Asia where it has not yet been achieved.

The desire for it is so vehement that there is sure to be dangerous unrest wherever one nation attempts to govern another. (FF 52)

What limits, if any, should be put on freedom?

Freedom is a principle to which there are very important limitations of which those in education are in a certain sense typical.

What people will do in given circumstances depends enormously upon their habits; and good habits are not acquired without discipline.

Most of us go through life without stealing, but many centuries of police discipline have gone into producing this abstention which now seems natural.

If children are taught nothing about manners they will snatch each others' food and the older children will get all the titbits.

In international affairs it will not be by prolonging interstate anarchy that the world will be brought back to a tolerable condition, but by the rule of international law, which will never prevail unless backed by international force.

In the economic sphere the old doctrine of *laissez faire* is not now held by any practical men, although a few dreamers still hanker after it.

As the world grows fuller, regulation grows more necessary. No doubt this is regrettable.

The world of the *Odyssey* is attractive.

One sails from island to island and always finds a lovely lady ready to receive one.

But nowadays immigration quotas interfere with this sort of life.

It was all very well for Odysseus, who was only one, but if a hundred million Chinese had descended on Calypso's island, life would have become rather difficult.

The broad rule is a simple one, that men should be free in what only concerns themselves, but that they should not be free when they are tempted to aggression against others.

But although the broad rule is simple, the carrying out of it in detail is very complex, and so the problem of the proper limitations on human freedom remains. (PFM 15)

Should there be freedom for groups that aim to destroy freedom?

Throughout the Western world, an acute question has arisen as to freedom for groups of which the purpose is to destroy freedom.

Should democracy tolerate attempts to replace it by despotism?

Should toleration extend to those who advocate intolerance?

Should freedom of the press extend to those who think a free press an abomination?

And, above all, should a nation permit the formation of powerful groups which aim at subjecting it to foreign domination?

Western nations have given a variety of answers to these questions.

Some have allowed more liberty, others less.

I do not think there is any clear principle by which such questions can be decided.

Broadly speaking, the greater the danger from such subversive groups, the more justification there is for interfering with their activities.

The danger is that frightened men will forget the general arguments in favor of liberty, and will carry suppression much further than is necessary in the interest of security.

I think that in Britain we have to a great extent avoided this danger.

I do not think that it has been avoided in the United States.

But since the matter is one in which arguments *pro* and *con* have to be balanced, it is difficult to advocate any clear-cut policy. (FF 55)

What is the status of individual freedom today?

Freedom for individuals as opposed to groups was formerly the most important part of freedom.

But in the modern world, very few individuals can have much influence except as members of organizations, and therfore the question of freedom for organizations is becoming more important than that of freedom for individuals.

In the late eighteenth century, many men believed in the Rights of Man, meaning individual man, but did not favor the rights of organizations in cases where these organizations had a purpose running contrary to that of the government or majority.

Although freedom for individuals is now relatively less important than it was in former times, it is still much more important than many people realize.

Buddhism, Christianity, and Marxism owe their origin to individuals, and no one of them could have arisen in a totalitarian state.

Galileo was ill-treated by the Inquisition, but half-heartedly as compared to modern methods. He was not put to death, his books were not burned, and his followers were not liquidated.

It is only in quite modern times, indeed only since the end of the First World War that persecution has become scientific and effective.

The harm done by persecution of individuals whose views are unpopular is that every progress, whether moral or intellectual, is at first considered shocking. For this reason, a society which cannot put up with unusual opinions necessarily becomes stereotyped and unprogressive.

Suppose, for example, that you hold that if a husband and wife hate each other, there is no great gain to mankind in perpetuating the legal tie, and divorce by mutual consent ought to be possible.

Or suppose you hold that a pregnant woman who, in the best medical opinion, is almost sure to die if her pregnancy is not interrupted, should not be forced to perish.

So long as you keep these opinions to yourself, no great harm will come to you; but if you give public expression to them, vast forces will be set in motion against you.

If you are a teacher in an American college, you will very likely not be allowed to go on teaching.

If you are a politician, you will not be elected.

If you are a journalist, only a few obscure Left Wing journals will employ you.

The forces of organized cruelty, disguised as morality, will crush you if they can.

They will not succeed if you have private means or happen to be a successful writer; but if you have neither of these pieces of good fortune, your life will become very painful.

People imagine that the battle for religious toleration has been won because we tolerate all sects that existed in the eighteenth century, but heresies which have arisen since that time may be called political, economic, and mental. (FF 56)

FREETHOUGHT

What is a freethinker?

To be worthy of the name, [a freethinker] must be free of two things, the force of tradition and the tyranny of his own passions.

No one is completely free from either.

What makes a freethinker is not his beliefs but the way in which he holds them.

If he holds them because his elders told him they were true when he was young, or if he holds them because if he did not he would be unhappy, his thought is not free; but if he holds them because, after careful thought, he finds a balance of evidence in their favor, then his thought is free, however odd his conclusions may seem.

Freedom from the tyranny of passion is as essential as freedom from the influence of tradition.

The jealous husband who suspects his wife of infidelity on inadequate grounds, and the complacent optimist, who refuses to suspect her when the evidence is overwhelming, are alike permitting passion to enslave their thought; in neither of them is thought free. (RGR 239)

GENTLEMAN

What is a "gentleman," and what produced him?

Hereditary power has given rise to our notion of a "gentleman."

This is a somewhat degenerate form of a conception which has a long history, from magic properties of chiefs, through divinity of kings, to knightly chivalry and the blue-blooded aristocrat.

The qualities that are admired, where power is hereditary, are such as result from leisure and unquestioned superiority.

Where power is aristocratic rather than monarchical, the best manners include courteous behavior towards equals as an addition to bland self-assertion in dealing with inferiors.

But whatever the prevalent conception of manners may be, it is only where power is (or lately was) hereditary that men will be judged by their manners.

The *bourgeois gentilhomme* is only laughable when he intrudes into a society of men and women who have never had anything better to do than study social niceties.

What survives in the way of admiration of the "gentleman" depends upon inherited wealth, and must rapidly disappear if economic as well as political power ceases to pass from father to son. (P 42)

Why was the gentleman held in high esteem for so long?

The gentleman has had a long inning in philosophical theory, because he is associated with Greek genius, because the virtue of contemplation acquired theological endorsement, and because the ideal of disinterested truth dignified the academic life.

The gentleman is to be defined as one of a society of equals who live on slave labor, or at any rate upon the labor of men whose inferiority is unquestioned.

It should be observed that this definition includes the saint and the sage, insofar as these men's lives are contemplative rather than active. (HWP 34)

GOD

Does God exist?

God and immortality, the central dogmas of the Christian religion, find no support in science.

It cannot be said that either doctrine is essential to religion, since neither is found in Buddhism.

But we in the West have come to think of them as the irreducible minimum of theology.

No doubt people will continue to entertain these beliefs because they are pleasant, just as it is pleasant to think ourselves virtuous and our enemies wicked.

But for my part, I cannot see any ground for either.

I do not pretend to be able to prove that there is no God.

I equally cannot prove that Satan is a fiction.

The Christian God may exist; so may the gods of Olympus, or of ancient Egypt, or of Babylon.

But no one of these hypotheses is more probable than any other: they lie outside the region of even probable knowledge, and therefore there is no reason to consider any of them. (WIB 5)

Most of us have been brought up to believe that the universe owes its existence to an all-wise and all-powerful creator, whose purposes are beneficent even in what to us may seem evil.

I do not think it is right to refuse to apply to this belief the kind of tests that we should apply to one that touches our emotions less intimately and profoundly.

Is there any evidence of the existence of such a being?

Undoubtedly belief in him is comforting and sometimes has some good moral effects on character and behavior. But this is no evidence that the belief is true. (RGR 89)

Is there evidence of an all-powerful and loving God?

There is a rather repulsive smugness and self-complacency in the argument that man is so splendid as to be evidence of infinite wisdom and infinite power in his creator.

Those who use this kind of reasoning always try to concentrate our attention on the few saints and sages; they try to make us forget the Neros and Attilas and Hitlers and the millions of mean poltroons to whom such men owed their power.

And even what is best in us is apt to lead to disaster. Religions that teach brotherly love have been used as an excuse for persecution, and our profoundest scientific insight is made into a means of mass destruction.

I can imagine a sardonic demon producing us for his amusement, but I cannot attribute to a being who is wise, beneficent, and omnipotent, the terrible weight of cruelty, suffering, and ironic degradation of what is best: that has marred the history of man in increasing measure as he has become more master of his fate. (from *The Listener,* May 29, 1947) (RGR 89)

What is the Christian attitude toward God?

The whole attitude of the Christian toward God is based on Oriental tyrannies, monarchies.

It's the attitude one took toward the King.

And it's an attitude which a modern man should consider abject and contemptible. (SP)

GOOD LIFE

What is a good rule for leading the good life?

The good life is one inspired by love and guided by knowledge. (WIB 20)

What is required in order to lead "the good life"?

To live the good life in the fullest sense a man must have a good education, friends, love, children (if he desires them), a sufficient income to keep him from want and grave anxiety, good health, and work which is not uninteresting.

All these things, in varying degree, depend upon the community, and are helped or hindered by political events.

The good life must be lived in a good society and is not fully possible otherwise. (WIB 60)

Can aristocrats achieve the good life?

Certain good things, such as art and science and friendship, can flourish very well in an aristocratic society.

They existed in Greece on a basis of slavery; they exist among ourselves on a basis of exploitation.

But love, in the form of sympathy, or benevolence, cannot exist freely in an aristocratic society.

The aristocrat has to persuade himself that the slave or proletarian or coloured man is of inferior clay, and that his sufferings do not matter.

The limitation of sympathy involved in the aristocratic ideal is its condemnation. (WIB 61)

GOVERNMENT

What makes a society hold together?

It is almost necessary that all the parties concerned should acknowledge a common loyalty to something outside all of them.

In China family businesses often succeed because of Confucian loyalty to the family; but impersonal joint stock companies are apt to prove unworkable, because no one has any compelling motive for honesty toward the other shareholders.

Where there is government by deliberation, there must, for success, be a general respect for the law, or for the nation, or for some principle which all parties respect.

A sense of solidarity sufficient to make government by discussion possible can be generated without much difficulty in a family, such as the Fuggers or Rothschilds, in a small religious body like the Quakers, in a barbarous tribe, or in a nation at war or in danger of war.

But outside pressure is all but indispensable: the members of a gang hang together for fear of hanging separately.

A common peril is much the easiest way of producing homogeneity. (P 24)

Modern loyalty to the vast groups of our time, insofar as it is strong and subjectively satisfying, makes use still of the old psychological mechanism evolved in the days of small tribes.

Congenital human nature, as opposed to what is made of it by schools and religions, by propaganda and economic organizations, has not changed much since the time when men first began to have brains of the size to which we are accustomed.

Instinctively we divide mankind into friends and foes—friends, toward whom we have the morality of co-operation; foes, toward whom we have that of competition.

But this division is constantly changing; at one moment, a man hates his business competitor; at another, when both are threatened by Socialism or by an external enemy, he suddenly begins to view him as a brother.

Always, when we pass beyond the limits of the family, it is the external enemy which supplies the cohesive force. In times of safety, we can afford to hate our neighbor, but in times of danger we must love him. People do not, at most times, love those whom they find sitting next to them in a bus, but during the blitz they did. (AI 6)

What is needed to produce national loyalty?

Social cohesion demands a creed, or a code of behavior, or a prevailing sentiment, or, best, some combination of all three; without something of the kind, a community disintegates, and becomes subject to a tyrant or a foreign conqueror.

But if this means of cohesion is to be effective, it must be deeply felt.

Loyalty to a leader, national pride, and religious fervor have proved, historically, the best means of securing cohesion; but loyalty to a leader is less permanently effective than it used to be, owing to the decay of hereditary sovereignty, and religious fervor is threatened by the spread of freethought. Thus national pride is left, and has become relatively more important than in former times. (P 157)

What dangers does Liberalism aim to cope with?

Social cohesion is a necessity, and mankind has never yet succeeded in enforcing cohesion by merely rational arguments.

Every community is exposed to two opposite dangers: ossification through too much discipline and reverence for tradition, on the one hand; on the other hand, dissolution, or subjection to foreign conquest, through the growth of an individualism and personal independence that makes co-operation impossible.

In general, important civilizations start with a rigid and superstitious system, gradually relaxed, and leading, at a certain stage, to a period of brilliant genius, while the good of the old tradition remains and the evil inherent in its dissolution has not yet developed.

But as the evil unfolds, it leads to anarchy, thence, inevitably, to a new tyranny, producing a new synthesis secured by a new system of dogma.

The doctrine of Liberalism is an attempt to escape from the endless oscillation.

The essence of Liberalism is an attempt to secure a social order not based on irrational dogma, and insuring stability without involving more restraints than are necessary for the preservation of the community.

Whether this attempt can succeed only the future can determine. (HWP xxiii)

What source of social cohesion is also a source of great danger?

A common peril is much the easiest way of producing homogeneity.

This, however, affords no solution to the problem of power in the world as a whole.

We wish to prevent the perils—e.g., war—which at present cause cohesion, but we do not wish to destroy social cooperation.

This problem is difficult psychologically as well as politically, and if we may judge by analogy, it is likely to be solved, if at all, by an initial despotism of some one nation.

Free cooperation among nations, accustomed as they are to the *liberum veto* is as difficult as among the Polish aristocracy before the partition.

Extinction, in this case as in that, is likely to be thought preferable to common sense.

Mankind needs government, but in regions where anarchy has prevailed, they will, at first, submit only to despotism.

We must therefore seek first to secure government, even though despotic, and only when government has become habitual can we hope successfully to make it democratic.

"Absolute power is useful in building the organization. More slow, but equally sure, is the development of social pressure demanding that the power shall be used for the benefit of all concerned.

"This pressure, constant in ecclesiastical and political history, is already making its appearance in the economic field." Berle and Means, *The Modern Corporation and Private Property,* p. 353. They are speaking of industrial corporations. (Italics added) (P 24)

What should we not learn from the ants and bees?

In all social animals, including Man, cooperation and the unity of a group has some foundation in instinct.

This is most complete in ants and bees, which apparently are never tempted to antisocial actions and never deviate from devotion to the nest or the hive.

Up to a point we may admire this unswerving devotion to public duty, but it has its drawbacks: ants and bees do not produce great works of art, or make scientific discoveries, or found religions teaching that all ants are sisters.

Their social life, in fact, is mechanical, precise and static.

We are willing that human life shall have an element of turbulence if thereby we can escape such evolutionary stagnation. (AI 2)

Does the power of government need curbing?

Yes, one needs the possibility of pulling up the holders of immediate power if they do wrong. That was the idea of the power of impeachment. (P 62)

Should government power be curbed by referendums?

Questions of peace and war, which are the most important of all, have to be decided quickly.

It would require a very great change in the institutions of the whole world to make the decision of peace or war one which could be taken slowly and deliberated on again.

It would be a very good thing if you could. (SHM 64)

We are very much better than totalitarian governments, for the reason that we have certain ultimate curbs on power.

But I think there ought to be some rather more immediate curb than very occasional general elections.

In the modern world, where things are so closely integrated, that is hardly enough, and we ought to have more in the way of referendums.

They'd be clumsy and slow but I think they might be better than a system in which it's possible at any moment for a government to plunge its country into utter and total disaster without consulting anybody. (SHM 68)

What deserves to be called "scientific government"?

I do not mean merely a government composed of men of science. There were many men of science in the government of Napoleon, including Laplace, who, however, proved so incompetent that he had to be dismissed in a very short time.

I should define a government as in a greater or less degree scientific in proportion as it can produce intended results, the greater the number of results that it can both intend and produce, the more scientific it is.

The framers of the American Constitution, for example, were scientific in safeguarding private property, but unscientific in attempting to introduce a system of indirect election for the presidency. The governments which made the Great War [World War I] were unscientific since they all fell during the course of it. (SO 227)

How might we get wise men to govern?

Even if we suppose that there is such a thing as "wisdom," is there any form of constitution which will give the government to the wise?

It is clear that majorities, like general councils, may err, and in fact have erred.

Aristocracies are not always wise; kings are often foolish; Popes, in spite of infallibility, have committed grievous errors.

Would anybody advocate entrusting the government to university graduates, or even to doctors of divinity?

Or to men who, having been born poor, have made a great fortune?

It is clear that no legally definable selection of citizens is likely to be wiser, in practice, than the whole body.

It might be suggested that men could be given political wisdom by suitable training.

But the question would arise, what is suitable training? And this would turn out to be a party [political] question.

The problem of finding a collection of "wise" men and leaving the government to them is thus an insoluble one. That is the ultimate reason for democracy. (HWP 107)

What's wrong with lending money to the government?

In view of the fact that the bulk of the public expenditure of most civilized governments consists in payment for past wars or preparations for future wars, the man who lends money to a government is in the same position as the bad men in Shakespeare who hire murderers.

The net result of the man's economical habits is to increase the armed forces of the state to which he lends his savings.

Obviously it would be better if he spent the money, even if he spent it in drink or gambling. (IPI 10)

GREEKS

What's the most surprising thing in all of history?

In all history, nothing is so surprising or so difficult to account for as the sudden rise of civilization in Greece.

Much of what makes civilization had already existed for thousands of years in Egypt and in Mesopotamia, and had spread thence to neighboring countries.

But certain elements had been lacking until the Greeks supplied them.

What they achieved in art and literature is familiar to everybody, but what they did in the purely intellectual realm is even more exceptional.

They invented mathematics and science and philosophy; they first wrote history as opposed to mere annals; they speculated freely about the nature of the world and the ends of life, without being bound in the fetters of any inherited orthodoxy.

What occurred was so astonishing that, until very recent times, men were content to gape and talk mystically about the Greek genius.

It is possible, however, to understand the development of Greece in scientific terms, and it is well worthwhile to do so. (HWP 3)

Why did the ancient Greeks take to philosophy?

Philosophy began among the Greeks as a revolt against religion, embodying the skepticism of men who, in the course of commerce, had been brought into contact with many beliefs and customs, and had therefore come to demand something more than tribal tradition as a basis for their own creed.

Their rationalism was, of course, imperfect; even the most freethinking among them retained the belief in Fate or cosmic justice.

But their rationality, where it existed, was more surprising than their irrationality where it survived.

They rejected the Olympian gods, they formed the conception of universal causation, and they tried to discover ways in which the existing universe could have evolved in accordance with natural laws.

For the first time in human history, Reason was proclaimed to be paramount, and everything was submitted to its scrutiny, in principle if not in fact.

Surviving prejudices survived because they were unnoticed; if anyone had pointed out that they were prejudices, the early Ionian philosophers would have abandoned them. (UH 41)

What are the good and bad results of ancient Greek thought?

They discovered mathematics and the art of deductive reasoning.

Geometry, in particular, is a Greek invention, without which modern science would have been impossible.

But in connection with mathematics, the one-sidedness of the Greek genius appears: it reasoned deductively from what appeared self-evident, not inductively from what had been observed.

Its amazing successes in the employment of this method misled not only the ancient world, but the greater part of the modern world also.

It has only been very slowly that scientific method, which seeks to reach principles inductively from observation of particular facts, has replaced the Hellenic belief in deduction from luminous axioms derived from the mind of the philosopher.

For this reason, apart from others, it is a mistake to treat the Greeks with superstitious reverence.

Scientific method, though some few among them were the first men who had an inkling of it, is, on the whole, alien to their temper of mind, and the attempt to glorify them by belittling the intellectual progress of the last four centuries has a cramping effect on modern thought. (Italics added) (HWP 39)

What happened to Greek philosophy after Democritus?

Democritus—such, at least, in my opinion—is the last of the Greek philosophers to be free from a certain fault which vitiated all later ancient and medieval thought.

All the philosophers we have been considering so far were engaged in a disinterested effort to understand the world.

They thought it easier to understand than it is, but without this optimism they would not have had the courage to make a beginning.

Their attitude, in the main, was genuinely scientific whenever it did not merely embody the prejudices of their age. But it was not *only* scientific; it was imaginative and vigorous and filled with the delight of adventure.

They were interested in everything—meteors and eclipses, fishes and whirlwinds, religion and morality; with a penetrating intellect they combined the zest of children.

From this point onwards, there are first certain seeds of decay, in spite of previously unmatched achievement, and then a gradual decadence.

What is amiss, even in the best philosophy after Democritus, is an undue emphasis on man as compared with the universe.

First comes skepticism, with the Sophists, leading to a study of *how* we know rather than an attempt to acquire fresh knowledge.

Then comes, with Socrates, the emphasis on ethics; with Plato, the rejection of the world of sense in favor of the self-created world of pure thought; with Aristotle, the belief in purpose as the fundamental concept in science.

In spite of the genius of Plato and Aristotle, their thought has vices which proved infinitely harmful. After their time, there was a decay of vigor, and a gradual recrudescence of popular superstition.

A partially new outlook arose as a result of the victory of Catholic orthodoxy; but it was not until the Renaissance that philosophy regained the vigor and independence that characterize the predecessors of Socrates. (HWP 72)

How should we view the Greeks of antiquity today?

Two opposite attitudes toward the Greeks are common at the present day.

One, which was practically universal from the Renaissance until very recent times, views the Greeks with almost superstitious reverence, as the inventors of all that is best, and as men of superhuman genius whom the moderns cannot hope to equal.

The other attitude, inspired by the triumphs of science and by an optimistic belief in progress, considers the authority of the ancients an incubus, and maintains that most of their contributions to thought are now best forgotten.

I cannot myself take either of these extreme views; each, I should say, is partly right and partly wrong. Before entering upon any detail, I shall try to say what sort of wisdom we can still derive from the study of Greek thought.

As to the nature and structure of the world, various hypotheses are possible.

To learn to conceive the universe according to each of these systems is an imaginative delight and an antidote to dogmatism. Moreover, even if no one of the hypotheses can be demonstrated, there is genuine knowledge in the discovery of what is involved in making each of them consistent with itself and with known facts.

Now almost all the hypotheses that have dominated modern philosophy were first thought of by the Greeks; their imaginative inventiveness in abstract matters can hardly be too highly praised. I regard them as giving birth to theories which have had an independent life and growth, and which, though at first somewhat infantile, have proved capable of surviving and developing throughout more than two thousand years. (HWP 38)

HAPPINESS

Does philosophy contribute to happiness?

Yes, if you happen to be interested in philosophy and good at it, but not otherwise—but so does bricklaying. Anything you're good at contributes to happiness. (SHM 76)

What ingredients make for happiness?

Four are the most important.

The first is health; the second, sufficient means to keep you from want; third, happy personal relations; and fourth, successful work. (SHM 72)

What works against happiness?

One thing is worry, and that's one respect in which I've become much happier as I've grown older.

I worry much less and I found a very useful plan in regard to worry, which is to think, "Now what is the very worst thing that could happen?" . . . And then think, "Well, after all, it wouldn't be so very bad a hundred years hence; it probably wouldn't matter."

After you've really made yourself think that, you won't worry so much. Worry comes from not facing unpleasant possibilities. (SHM 76)

Envy is a terrible source of unhappiness to many.

They think someone else has a better car or a better garden, or how nice it would be to live in a happier climate, or how much more recognition so-and-so's work gets—things like that.

Instead of enjoying what is there for them to enjoy, the pleasure of it is taken away by the thought that perhaps somebody else has more. (SHM 77)

Does it make people happy to have some cause to live for?

Yes, provided they can succeed more or less.

If it's a cause in which there is no success, they don't get happy.

But if they can get a measure of success from time to time, then it does help. (SHM 79)

What contributes to happiness in old age?

Side interests, especially as one gets older, are a very important element in happiness.

The more your interests are impersonal and extend beyond your own life, the less you will mind the prospect that your own life may be going to come to an end before very long.

I think that's a very important element of happiness in old age. (SHM 79)

HEGEL

Why did Russell call Hegel one of philosophy's misfortunes?

I think Hegel's *Philosophy of History* is a very important book indeed, judged by the effects it has had, and a totally unimportant book judged by any truth it may contain. [One effect is that it influenced Marx, who, of course, had an enormous effect.]

[It is] important, partly because it presented a pattern in history—a scheme, a system—according to which historical events were supposed to have developed, which of course people like.

It is a simple formula and they think "now we understand it all"; if it is false, they do not notice it.

I do not object to a man writing universal history, if he has the time; but I do object to the notion that there is a simple scheme or thread running through it all.

You can get Marx out of Hegel by just a few transformations. Where Hegel talks of nations, Marx talks of classes. Where Hegel talks about the Idea, Marx talks about methods of production. With those two changes, the two are practically identical.

I do not say that Hegel is responsible [for the sins of his disciple, Marx], but I say that the same sin is there in both cases, of thinking there is a simple formula.

I think the course of history is subject to laws and is probably for a sufficiently wise person deterministic; but nobody is wise enough.

It is far too complicated and nobody can work it out; and the person who says he has done so is a charlatan. (ITL 410)

HEROES

Why is it worthwhile to remember heroic individuals?

There is a tendency in our time to pay too little attention to the individual and too much to the mass.

We are so persuaded that we live in the Age of the Common Man that men become common even when they might be otherwise.

There has been a movement, especially in teaching history to the young, towards emphasis on types of culture as opposed to the doings of individual heroes.

Up to a point, this is entirely praiseworthy.

We get a better sense of the march of events if we are told something about the manner of life of Cro-Magnon man or Neanderthal man, and it is wholesome to know about the tenement houses in Rome where the Romans lived whom Plutarch does not mention.

A book like the Hammond's *Village Laborer* presents a whole period from a point of view of which there is nothing in the older conventional histories.

All this is true and important.

But what, though important, is not true, but perniciously false, is the suggestion, which easily grows up when history is studied *only* in this way, that individuals do not count and that those who have been regarded as heroes are only embodiments of social forces, whose work would have been done by someone else if it had not been done by them, and that, broadly speaking, no individual can do better than let himself be borne along by the current of his time.

What is worst about this view is that, if it is held, it tends to become true.

Heroic lives are inspired by heroic ambitions, and the young man who thinks there is nothing important to be done is pretty sure to do nothing important.

For such reasons I think the kind of history that is exemplified by Plutarch's *Lives* is quite as necessary as the more generalized kind.

Very few people can make a community: Lenin and Stalin are the only ones who have achieved it in modern times.

But a very much larger number of men can achieve an individual life which is significant.

This applies not only to men whom we may regard as models to be imitated, but to all those who afford new material for imagination.

The Emperor Frederick II, for example, most certainly does not deserve to be imitated, but he makes a splendid piece in one's mental furniture.

The Wonder of the World, tramping hither and thither with his menagerie, completed at last by his Prime Minister in a cage, debating with Moslem sages, winning crusades in spite of being excommunicate, is a figure that I should be sorry not to know about.

We all think it worthwhile to know about the great heroes of tragedy—Agamemnon, Oedipus, Hamlet, and the rest—but there have been real men whose lives had the same quality as that of the great tragic heroes, and had the additional merit of having actually existed.

All forms of greatness, whether divine or diabolic, share a certain quality, and I do not wish to see this quality ironed out by the worship of mediocrity.

When I first visited America nearly sixty years ago, I made the acquaintance of a lady who had lately had a son.

Somebody remarked lightly, "Perhaps he will be a genius." The lady, in tones of heart-felt horror, replied, "Oh, I hope not!" Her wish, alas, was granted. (PFM 187)

HISTORY

Why read history?

There is history in the large and history in the small, each has its value, but their values are different.

History in the large helps us to understand how the world developed into what it is; history in the small makes us know interesting men and women, and promotes a knowledge of human nature. (UH 19)

There are things to be learned from history, but they are not simple general formulae, which can only be made plausible by missing out half the facts.

The men who make up philosophies of history [such as Hegel, Marx, and Spengler] may be dismissed as inventors of mythologies.

There remain two very different functions that history can perform.

On the one hand it may seek for comparatively small and humble generalizations such as might form a beginning of a science (as opposed to a philosophy) of history.

On the other hand, it can, by the study of individuals, seek to combine the merits of drama or epic poetry with the merit of truth.

They are very different, they appeal to different types of mind, and they demand different methods.

One might take *Middletown* and Plutarch's *Lives* as illustrative of the two types of history.

I should not wish to be deprived of either, but the satisfactions that they offer are as far asunder as the poles.

The one views man objectively, as the heavenly bodies are viewed by an astronomer; the other appeals to imagination, and aims at giving us the kind of knowledge of men that a practiced horseman has of horses—a knowledge felt rather than expressed, which it would be impossible to translate into the language of science, but which is nonetheless useful in practical affairs. (UH 17-18)

Why should the general reader read history?

[This is] what history can do and should do for the general reader:

I am not thinking of what history does for historians; I am thinking of history as an essential part of the furniture of an educated mind.

We do not think that poetry should be read only by poets, or that music should only be heard by composers.

And, in like manner, history should not be known only to historians.

But clearly the kind of history which is to contribute to the mental life of those who are not historians must have certain qualities that more professional work need not have, and, conversely, does not require certain things which one would look for in a learned monograph.

I will try to say—though I find it very difficult—what I feel that I personally have derived from the reading of history.

I should put first and foremost something like a new dimension in the individual life, a sense of being a drop in a great river rather than a tightly bounded separate entity.

The man whose interests are bounded by the short span between his birth and death has a myopic vision and a limitation of outlook which can hardly fail to narrow the scope of his hopes and desires.

And what applies to an individual man applies also to a community.

Those communities that have as yet little history make upon a European a curious impression of thinness and isolation.

They do not feel themselves the inheritors of the ages, and for that reason what they aim at transmitting to their successors seems jejune and emotionally poor to one in whom the past is vivid and the future is illuminated by knowledge of the slow and painful achievements of former times.

History makes one aware that there is no finality in human affairs; there is not a static perfection and an unimprovable wisdom to be achieved.

Whatever wisdom we may have achieved is a small matter in comparison with what is possible.

Whatever beliefs we may cherish, even those that we deem most important, are not likely to last forever; and, if we imagine that they embody eternal verities, the future is likely to make a mock of us.

Cocksure certainty is the source of much that is worst in our present world, and it is something of which the contemplation of history ought to cure us, not only or chiefly because there were wise men in the past, but because so much that was thought wisdom turned out to be folly—which suggests that much of our own supposed wisdom is no better.

I do not mean to maintain that we should lapse into a lazy skepticism.

We should hold our beliefs, and hold them strongly. Nothing great is achieved without passion, but underneath the passion should always be that large impersonal survey which sets limits to actions that our passions inspire.

If you think ill of Communism or Capitalism, should you exterminate the human race in order that there may be no more Communists or Capitalists as the case may be?

Few people would deliberately assert that this would be wise, and yet it is a consummation towards which some politicians who are not historically minded seem to be leading mankind.

This is an extreme example, but it is by no means difficult to think of innumerable others. (PFM 181)

Why has the general reader's interest in history declined?

There are a number of reasons for it.

In the first place, reading altogether has declined.

People go to the movies, or listen to the radio, or watch television.

History has ceased to be as interesting as it used to be, partly because the present is so full of important events, and so packed with quick-moving changes, that many people find neither time nor inclination to turn their attention to former centuries.

A life of Hitler or Lenin or Stalin or Trotsky can be quite as interesting in itself as a life of Napoleon, and has, in addition, more relevance to present problems.

But I am afraid we must admit that there is another cause for the decline of historical reading, and that is the decline of historical writing in the grand manner.

I do not know how eagerly their contemporaries lapped up Herodotus or Thucydides or Polybius or Plutarch, but we all know the eagerness with which historians were welcomed in the eighteenth and nineteenth centuries.

In Britain there was a long procession from Clarendon's *History of the Rebellion* to Macaulay.

In France, from the time of Voltaire onwards, history was a battleground of rival philosophies.

In Germany, under the inspiration of Hegel, historians combined brilliance with wickedness in equal proportions. (PFM 189)

How should history be written for the general reader?

Let us come to the question how history should be written if it is to produce the best possible result in the nonhistorical reader.

Here there is first of all an extremely simple requirement: it must be interesting.

I mean that it must be interesting not only to men who for some special reason wish to know some set of historical facts, but to those who are reading in the same spirit in which one reads poetry or a good novel.

This requires first and foremost that the historian should have feelings about the events that he is relating and the characters that he is portraying.

It is of course imperative that the historian should not distort facts, but it is not imperative that he should not take sides in the clashes and conflicts that fill his pages.

An historian who is impartial, in the sense of not liking one party better than another and not allowing himself to have heroes and villains among his characters, will be a dull writer.

If the reader is to be interested, he must be allowed to take sides in the drama.

If this causes an historian to be one-sided, the only remedy is to find another historian with an opposite bias.

The history of the Reformation, for example, can be interesting when it is written by a Protestant historian, and can be equally interesting when it is written by a Catholic historian.

If you wish to know what it felt like to live at the time of the Wars of Religion you will perhaps succeed if you read both the Protestant and Catholic histories, but you will not succeed if you read only men who view the whole series of events with complete detachment.

Carlyle said about his history of the French Revolution that his book was itself a kind of French Revolution.

This is true, and it gives the book a certain abiding merit in spite of its inadequacy as an historical record.

As you read it you understand why people did what they did, and this is one of the most important things that a history ought to do for a reader.

At one time I read what Diodorus Siculus has to say about Agathocles, who appeared as an unmitigated ruffian.

I looked up Agathocles afterwards in a modern reference book and found him represented as bland and statesmanlike and probably innocent of all the crimes imputed to him.

I have no means of knowing which of these two accounts is the more true, but I know that the whitewashing account was completely uninteresting.

I do not like a tendency, to which some modern historians are prone, to tone down everything dramatic and make out that heroes were not so very heroic, villains not so very villainous.

No doubt a love of drama can lead a historian astray, but there is drama in plenty that requires no falsification, though only literary skill can convey it to the reader. (PFM 183)

Why read memoirs and biographies?

Much that is important, much that is delightful and amusing, is only to be discovered by discursive reading of biographies and memoirs.

The professors must not prevent us from realizing that history is full of fun, and that the most bizarre things really happen.

I have found that the greatest pleasures to be derived from history come only after one knows some period rather well, for then each new fact fits into its place in the jigsaw puzzle. (UH 22)

Not only do they [letters and memoirs] contain much intimate detail, which makes it possible to realize that the men concerned really lived, but there is the advantage that the writers did not know what was going to happen, as the historians do.

Historians are apt to represent what occurred as inevitable, so that it comes to seem as if contemporaries must have foreseen coming events.

Everything becomes much more vivid when one sees the mistakes and perplexities of those who could only guess at the outcome, and often guessed wrong. (UH 26)

How does one's autobiography differ from a nation's official history?

When a man writes his autobiography, he is expected to show a certain modesty, but when a nation writes its autobiography, there is no limit to its boasting and vainglory.

Elementary education, in all advanced countries, is in the hands of the State.

Some of the things taught are known to be false by the officials who prescribe them, and many others are known to be false, or at any rate very doubtful, by every unprejudiced person.

Take, for example, the teaching of history.

Each nation aims only at self-glorification in the school textbooks of history.

When I was young, schoolbooks taught that the French were wicked and the Germans virtuous; now they teach the opposite.

In neither case is there the slightest regard for truth.

German schoolbooks, dealing with the battle of Waterloo, represent Wellington as all but defeated when Blücher saved the situation; English books represent Blücher as having made very little difference.

The writers of both the German and the English books know that they are not telling the truth.

American schoolbooks used to be violently anti-British; since the war they have become equally pro-British, without aiming at truth in either case.

Both before and since, one of the chief purposes of education in the United States has been to turn the motley collection of immigrant children into "good Americans."

A "good American" is a man or woman imbued with the belief

that America is the finest country on earth, and ought always to be enthusiastically supported in any quarrel.

It is just possible that these propositions are true; if so, a rational man will have no quarrel with them.

But if they are true, they ought to be taught everywhere, not only in America.

Meanwhile the whole machinery of the State, in all the different countries, is turned on to making defenseless children believe absurd propositions, the effect of which is to make them willing to die in defense of sinister interests under the impression that they are fighting for truth and right. (SE 157)

What is the value of having an historical perspective?

The perspective of history enables us to see more clearly what events and what sorts of activities have permanent importance.

Most of the contemporaries of Galileo saw far more significance in the Thirty Years War than in his discoveries, but to us it is evident that the war was a thirty years' futility, while his discoveries began a new era.

When Gladstone visited Darwin, Darwin observed afterwards: "What an honor to be visited by so great a man."

His modesty was amiable, but showed a lack of historical perspective.

Many occurrences—party contests, for example—rouse at the time an excitement quite out of proportion to their real importance, whereas the greatest events, like the summits of high mountains, though dominant from far away, are screened by the foreground from a nearer view.

It is a help towards sanity and calm judgment to acquire the habit of seeing contemporary events in their historical setting, and of imagining them as they will appear when they are in the past.

Theologians assure us that God sees all time as though it were present; it is not in human power to do this except to a very limited degree, but in so far as we can do it, it is a help towards wisdom and contemplative insight.

We live in the present, and in the present we must act; but life is not all action, and action is best when it proceeds from a wide survey in which the present loses the sharpness of its emotional insistence.

Men are born and die; some leave hardly a trace, others transmit something of good or evil to future ages.

The man whose thoughts and feelings are enlarged by history will wish to be a transmitter, and to transmit, so far as may be, what his successors will judge to have been good. (UH 55)

[There are] various ways in which history can be interesting and instructive, but in addition to these it has a more general function, perhaps more important than any of them.

Our bodily life is confined to a small portion of time and space, but our mental life need not be thus limited.

What astronomy does to enlarge the spatial habitat of the mind, history does to increase its temporal domain.

Our private lives are often exasperating, and sometimes almost intolerably painful.

To see them in perspective, as an infinitesimal fragment in the life of mankind, makes it less difficult to endure personal evils which cannot be evaded.

Although history is full of ups and downs, there is a general trend in which it is possible to feel some satisfaction: we know more than our ancestors knew, we have more command over the forces of nature, we suffer less from disease and from natural cataclysms.

It is true that we have not yet learnt to protect ourselves from each other: man is as dangerous to man as he ever was.

But even in this respect there are at least the preliminaries of improvement.

Violence is now mainly organized and governmental, and it is easier to imagine ways of ending this than of ending the sporadic unplanned violence of more primitive times. (UH 54)

Why read Plutarch?

Plutarch, ever since the Renaissance, has been the most influential of ancient historians, not indeed among the writers on history, for he is by no means reliable, but among practical statesmen and political theorists.

To take only two examples, Rousseau and Alexander Hamilton owed the bent of their minds largely to him; his maxims supplied Rousseau with doctrines, and his heroes supplied Hamilton with ambitions.

A reader to whom he has hitherto been merely a great name is likely to be surprised to find that he is an easygoing gossipy writer, who cannot resist a good story, and except in a few instances, is quite willing to relate and even exaggerate the weaknesses of his heroes.

He tells for instance how Mark Antony, when he was already an important official, gave offense by traveling everywhere with a third-rate actress, whom he inflicted even upon the most rigidly respectable provincials.

(This was before he had reached the point at which he could aspire to Queens.)

He tells how Caesar, as a young man, got into trouble for reading a love letter from Brutus's mother during a meeting of the Senate, where no one was allowed to read anything.

And then he goes on to portray Caesar in the aspect of slightly ridiculous pomposity that Shakespeare has preserved.

His heroes are not statuesque figures of perfection; they are concrete men, who could have existed even if they never in fact did. (UH 20)

Why read Herodotus?

Herodotus, who is called the Father of History, is worth reading for a number of reasons.

In the first place, he is full of amusing stories.

Almost at the beginning of the book, there is the story of the vain king, Candaules, who regretted that no one but himself knew fully the beauty of his Queen, for which he wished to be envied.

So he hid his Prime Minister Gyges behind a curtain, where he could see the Queen going naked to the bath. But she saw his feet sticking out, and complained that he had offered her a mortal indignity. Then and there she made him a speech, "Only two courses are open to you to expiate your offense," she said, "either you must die or you must kill the King and marry me." Gyges had no difficulty in making his choice, and became the founder of the dynasty that ended with Croesus.

Herodotus is full of such stories, from which he is not deterred by any scruples as to the dignity of history.

Nor does respect for fact cause him to abstain from drama; the account of the defeat of Croesus by Cyrus is a fascinating tale, though obviously in part legend rather than history.

To anyone who enjoys anthropology Herodotus is interesting from his description of various barbarian customs as they existed in his day. Sometimes he is merely repeating traveler's tales, but very often he is confirmed by modern research. His survey of the nations and races known to him is leisurely and ample, and affords an admirable intro-duction to the ancient world for a previously ignorant reader.

The main theme of his history is the conflict of Europe and Asia, culminating, for his time, in the defeats of the Persians at Marathon and Salamis.

Throughout all the subsequent centuries, this swaying battle has continued.

Salamis marked the end of the westward expansion of the Asiatics in Greek times; then came European conquest of Asia by the Macedonians and Romans, culminating in the time of Trajan, and followed by a long period of Asiatic ascendency.

Limits were set to the extent of Asiatic conquest by the defeat of Attila at Chalons in the fifth century and of the Moors at Tours in the eighth; the last great Asiatic victory was the conquest of Con-stantinople in 1453.

In subsequent centuries, Europe had unquestioned superiority through scientific technique. The first sign of a contrary movement was the defeat of Russia by the Japanese in the war of 1904–5.

How far this contrary movement will go it is impossible to guess, for, though Japan will no doubt be defeated, China and India will succeed to it as champions of Asia.

All these vast secular movements come within the framework suggested by Herodotus [1943]. (UH 18)

Why read Thucydides?

Thucydides, the second of the great historians, has a smaller theme than that of Herodotus, but treats it with more art and also with a more careful regard for accuracy.

His subject is the conflict of Athens and Sparta in the Pelopon-nesian War.

His history, as Cornford has pointed out, is modeled on Greek tragedy: Athens, his own beloved city, which was finally defeated, is like the typical hero, driven by Fate and overweening pride to a disastrous but not inglorious end.

His writing is severe, and confined strictly to what is relevant; there are no gossipy digressions, and there is little that is amusing.

But there is a presentation, full of epic grandeur, of the spectacle of men driven by destiny into folly, choosing wrongly over and over again when a right choice would have brought victory, becoming wicked through exasperation; and falling at last into irretrievable ruin.

The theme is one that appealed to the Greek mind. A great impersonal Power, called indifferently Fate or Justice or Necessity, ruled the world, and was superior to the gods. Whatever person or country or thing over-stepped the ordained boundaries, suffered the punishment of pride.

This was the real religion of the Greeks, and Thucydides in his history magnificently illustrated it. (UH 20)

Why read Gibbon?

Gibbon, it must be admitted, has grave defects.

His erudition, by modern standards, is inadequate; his characters, even when they are barbarians, have an eighteenth-century flavor, like Voltaire's cannibals; princes, wars, and politics crowd out common men and economic facts more than the modern reader could wish.

But when all this is allowed, he remains both a great and a delightful writer.

His wit and irony—particularly when he uses them to contemn superstition—are inimitable.

But his chief virtue is that, although his portraits of individuals are often disappointing, his sense of the march of great events is sure and unerring.

No one has ever presented the pageant of history better than he has done.

To treat in one book the whole period from the second century to the fifteenth was a colossal undertaking, but he never lost sight of the unity of his theme, or of the proportions to be presented among its several parts.

This required a grasp of a great whole which is beyond the power of most men, and which, for all his shortcomings, puts Gibbon in the first rank among historians. (UH 21)

How did the nineteenth century mislead the Victorians?

The land of Europe had rest ninety-nine years, from 1815 to 1914.

True, there were several Russo-Turkish wars, there was the Crimean War, there were Bismarck's three wars, there was the Boer War, and at the end of the period, there was the Russo-Japanese War; but none of these produced at the time any profound upheaval, and none of them gave rise to a feeling of general insecurity such as now haunts us even in our dreams.

I was 42 when this era of tranquility ended.

All of us who grew up at that time took for granted, almost without conscious thought, that the nineteenth century had set the pattern for the future.

It had seen great changes, almost all beneficent; we expected more changes of the same sort.

The practice of toleration, liberty, and enlightenment had spread with astonishing rapidity.

Nobody thought of the nineteenth century as a brief and exceptional interlude between two dark ages.

Looking back, it is clear that we ought to have foreseen coming troubles: overpopulation, the end of great undeveloped food-producing areas, the bitter competition produced by the spread of industrialism in a number of countries all avid for power, the intoxication caused by Western ideas in intellectuals belonging to countries with other traditions and other circumstances.

All this we ought to have foreseen, but we did not, and so when war came, we found ourselves in a world for which we were intellectually and imaginatively unprepared.

Our statesmen found old maxims inapplicable, but could not think of new ones.

Blindly the nations blundered on from folly to folly.

If we are to understand our own time, we must find the key to it, not in the eighteenth and nineteenth centuries, but in earlier, wilder, and darker epochs. (NHCW 114)

What kind of man was Napoleon?

Until one knows much intimate detail about a prominent man, it is impossible to judge whether he was really as great as he appears or not.

Some great men become greater the more they are studied; I should mention Spinoza and Lincoln as instances.

Napoleon, on the other hand, becomes, at close quarters, a ridiculous figure.

Perhaps it was not his fault that on the night of his wedding to Josephine, her pug dog bit him in the calf as he was getting into bed, but on many occasions on which he appeared in an unfavorable light, the whole blame was clearly his.

In the course of one of his many quarrels with Talleyrand, he twitted his foreign secretary with being a cripple and having an unfaithful wife.

After he was gone, Talleyrand shrugged his shoulders, turned to the bystanders, and remarked: "What a pity that such a great man should have such bad manners."

His marriage to Marie Louise was celebrated by proxy, and he traveled to the frontiers of France to meet her.

A magnificent ceremonial was arranged, including a state banquet at which all the great men and grand ladies in Napoleon's orbit were to be present.

The dinner hour came; it passed, and still the Emperor and Empress did not appear. The Court Chamberlain was in perplexity and despair.

At last, by discreet inquiries, he discovered that Napoleon could not wait till after dinner to enjoy the favors of an Emperor's daughter.

The Czar Alexander took his measure, and deceived him completely by pretending to be a simple-minded youth.

At the height of his apparent friendship with Napoleon, he wrote to his mother to say, "He laughs best who laughs lasts."

In the correspondence of the two Emperors, all the skill is on the side of Alexander, all the bombast on the side of Napoleon.

It is a pity that historians have failed to emphasize the ridiculous sides of Napoleon, for he became a myth and a legend, inspiring the admiration of military conquest and the cult of the military superman.

His effect was particularly bad on the Germans, who at the same time admired him and wished for revenge on account of the humiliations which he had inflicted on them.

If they could have laughed at him, they could have had their revenge at less cost to mankind. (UH 22)

Napoleon is the supreme example of the soldier of fortune.

The Revolution suited him, since it made his opportunity, but otherwise he was indifferent to it.

Though he gratified French patriotism and depended upon it, France, like the Revolution, was to him merely an opportunity; he had even, in his youth, toyed with the idea of fighting for Corsica against France.

His success was due, not so much to any exceptional qualities of character, as to his technical skill in war; when other men would have been defeated, he was victorious.

The French revolutionary armies conceived of themselves as the liberators of Europe, and were so regarded in Italy as well as by many in Western Germany, but Napoleon himself never brought any more liberation than seemed useful for his own career. (P 21–22)

Did important men always have their minds on important things?

One is surprised, often, by preoccupation with small matters when great things are happening.

When Napoleon's return from Elba compelled the Bourbons to fly, Louis Philippe wrote innumerable letters of lamentation, not about public affairs, but about his children's whooping cough.

When Lord Cranville Levison Gower had to fly from Austerlitz, what worried him most was that the roads were rough and his coach had defective springs.

When Cicero sailed from Italy to escape the proscription of the Second Triumvirate, he turned back because he decided that seasickness was worse than death. (UH 26)

How serene were the great men of the past?

The pedant is convinced that the truly great men are always "serene," that they see how, in mysterious ways, good comes out of evil, and that, speaking generally, they help us to bear with fortitude the misfortunes of others.

The generous young, exposed in almost every university of the world to this desiccated abomination, are apt to reject with scorn all the conventionally great names.

Take, for example, Shakespeare, whose supposed "serenity" is the theme of endless academic nonsense. Here are a few examples of his "serenity":

> When we are born we cry, that we are come
> To this great stage of fools.

Again,

> As flies to us are we to the gods,
> They kill us for their sport.

Again,

> You taught me language, and my profit on't
> Is, I know to curse.

No, the greatest men have not been "serene."

They have had, it is true, an ultimate courage, a power of creating beauty where nature has put only horror, which may, to a petty mind, appear like serenity.

But their courage has had to surpass that of common men, because they have seen deeper into the indifference of nature and the cruelty of man.

To cover up these things with comfortable lies is the business of cowards; the business of great men is to see them with inflexible clarity, and yet to think and feel nobly.

And in the degree in which we can all be great, this is the business of each of us. (UH 39)

What is the anarchy/dictatorship seesaw?

The question of combining discipline with freedom in the best proportions is one which our age must solve, and solve quickly, if it is to avoid the opposite dangers of anarchy and dictatorship.

There has been, ever since the rise of Greece, an oscillation in this respect, both in the large and in the small, but an endless seesaw is surely not the best that human intelligence can compass.

What has happened hitherto has been something like this: a tribe or nation, under a rigid traditional system, slowly builds up a compressed energy which at last breaks its bonds; old habits break down first in the sphere of opinion, and then in the sphere of conduct.

The greatest creative ages are those where opinion is free, but behavior is still to some extent conventional.

Ultimately, however, skepticism breaks down moral taboos, society becomes impossibly anarchic, freedom is succeeded by tyranny, and a new tight tradition is gradually built up.

In Greece, the Homeric heroes have a fixed pattern of behavior, and a moral code which even transgressors do not question.

In Aeschylus the old rigidity, somewhat softened, still exists, but the sophists generated doubt, and Euripides is perplexed and uncertain.

The result, after a period of extraordinary brilliance, was a general decay, first of morals, and then of other forms of excellence.

The rigid Romans imposed their yoke, but in turn became first intelligent and then soft.

Christianity, more severe than any previous religion, again created a system in which the energies of the community were husbanded but the individual was stifled.

In the Italian renaissance the Christian discipline broke down, to be succeeded by a brief period of genius and individualism, soon extinguished by the Spaniards, and the counterreformation.

Similarly the romantic movement led up to the dictatorships of our own day.

The English-speaking nations, it must be said, have been less subject to these oscillations than the nations of the Continent of Europe. (UH 51)

Does being aware of history always produce good results?

When we speak of the importance of history, we must admit its importance for evil as well as for good.

This applies equally to the popular myths which have gradually become a part of folklore.

I went to Ireland once with my two young children. My daughter, aged five, made friends with a peasant woman who treated her with great kindness.

But, as we went away, the woman said, "She's a bonny girl, in spite of Cromwell."

It seemed a pity that the woman did not know either more history or less. (PFM 190)

HUMAN NATURE

Can human nature be changed?

I don't know what human nature is supposed to be.

But your nature is infinitely malleable, and that is what people don't realize.

If you compare a domestic dog with a wild wolf you will see what training can do.

The domestic dog is a nice comfortable creature, barks occasionally, and he may bite the postman, but on the whole, he's all right; whereas the wolf is quite a different thing.

You can do exactly the same thing with human beings.

Human beings, according to how they're treated, will turn out totally different, and I think the idea that you can't change human nature is silly. (SHM 35)

IDEAL

Lord Russell, what things do you hope to see the world achieve?

I think I should put first, security against extreme disaster such as threatened by modern war.

I should put second, the abolition of abject poverty throughout the world.

Third, as a result of security and economic well-being, a general growth of tolerance and kindly feeling.

Fourth, the greatest possible opportunity for personal initiative in ways not harmful to the community.

All these things are possible, and all would come about if men chose.

In the meantime, the human race lives in a welter of organized hatreds and threats of mutual extermination.

I cannot but think that sooner or later people will grow tired of this very uncomfortable way of living.

A person who lived so in private life would be considered a lunatic.

If I bought a revolver and threatened to shoot my next-door neighbor, he would also no doubt buy a revolver to protect himself if he lived in a community where law and police did not exist.

He and I would both find life much more unpleasant than it is at present, but we should not be acting any more absurdly than the present States which are supposedly guided by the best wisdom that human beings can provide. (PFM 48)

IDEOLOGY

What have ideologies done to the present world? [1951]

So far as ideologies are concerned, the troubles of our time show themselves in an increase of fanaticism.

There was, of course, some fanaticism in the period which now seems in retrospect to have been comparatively free from it.

There was fanaticism in the French Revolution, but it was in control for only about two years.

There was fanaticism in the German resistance to Napoleon, but it seemed to die down after 1815. There was fanaticism on both sides in the American Civil War and in the struggle between Russian revolutionaries and the czardom.

But except in Russia, the fanatics never seemed to gain control for any length of time.

Since 1914—largely, I think, as a result of sufferings caused by war—we have seen fanaticisms of various kinds controlling governments and making sensible statesmanship impossible.

There was anti-German fanaticism in the years after the First World War; there was answering German fanaticism, leading to the victory of the Nazis.

There was anti-Semitic fanaticism, with the inevitable response of Zionist fanaticism.

Most important of all, there was, and is, Communist and anti-Communist fanaticism.

While mankind remains in this temper, the sort of cooperation required for the inauguration of world government is clearly out of the question. (NHCW 115)

IMPERMANENCE

Nothing lasts forever. What thoughts does that give rise to, Lord Russell?

The flight of time, the transitoriness of all things, the empire of death, are the foundations of tragic feeling.

Ever since men began to reflect deeply upon human life, they have sought various ways of escape: in religion, in philosophy, in poetry, in history—all of which attempt to give eternal value to what is transient.

Kings engrave their victories on monuments of stone, poets relate old sorrows in words whose beauty (they hope) will make them immortal, and philosophers invent systems proving that time is no more than an illusion.

Vain effort!

The stone crumbles, the poet's words become unintelligible, and the philosopher's systems are forgotten.

Nonetheless, striving after eternity has ennobled the passing moment. (MAO 151)

INCEST

Why is the incest taboo important?

Whatever the dominant social unit at any stage of social evolution, there were two opposite patterns of behavior: one towards members of the same tribe, the other towards outsiders.

Within the group, cooperation was the rule; friendly feeling was expected and usually achieved.

To this, however, there were limits, especially owing to sexual rivalry; if at any time the number of females happened to be less than the number of males, it was to be expected that there would be vehement combats between the males of a single tribe.

Such combats would occur even when the numbers of men and women were equal if polygamy was tolerated; and as soon as tribes came to have chiefs, it was to be expected that the chiefs would permit themselves many wives.

This is one of the ways in which harmony within the tribe required the support of custom and the moral law.

Within the family the same result had been achieved at a very early date by means of the incest taboo; and the various complex rules of exogamy which are common in savage tribes must have been intended to extend beyond the family the same rule of law that had been secured by the prohibition of incest.

The incest taboo is perhaps the most successful example known of the victory of custom over instinct.

The great majority of mankind at the present day go through life without at any moment experiencing any conscious impulse towards incest.

There are, it is true, savage tribes where the impulse is still difficult to resist, and where adult brothers and sisters take pains not to meet.

But in the main the prohibition has proved effective not only outwardly but inwardly, presumably because it is ancient and absolute and does not demand anything superhumanly difficult.

To the social psychologist it is important, since it shows what custom can achieve. (NHCW 54)

INDIVIDUALS

How does the role of the scientist today differ from that of past centuries?

A great many very important and very useful activities which have hitherto been carried out by individuals without the help of an organization are coming more and more to depend upon organizations.

The great men of science of the past didn't depend on very expensive apparatus—great men like Copernicus, Galileo, Newton, Darwin.

They did their work as individuals, and they were able to.

But take a modern astronomer. I met a very eminent astronomer of the present day, and his work, which is very useful, depends entirely upon very powerful telescopes, which had been contributed by a very rich man.

He was only able to do his work because he was on good terms with certain very rich men. (SHM 107)

Have remarkable individuals made much of a difference?

I do not mean to subscribe to Carlyle's cult of heroes, still less to Nietzsche's exaggerations of it.

I do not wish for one moment to suggest that the common man is unimportant, or that the study of masses of men is less worth pursuing than the study of notable individuals.

I wish only to preserve the balance between the two.

I believe that remarkable individuals have done a great deal to mold history.

I think that, if the hundred ablest men of science of the seventeenth century had all died in infancy, the life of the common man in every industrial community would now be quite different from what it is.

I do not think that if Shakespeare and Milton had not existed someone else would have composed their works.

And yet this is the sort of thing that some "scientific" historians seem to wish one to believe.

I will go a step further in agreement with those who emphasize the individual.

I think that what is most worthy to be known and admired in human affairs has to do with individuals rather than with communities.

I do not believe in the independent value of a collection of human beings over and above the value contained in their several lives, and I think it is dangerous if history neglects individual value in order to glorify a State, a Nation, a Church, or any other such collective entity.

But I will not pursue this theme further for fear of being led into politics. (PFM 188)

INNOVATION

Why have great scientific discoveries scared people?

Because they made people feel unsafe.

Every human being, like every animal, wants to live in what is felt to be a safe environment—an environment where you won't be exposed to unexpected peril.

Now when a man tells you that something you've always believed was in fact not true, it gives you a frightful shock, and you think, "Oh!

I don't know where I am. When I think I'm planting my foot upon the ground, perhaps I'm not." And you get into a terror. (SHM 110)

Why is there resistance to new ideas?

To attain complete truth is not given to mortals, but to advance toward it by successive steps is not impossible. On any matter of general interest, there is usually, in any given community, a received opinion, which is accepted as a matter of course, by all who give no special thought to the matter.

Any questioning of the received opinion rouses hostility for a number of reasons.

The most important of these is the instinct of conventionality, which exists in all gregarious animals and often leads them to put to death any markedly peculiar member of the herd.

The next most important is the feeling of insecurity aroused by doubt as to the beliefs by which we are in the habit of regulating our lives.

Whoever has tried to explain the philosophy of Berkeley to a plain man in its unadulterated form will have seen the anger aroused by this feeling.

What the plain man derives from Berkeley's philosophy at a first hearing is an uncomfortable suspicion that nothing is solid, so that it is rash to sit on a chair or to expect the floor to sustain us.

Because this suspicion is uncomfortable, it is irritating, except to those who regard the whole argument as merely nonsense.

And in a more or less analogous was, any questioning of what has been taken for granted destroys the feeling of standing on solid ground, and produces a condition of bewildered fear.

A third reason which makes men dislike novel opinions is that vested interests are bound up with old beliefs.

The long fight of the Church against science, from Giordano Bruno to Darwin, is attributable to this motive, among others.

The horror of socialism which existed in the remote past was entirely attributable to this cause.

But it would be a mistake to assume, as is done by those who seek economic motives everywhere [Marxists], that vested interests are the principal source of anger against novelties in thought.

If this were the case, intellectual progress would be much more rapid than it is.

The instinct of conventionality, horror of uncertainty, and vested interests, all militate against the acceptance of a new idea.

And it is even harder to think of a new idea than to get it accepted; most people might spend a lifetime in reflection without ever making a genuinely original discovery.

In view of all these obstacles, it is not likely that any society will suffer from a plethora of heretical opinions. (PI 64)

What was the source of the power of intellectuals in the past?

A very different type of character comes to the fore where power is achieved through learning or wisdom, real or supposed.

The two most important examples of this form of power are traditional China and the Catholic Church.

There is less of it in the modern world than there has been at most times in the past; apart from the Church in England, very little of this type of power remains.

Oddly enough, the power of what passes for learning is greatest in the most savage communities, and steadily decreases as civilization advances.

When I say "learning" I include, of course, reputed learning, such as that of magicians and medicine men.

Twenty years of study are required in order to obtain a Doctor's Degree at the University of Lhassa, which is necessary for all the higher posts except that of the Dalai Lama.

This position is much what it was in Europe in the year 1000, when Pope Silvester II was reputed a magician because he read books, and was consequently able to increase the power of the Church by inspiring metaphysical terrors.

The intellectual, as we know him, is a spiritual descendent of the priest; but the spread of education has robbed him of his power.

The power of the intellectual depends upon superstition, reverence for a traditional incantation or a sacred book.

Of these, something survives in English-speaking countries, as seen in the English attitude to the Coronation Service and the American reverence for the Constitution; accordingly, the Archbishop of Canterbury and the Supreme Court Judges still have some of the traditional power of learned men.

But this is only a pale ghost of the power of Egyptian priests or Chinese Confucian scholars. (P 43)

ISLAM

What was the cause of Islam's rise to power?

The power of a community depends not only upon its numbers and its economic resources and its technical capacity, but also on its beliefs.

A fanatical creed, held by all the members of a community, often greatly increases its power; sometimes, however, it diminishes it. As fanatical creeds are much more in the fashion than they were during the nineteenth century, the question of their effect on power is one of great practical importance.

One of the arguments against democracy is that a nation of united fanatics has more chance of success in war than a nation containing a large proportion of sane men.

It should be observed that the cases in which fanaticism has led to success are naturally better known than those in which it has led to failure, since the cases of failure have remained comparatively obscure. Thus a too rapid survey is apt to be misleading; but if we are aware of this possible source of error, it is not difficult to avoid.

The classic example of power through fanaticism is the rise of Islam.

Mohammad added nothing to the knowledge or to the material resources of the Arabs, and yet, within a few years of his death, they had acquired a large empire by defeating their most powerful neighbors. Undoubtedly, the religion founded by the Prophet was an essential element in the success of his nation. At the very end of his life, he declared war on the Byzantine Empire. "The Moslems were discouraged, they alleged the want of money, or horses, or provisions, the season of harvest, and the intolerable heat of the summer. 'Hell is much hotter,' said the indignant prophet. He disdained to compel their service; but on his return, he admonished the most guilty, by an excommunication of fifty days" (Gibbon, Chap. L).

Fanaticism, while Mohammad lived, and for a few years after his death, united the Arab nation, gave it confidence in battle, and promoted courage by the promise of Paradise to those who fell fighting the infidel. (P 149)

JUSTICE

What is a just way to distribute the necessities of life?

Such things as food, houses, and clothes are necessaries of life, about the need of which there is not much controversy or much difference between one man and another.

Therefore they are suitable for governmental action in a democracy.

In all such matters, justice should be the governing principle.

In a modern democratic community, justice means equality. But it would not mean equality in a community where there was a hierarchy of classes, recognized and accepted by inferiors as well as superiors.

Even in modern England, a large majority of wage earners would be shocked if it were suggested that the King should have no more pomp than they have.

I should therefore define justice as the arrangement producing the least envy.

This would mean equality in a community free from superstition, but not in one which firmly believed in social inequality. (SE 185)

Why is it difficult to define justice except in terms of equality?

There is a conception of justice, which is associated in people's minds with law, but is, in fact, a very different thing.

Justice is conceived by modern democrats in a way quite different from that in which it was conceived in former times.

Plato's *Republic* is, in form, an attempt to define justice, and after an immense discussion, it arrives at the interesting result that justice consists in giving every man his due, i.e., what it is just to give him.

This remarkable piece of work has been greeted by almost all of Plato's successors as showing stupendous profundity; but if any lesser man had said it, somebody would have pointed out that the definition is circular.

One could, of course, avoid the circularity by saying that a man's due is to be measured by his services to the community, but I cannot imagine how his services to the community are to be estimated.

Compare a baker and an opera singer.

You could live without the services of the opera singer, but not without the services of the baker.

On this ground you might say that the baker performs a greater service to the community; but no lover of music would agree.

The whole conception of desert, which underlies any other conception of justice than one of equality, is impossible to carry out in any systemic manner. (NHCW 79)

On what besides equality should justice be based?

But although equality is the main concept that modern believers in democracy use in defining "justice," there is always some admixture of the idea of desert.

Most people would consider that an exceptional degree of either merit or demerit justifies exceptional treatment.

They do not disapprove of rewards for public servants who have performed some conspicuous service, and their belief that it is right to punish criminals is seldom based entirely upon a deterrent view of punishment.

In general, it must be admitted that society gains if there are rewards for useful actions, and the opposite for such as are harmful.

I do not think, therefore, that flat equality can be recommended; what can be said, I think with truth, is that all inequality must be justified by its useful effects, and not by some abstract concept of merit or demerit. (NHCW 80)

What's wrong with accepting confessions of guilt, in criminal cases?

The desire to obtain a confession was the basis of the torture of the Inquisition.

In Old China, torture of suspected persons was habitual, because a humanitarian emperor had decreed that no man should be condemned except on his own confession.

For the taming of the power of the police, one essential is that a confession shall never, in any circumstances, be accepted as evidence. (P 295)

KANT

Why did Russell call Kant one of philosophy's misfortunes?

Kant (1724–1804) is generally considered the greatest of modern philosophers. I cannot myself agree with this estimate. . . .

His philosophy allowed an appeal to the heart against the cold dictates of theoretical reason.

In Kant . . . the subjectivist tendency that begins with Descartes was carried to new extremes.

There is an emphasis upon mind as opposed to matter, which leads in the end to the assertion that only mind exists. (HWP 704)

KILLING

What is the conventional view about taking human life?

Questions of practical morals raise more difficult problems than questions of mere opinion.

The thugs honestly believe it their duty to commit murders, but the government does not acquiesce.

The conscientious objectors honestly hold the opposite opinion, and again the government does not acquiesce.

Killing is a state prerogative; it is equally criminal to do it unbidden and not to do it when bidden. (PI 66)

KNOWLEDGE

Will enough knowledge produce the perfect human?

Some of the Greeks, notably Socrates, thought that knowledge alone would suffice to produce the perfect man.

According to Socrates, no one sins willingly, and, if we all had enough knowledge, we should all behave perfectly. I do not think that this is true.

One could imagine a satanic being with immense knowledge and equally immense malevolence—and, alas, approximations to such a being have actually occurred in human history.

It is not enough to seek knowledge rather than error.

It is necessary, also, to feel benevolence rather than its opposite.

But, although knowledge alone is not enough, it is a very essential ingredient of wisdom. (BW 397)

How is "useless" knowledge useful?

Perhaps the most important advantage of "useless" knowledge is that it promotes a contemplative habit of mind.

A contemplative habit of mind has advantages ranging from the most trivial to the most profound.

To begin with minor vexations, such as fleas, missing trains, or cantankerous business associates.

Such troubles seem hardly worthy to be met by reflections on the excellence of heroism or the transitoriness of all human ills, and yet the irritation to which they give rise destroys many people's good temper and enjoyment of life.

On such occasions, there is much consolation to be found in out of the way bits of knowledge which have a real or fancied connection with the trouble of the moment; or even if they have none, they serve to obliterate the present from one's thoughts.

When assailed by people who are white with fury, it is pleasant to remember the chapter in Descartes' *Treatise of the Passions* entitled, "Why those who grow pale with rage are more to be feared than those who grow red."

When the rapacity of capitalists grows oppressive, one may be suddenly consoled by the recollection that Brutus, that exemplar of republican virtue, lent money to a city at 40 percent, and hired a private army to besiege it when it failed to pay the interest.

Curious learning not only makes unpleasant things less unpleasant, but also makes pleasant things more pleasant.

I have enjoyed peaches and apricots more since I have known that they were first cultivated in China in the early days of the Han dynasty;

that Chinese hostages held by the great King Kaniska introduced them to India, whence they spread to Persia, reaching the Roman Empire in the first century of our era; the the word, "apricot," is derived from the same Latin root as the word, "precocious," because the apricot ripens early; and that the A at the beginning was added by mistake, owing to a false etymology.

All this makes the fruit taste much sweeter. (IPI 29)

LANGUAGE

How can a writer appeal to reason without being dull?

Jeremy Bentham made a table of the springs of action, where every human desire was named in three parallel columns, according as men wish to praise it, to blame it, or to treat it neutrally.

Thus we find in one column "gluttony," and opposite it, in the next column, "love of the pleasures of the social board." And again, we find in the column giving eulogistic names to impulses, "public spirit," and opposite to it, in the next column, we find "spite."

I recommend that anybody who wishes to think clearly on any ethical topic to imitate Bentham in this particular, and after accustoming himself to the fact that almost every word conveying blame has a synonym conveying praise, to acquire a habit of using words that convey neither praise nor blame.

Both "adultery" and "fornication" are words conveying such immensely strong moral reprobation that so long as they are employed it is difficult to think clearly.

There are, however, other words used by those lascivious writers who wish to corrupt our morals: such writers will speak of "gallantry," of "love unfettered by the cold bonds of law."

Both sets of terms are designed to arouse prejudices; if we wish to think dispassionately, we must eschew the one set just as much as the other.

Unfortunately this must inevitably ruin our literary style.

Both words of praise and words of blame are colorful and interesting. The reader can be carried along by an invective or panegyric, and with a little skill his emotions can be aroused by the author in any desired direction.

We, however, wish to appeal to reason, and we must therefore employ dull neutral phrases, such as "extramarital sexual relations."

Yet perhaps this is too austere a precept, for after all we are dealing with a matter in which human emotions are very strongly involved, and if we eliminate emotions too completely from our writing, we may fail to convey the nature of the subject matter with which we are dealing.

In regard to all sexual matters there is a polarity according as they are described from the point of view of the participants or from that of jealous outsiders. What we do ourselves is "gallantry"; what others do is "fornication."

We must, therefore, remember the emotionally colored terms, and we may employ them on occasion, but we must do so sparingly, and, in the main, we must content ourselves with neutral and scientifically accurate phraseology. (MM 39)

LAW

Is Law an alternative to force?

Law is often represented as an alternative to force, but this is a mistake.

Law is only a way of organizing and concentrating force and transferring it from individuals to groups, or from small groups to larger ones.

In a civilized community it is held that force should not be employed by private individuals, but should be excercised only by the State in accordance with certain rules.

These rules constitute law.

There are always exceptions; a man is allowed to exercise force in self-defense; in many countries he is allowed to commit murder if he finds his wife committing adultery.

Law in origin was merely a codification of the power of dominant groups, and did not aim at anything that to a modern man would appear to be justice.

In many Germanic tribes, for example, if you committed a murder, you were fined, and the fine depended upon the social status of your victim.

Wherever aristocracy existed, its members had various privileges which were not accorded to plebs.

In Japan before the Meiji era began, a man who omitted to smile in the presence of a social superior could legally be killed then and there by the superior in question.

This explains why European travelers find the Japanese a smiling race. (NHCW 74)

On what does law enforcement depend besides the police?

The ultimate power of the Law is the coercive power of the State.

It is the characteristic of civilized communities that direct physical coercion is (with some limitations) the prerogative of the State, and the Law is a set of rules according to which the State exercises this prerogative in dealing with its own citizens.

The Law is almost powerless when it is not supported by public sentiment, as might be seen in the United States during prohibition, or in Ireland in the 1880s, when moonlighters had the sympathy of a majority of the population.

Law, therefore, as an effective force, depends upon opinion and sentiment even more than upon the powers of the police.

The degree of feeling in favor of Law is one of the most important characteristics of a community. (P 37)

LEADERS

Are some people always leaders and others always followers?

Some men's characters lead them always to command, others always to obey; between these extremes lie the mass of average human beings, who like to command in some situations, but in others prefer to be subject to a leader. (P 16)

LEISURE

Is it right to enjoy leisure when the world is so full of threatening problems?

Whatever may be in store for us and for the world, it is well that our leisure should be spent in enjoying whatever can be enjoyed without injury to others. (RSN52 5)

LIBERALISM

When and where did modern Liberalism start?

Modern Liberalism begins in Milan in the conflicts of that city with its Archbishop and the Emperor.

It was a very limited form of democracy, consisting chiefly of independence from feudal magnates and ecclesiastical dignitaries.

It had immense historical importance as giving opportunity for revival of political speculation and freedom of thought. Democratic forms of government, it is true, did not last very long.

They gave way in Venice to aristocracy, and in Milan and Florence to the rule of plutocratic bosses.

But there were always limits to what these men could practice in the way of abominations, since they had no traditional claim to power and were liable to be expelled if they behaved too badly. (FF 81)

Where did Liberalism flourish and what did it represent?

Early Liberalism was a product of England and Holland, and had certain well-marked characteristics.

It stood for religious toleration; it was Protestant, but of the latitudinarian rather than of a fanatical kind; it regarded the wars of religion as silly.

It valued commerce and industry, and favored the rising middle class rather than the monarchy and the aristocracy; it had immense respect for the rights of property, especially when accumulated by the labors of the individual possessor.

The hereditary principle, though not rejected, was restricted in scope more than it had previously been; in particular, the divine right of kings was rejected in favor of the view that every community has a right, at any rate initially, to choose its own form of government.

Implicitly, the tendency of early liberalism was towards democracy tempered by the rights of property.

There was a belief—not at first wholly explicit—that all men are born equal, and that their subsequent inequality is a product of circumstances.

This led to a great emphasis upon the importance of education as opposed to congenital characteristics.

There was a certain bias against government, because governments almost everywhere were in the hands of kings or aristocracies, who seldom either understood or respected the needs of merchants, but this bias was held in check by the hope that the necessary understanding and respect would be won before long.

Early liberalism was optimistic, energetic, and philosophic, because it represented growing forces which appeared likely to become victorious without great difficulty, and to bring by their victory great benefits to mankind.

It was opposed to everything medieval, both in philosophy and in politics, because medieval theories had been used to sanction the powers of the Church and King, to justify persecution, and to obstruct the rise of science; but it was equally opposed to the modern fanaticisms of Calvinists and Anabaptists.

It wanted an end to political and theological strife, in order to liberate energies for the exciting enterprises of commerce and science, such as the East India Company and the Bank of England, the theory of gravitation and the discovery of the circulation of the blood.

Throughout the Western world bigotry was giving place to enlightenment, the fear of Spanish power was ending, all classes were increasing in prosperity, and the highest hopes appeared to be warranted by the most sober judgment.

For a hundred years nothing appeared to dim these hopes; then, at last, they themselves generated the French Revolution, which led directly to Napoleon and thence to the Holy Alliance.

After these events, liberalism had to acquire its second wind before the renewed optimism of the nineteenth century became possible. (HWP 597)

LOVE

Can love and rationality be reconciled?

I regard love as one of the most important things in human life, and I regard any system as bad which interferes unnecessarily with its free development.

Love, when the word is properly used, does not denote any and every relation between the sexes, but only one involving considerable emotion, and a relation which is psychological as well as physical.

It may reach any degree of intensity. Such emotions as are expressed in "Tristan and Isolde" are in accordance with the experience of countless men and women. The power of giving artistic expression to the emotion of love is rare, but the emotion itself, at least in Europe, is not.

It is much commoner in some societies than in others, and this depends, I think, not upon the nature of the people concerned but upon their conventions and institutions.

In China it is rare, and appears in history as a characteristic of bad emperors who are misled by wicked concubines; traditional Chinese culture objected to all strong emotions and considered that a man should in all circumstances preserve the empire of reason.

In this it resembled the early eighteenth century.

We, who have behind us the romantic movement, the French Revolution, and the Great War [World War I] are conscious that the part of reason in human life is not so dominant as was hoped in the reign of Queen Anne. And reason itself has turned traitor in creating the doctrine of psychoanalysis.

The three main extra-rational activities in modern life are religion, war, and love; all these are extra-rational, but love is not anti-rational, that is to say, a reasonable man may reasonably rejoice in its existence. (MM 80–81)

Does romantic love have value?

Love poetry, however, is not the only purpose of love, and romantic love may flourish even where it does not lead to artistic expression.

I believe myself that romantic love is the source of the most intense delights that life has to offer.

In the relations of a man and woman who love each other with passion and imagination and tenderness, there is something of inestimable value, to be ignorant of which is a great misfortune to any human being.

I think it important that a social system should be such as to permit this joy, although it can only be an ingredient in life and not its main purpose. (MM 50)

How is a drive for business-success antagonistic to love?

In the modern world, however, love has an enemy more dangerous than religion, and that is the gospel of work and economic success.

It is generally held, especially in America, that a man should not allow love to interfere with his career, and that if he does, he is silly.

But in this as in all human matters a balance is necessary. It would be foolish, though in some cases it might be tragically heroic, to sacrifice career completely for love, but it is equally foolish and in no degree heroic to sacrifice love completely for career. Nevertheless this happens, and happens inevitably, in a society organized on the basis of a universal scramble for money.

Consider the life of a typical businessman of the present day, especially in America: from the time he is first grown-up he devotes all his best thoughts and all his best energies to financial success; everything else is merely unimportant recreation.

In his youth he satisfies his physical needs from time to time with prostitutes; presently he marries, but his interests are totally different from his wife's, and he never becomes really intimate with her.

He comes home late and tired from the office; he gets up in the morning before his wife is awake; he spends Sunday playing golf because exercise is necessary to keep him fit for the money-making struggle.

His wife's interests appear to him essentially feminine, and while he approves of them, he makes no attempt to share them.

He has no time for illicit love any more than for love in marriage, though he may, of course, occasionally visit a prostitute when he is away from home on business.

His wife probably remains sexually cold towards him, which is not to be wondered at, since he never has time to woo her.

Subconsciously he is dissatisfied, but he does not know why. He drowns his dissatisfaction mainly in work, but also in other less desirable ways, for example, by the sadistic pleasure to be derived from watching prize-fights or persecuting radicals.

His wife, who is equally unsatisfied, finds an outlet in second-rate culture, and in upholding virtue by harrying all those whose lives are generous and free.

In this way the lack of sexual satisfaction in both husband and wife turns to hatred of mankind disguised as public spirit and a high moral standard. (MM 81)

What's wrong with St. Paul's views on marriage and sex?

St. Paul apparently thought that the only thing needed in a marriage was opportunity for sexual intercourse, and this view has been on the whole encouraged by the teaching of Christian moralists. Their dislike of sex has blinded them to all the finer aspects of the sexual life, with the result that those who have suffered their teaching in youth go about the world blind to their own best potentialities.

Love is something more than desire for sexual intercourse; it is the principal means of escape from the loneliness which afflicts most men and women throughout the greater part of their lives. There is a deep-seated fear, in most people, of the cold world and the possible cruelty of the herd; there is a longing for affection, which is often concealed by roughness, boorishness or a bullying manner in men, and by nagging and scolding in women.

Passionate mutual love while it lasts puts an end to this feeling; it breaks down the hard walls of the ego, producing a new being composed of two in one.

Nature did not construct human beings to stand alone, since they cannot fulfill her biological purpose except with the help of another; and civilized people cannot fully satisfy their sexual instinct without love.

The instinct is not completely satisfied unless a man's whole being, mental quite as much as physical, enters into the relation.

Those who have never known the deep intimacy and the intense companionship of happy mutual love have missed the best thing that life has to give; unconsciously, if not consciously, they feel this, and the resulting disappointment inclines them towards envy, oppression, and cruelty.

To give due place to passionate love should be therefore a matter which concerns the sociologists, since if they miss this experience men and women cannot attain their full stature, and cannot feel towards the rest of the world that kind of generous warmth without which their social activities are pretty sure to be harmful. (MM 82)

To Edith

> Through the long years I sought peace,
> I found ecstasy, I found anguish,
>   I found madness.
> I found loneliness
> I found the solitary pain
>   that gnaws the heart,
> But peace I did not find.
>
> Now, old and near my end,
>   I have known you.
> And, knowing you,
> I have found both ecstasy and peace.
>   I know rest,
> After so many lonely years,
> I know what life and love may be.
>
> Now, if I sleep,
> I shall sleep fulfilled. (A1)

MACHINES

How can the boring effects of mass production be overcome?

The only way of avoiding the evils at present associated with machinery is to provide breaks in the monotony, with every encouragement to high adventure during the intervals.

Many men would cease to desire war if they had opportunities to risk their lives in Alpine climbing; one of the ablest and most vigorous workers for peace that it has been my good fortune to know habitually spent his summer climbing the most dangerous peaks in the Alps.

If every working man had a month in the year during which, if he chose, he could be taught to work an aeroplane, or encouraged to hunt for sapphires in the Sahara, or otherwise enabled to engage in some dangerous and exciting pursuit involving quick personal initiative, the popular love of war would be confined to women and invalids. (SE 89)

MALEVOLENCE

What is the evidence that people are malevolent?

In the ordinary man and woman there is a certain amount of malevolence, both special ill-will directed to particular enemies and general impersonal pleasure in the misfortunes of others.

It is customary to cover this over with fine phrases; about half of conventional morality is a cloak for it.

But it must be faced if the moralists' aim of improving our actions is to be achieved.

It is shown in a thousand ways, great and small: in the glee with which people repeat and believe scandal, in the unkind treatment of criminals in spite of clear proof that better treatment would have more effect in reforming them, in the unbelievable barbarity with which all white races treat negroes, and in the gusto with which old ladies and clergymen pointed out the duty of military service to young men during the war [World War I].

Even children may be the objects of wanton cruelty: David Copperfield and Oliver Twist are by no means imaginary.

This active malevolence is the worst feature of human nature and the one which it is most necessary to change if the world is to grow happier. (WIB 67)

MARRIAGE

Under what conditions is marriage an essential social institution?

In quite modern times, that is to say since about the period of the French Revolution, an idea has grown up that marriage should be the outcome of romantic love. Most moderns, at any rate in English-speaking countries, take this for granted, and have no idea that not long ago it was a revolutionary innovation.

The novels and plays of a hundred years ago deal largely with the struggle of the younger generation to establish this new basis for marriage as opposed to the traditional marriage of parental choice.

Whether the effect has been as good as the innovators hoped may be doubted.

There is something to be said for Mrs. Malaprop's principle, that love and aversion both wear off in matrimony so that it is better to begin with a little aversion.

Certain it is that when people marry without previous sexual knowledge of each other and under the influence of romantic love, each imagines the other to be possessed of more than mortal perfection, and conceives that marriage is going to be one long dream of bliss. This is especially liable to be the case with the woman if she has been brought up ignorant and pure, and therefore incapable of distinguishing sex hunger from congeniality.

In America, where the romantic view of marriage has been taken more seriously than anywhere else, and where law and custom alike are based upon the dreams of spinsters, the result has been an extreme prevalence of divorce and an extreme rarity of happy marriages.

Marriage is something more serious than the pleasure of two people in each other's company; it is an institution which, through the fact that it gives rise to children, forms part of the intimate texture of society, and has an importance extending far beyond the personal feelings of the husband and wife.

It may be good—I think it is good—that romantic love should form the motive for a marriage, but it should be understood that the kind of love which will enable a marriage to remain happy and to fulfill its social purpose is not romantic but is something more intimate, affectionate, and realistic.

In romantic love the beloved object is not seen accurately, but through a glamorous mist.

The view that romantic love is essential to marriage is too anarchic, and, like St. Paul's view, though in an opposite sense, it forgets that children are what make a marriage important.

But for children there would be no need for any institution concerned with sex, but as soon as children enter in, the husband and wife, if they have any sense of responsibility or any affection for their offspring, are compelled to realize that their feelings towards each other are no longer what is of most importance. (MM 51)

What makes for happiness—or unhappiness—in marriage?

When we look round the world at the present day and ask ourselves what conditions seem on the whole to make for happiness in marriage and what for unhappiness, we are driven to a somewhat curious conclusion, that the more civilized people become the less capable they seem of lifelong happiness with one partner.

Irish peasants, although until recent times marriages were decided by the parents, were said by those who ought to know them to be on the whole happy and virtuous in their conjugal life.

In general, marriage is easiest where people are less differentiated.

When a man differs little from other men, and a woman differs little from other women, there is no particular reason to regret not having married someone else.

But people with multifarious tastes and pursuits and interests will tend to desire congeniality in their partners, and to feel dissatisfied when they find that they have secured less of it than they might have obtained.

The Church, which tends to view marriage solely from the point of view of sex, sees no reason why one partner should not do just as well as another, and can therefore uphold the indissolubility of marriage without realizing the hardship that this often involves.

Another condition which makes for happiness in marriage is paucity of unowned women and absence of social occasions when husbands meet other women. If there is no possibility of sexual relations with any woman other than one's wife, most men will make the best of the situation and, except in abnormally bad cases, will find it quite tolerable. The same thing applies to wives, especially if they never imagine that marriage should bring much happiness.

That is to say, a marriage is likely to be what is called happy if neither party ever expected to get much happiness out of it. (MM 91–92)

What are other causes of unhappiness in marriage?

Among civilized people in the modern world none of these conditions for what is called happiness exist, and accordingly one finds that very few marriages after the first few years are happy.

Some of the causes of unhappiness are bound up with civilization, but others would disappear if men and women were more civilized than they are. Let us begin with the latter. Of these the most important is bad sexual education, which is a far commoner thing among the well-to-do than it can ever be among peasants.

Peasant children early become accustomed to what are called the facts of life, which they can observe not only among human beings but among animals. They are thus saved from both ignorance and fastidiousness.

The carefully educated children of the well-to-do, on the contrary, are shielded from all practical knowledge of sexual matters, and even the most modern parents, who teach children out of books, do not give them that sense of practical familiarity which the peasant child early acquires.

The triumph of Christian teaching is when a man and a woman marry without either having had previous sexual experience. In nine cases out of ten where this occurs, the results are unfortunate. Sexual behavior among human beings is not instinctive, so that the inexperienced bride and bridegroom, who are probably not aware of this fact, find themselves overwhelmed with shame and discomfort. It is little better when the woman alone is innocent but the man has acquired his knowledge from prostitutes.

Most men do not realize that a process of wooing is necessary after marriage, and many well-brought-up women do not realize what harm they do in marriage by remaining reserved and physically aloof.

All this could be put right by better sexual education, and is in fact very much better with the generation now young than it was with their parents and grandparents.

There used to be a widespread belief among women that they were morally superior to men on the ground that they had less pleasure in sex. This attitude made frank companionship between husbands and wives impossible. It was, of course, in itself quite unjustifiable, since failure to enjoy sex, so far from being virtuous, is a mere physiological or psychological deficiency, like failure to enjoy food, which also a hundred years ago was expected of elegant females. (MM 92)

How has women's emancipation made marriage more difficult?

In the old days the wife had to adapt herself to the husband, but the husband did not have to adapt himself to the wife.

Nowadays many wives, on grounds of woman's right to her own individuality and her own career, are unwilling to adapt themselves to their husbands beyond a point, while men who still hanker after the old tradition of masculine domination see no reason why they should do all the adapting.

This trouble arises especially in connection with infidelity.

In old days the husband was occasionally unfaithful, but as a rule his wife did not know of it. If she did, he confessed that he had sinned and made her believe that he was penitent. She, on the other hand, was usually virtuous. If she was not, and the fact came to her husband's knowledge, the marriage broke up.

Where, as happens in many modern marriages, mutual faithfulness is not demanded, the instinct of jealousy nevertheless survives, and often proves fatal to the persistence of any deeply rooted intimacy even where no overt quarrels occur. (MM 94–95)

MARX

What is wrong in Marx's thinking?

My objections to Marx are of two sorts: one, that he was muddle-headed; and the other, that his thinking was almost entirely inspired by hatred.

The doctrine of surplus value, which is supposed to demonstrate the exploitation of wage earners under capitalism, is arrived at, (a) by surreptitiously accepting Malthus's doctrine of population, which Marx and all his disciples explicitly repudiate; (b) by applying Ricardo's theory of value to wages, but not to the prices of manufactured articles.

He is entirely satisfied with the result, not because it is in accordance with the facts or because it is logically coherent, but because it is calculated to rouse fury in wage earners.

Marx's doctrine that all historical events have been motivated by class conflicts is a rash and untrue extension to world history of certain features prominent in England and France a hundred years ago.

His belief that there is a cosmic force called Dialectical Materialism which governs human history independently of human volitions, is mere mythology.

His theoretical errors, however, would not have mattered so much but for the fact that, like Tertullian and Carlyle, his chief desire was to see his enemies punished, and he cared little what happened to his friends in the process. (PFM 211)

There is no alchemy by which a universal harmony can be produced out of hatred.

Those who have been inspired to action by the doctrine of class war will have acquired the habit of hatred, and will instinctively seek new enemies when the old ones have been vanquished. (WW 20)

What is the motive-power that drives Marxism?

Marx, as everyone knows, thought that the conflict of classes has always been the main cause of social change, and will continue to be so until his followers are victorious, after which people will live happily ever after, as at the end of a fairy tale.

Marx himself is not concerned with justice, but only with resentment.

It is inevitable, so he says, that the underprivileged should be resentful and should be a majority—hence instability, revolution, class wars, etc.

The motive of the whole process in his system is not any positive principle of justice, but the purely negative principle of hatred.

I do not think that out of such a principle a good social system can be created.

As we have seen in Soviet Russia, when men whose motive-power is hatred acquire authority, they still from habit continue to hate, and will therefore turn upon each other.

The only possible issue of such a psychology is dictatorship and a police State.

This illustrates a principle which Marxists are apt to forget, namely, that it matters not only what is done but why it is done, since all passions, good and bad alike, have a certain momentum and a tendency to self-perpetuation. (NHCW 81)

What was Marx's chief error?

The most important error in his theory, to my mind, is that it ignores intelligence as a cause.

Men and Apes in the same environment, have different methods of securing food: men practice agriculture, not because of some extra-human dialectic compelling them to do so, but because intelligence shows them its advantages.

The industrial revolution might have taken place in antiquity if Greek intelligence had remained what it was at its best.

To this it is customary to reply that slave labor, being cheap, removed the incentive to the invention of labor-saving devices.

The facts do not bear out this view.

Modern methods of production began in the cotton industry, not only in spinning and weaving, which employed "free" labor, but also in the gathering of cotton, which was the work of slaves.

Moreover, no slaves were ever cheaper than the wretched children whom the Lancashire manufacturers employed in the factories of the early nineteenth century, where they had to work 14 or 16 hours a day, for little more than board and lodging, till they died. (It must be remembered that the death of a slave was an economic loss to his owner, but the death of a wage earner is not.)

Yet it was these same ruthless employers who were the pioneers of the industrial revolution, because their heads were better than their hearts.

Without intelligence, men would never have learned to economize hand labor by the help of machines. (UH 35)

Did Marx put too much emphasis on economic power?

Marx, in the first place, put too much emphasis on economic as opposed to other forms of power.

Second, misled by the state of business in the 1840s in England, he thought it was ownership that gives power and not executive control.

Both those interpretations led him to propose a panacea for all the ills of the world which proved entirely fallacious. (SHM 65)

What did Marx fail to take into account?

In spite of the fundamental importance of econom
ing the politics and beliefs of an age or nation, I d
non-economic factors can be neglected without risks of err
be fatal in practice.

These four passions—acquisitiveness, rivalry, vanity, and lo
power—are, after the basic instincts, the prime movers of all that happen
in politics.

Only one, acquisitiveness, is concerned at all directly with men's
relations to their material conditions.

The other three—vanity, rivalry, love of power—are concerned with
social relations.

I think this is the source of what is erroneous in the Marxian interpretation of history, which tacitly assumes that acquisitiveness is the
source of all political actions. (WW 22)

How did Marx's intellectual error lead to tyranny?

Karl Marx, owing to a purely intellectual error, imagined that if private
property were abolished, economic injustice would cease.

He made this mistake because he did not realize that property is
only one form of power, and that to abolish private property while
concentrating power in the hands of a minority not only ensures an
intolerable tyranny, but also must lead to the greatest economic injustice.

The percentage difference between generals and privates is greater
in modern Russia than in any other civilized country.

The gulf between the pay of officers and the pay of privates in
the army is such as to horrify Americans, but that does not stop
Communists from speaking of America as the home of plutocracy and
of Russia as the country where the interests of the proletariat prevail.
(FF 68)

Why did Marx want to help the working class?

His devotion to the interests of the proletariat is perhaps somewhat
surprising, in view of his bourgeois origin and his academic education.

ion associated with feelings
ith social superiors, ruthless

ter that first led him to become

feeling of inferiority, but perhaps
race and a Christian by education.
had to endure the contempt of
nout being able to fall back upon
be possible to a Jew by religion.

MATH

How has math influenced ideas about religion, God, and mysticism?

Mathematics is, I believe, the chief source of the belief in eternal and exact truth, as well as in a supersensible intelligible world.

Geometry deals with exact circles, but no sensible object is *exactly* circular; however carefully we may use our compasses, there will be some imperfections and irregularities.

This suggests the view that all exact reasoning applies to ideal as opposed to sensible objects; it is natural to go further, and to argue that thought is nobler than sense, and the objects of thought more real than those of sense-perception.

Mystical doctrines as to the relation of time to eternity are also reinforced by pure mathematics, for mathematical objects, such as numbers, if real at all, are eternal and not in time.

Such eternal objects can be conceived as God's thoughts. Hence Plato's doctrine that God is a geometer, and Sir James Jean's belief that He is addicted to arithmetic.

The combination of mathematics with theology, which began with Pythagoras, characterized religious philosophy in Greece, in the Middle Ages and in modern times down to Kant.

In Plato, Saint Augustine, Thomas Aquinas, Descartes, Spinoza, and Kant, there is an intimate blending of religion and reasoning, of moral aspiration with logical admiration of what is timeless, which comes from Pythagoras, and distinguishes the intellectualized theology of Europe from the more straightforward mysticism of Asia.

It is only in quite recent times that it has been possible to say clearly where Pythagoras was wrong.

I do not know of any other man who has been as influential as he was in the sphere of thought. I say this because what appears as Platonism is, when analyzed, found to be in essence Pythagoreanism.

The whole conception of an eternal world, revealed to the intellect but not to the senses, is derived from him.

But for him, Christians would not have thought of Christ as the Word; but for him, theologians would not have sought logical *proofs* of God and immortality. (Italics added) (HWP 37)

How has geometry influenced philosophy and scientific method?

Geometry, as established by the Greeks, starts with axioms which are (or are deemed to be) self-evident, and proceeds, by deductive reasoning, to arrive at theorems that are very far from self-evident.

The axioms and theorems are held to be true of actual space, which is something given in experience.

It thus appeared to be possible to discover things about the actual world by first noticing what is self-evident and then using deduction.

This view influenced Plato and Kant, and most of the intermediate philosophers.

When the Declaration of Independence says "we hold these truths to be self-evident," it is modeling itself on Euclid.

The eighteenth-century doctrine of natural rights is a search for Euclidean axioms in politics.

The form of Newton's *Principia,* in spite of its admittedly empirical material, is entirely dominated by Euclid. (Italics added) (HWP 36)

MONEY

Why do most people want to have more money?

It may seem, at first sight, as though material goods were what we desire.

But, in fact, we desire these mainly in order to impress our neighbors.

When a man moves into a larger house in a more genteel quarter, he reflects that "better" people will call on his wife, and some unprosperous cronies of former days can be dropped.

When he sends his son to a good school or an expensive university, he consoles himself for the heavy fees by thoughts of the social kudos to be gained.

In every big city, whether of Europe or of America, houses in some districts are more expensive than equally good houses in other districts, merely because they are more fashionable.

One of the most powerful of all our passions is the desire to be admired and respected.

As things stand, admiration and respect are given to the man who seems to be rich.

This is the chief reason why people wish to be rich.

The actual goods purchased by their money play quite a secondary part.

Take, for example, a millionaire who cannot tell one picture from another, but has acquired a gallery of old masters by the help of experts. The only pleasure he derives from his pictures is the thought that others know how much they have cost; he would derive more direct enjoyment from sentimental chromos out of Christmas numbers, but he would not obtain the same satisfaction for his vanity.

All this might be different, and has been different in many societies.

In aristocratic epochs, men have been admired for their birth.

In some circles in Paris, men are admired for their artistic or literary excellence, strange as it may seem.

In a German university, a man may actually be admired for his learning.

In India, saints are admired; in China, sages.

The study of these differing societies shows the correctness of our analysis, for in all of them we find a large percentage of men who are indifferent to money so long as they have enough to keep alive on, but are keenly desirous of the merits by which, in their environment, respect is to be won. (SE 85)

MORALITY

What's wrong with the way conventional morality views the virtuous man?

The world has need of ways of thinking and feeling which are adapted to what we know, to what we can believe, and what we feel ourselves compelled to disbelieve.

There are ways of feeling that are traditional and that have all the prestige of the past and weighty authority, and yet that are not adapted to the world in which we live, where new techniques have made some new virtues necessary and some old virtues unnecessary.

The Hebrew prophets, surrounded by hostile nations, and determined that their race should not be assimilated by Gentile conquerors, developed a fierce doctrine in which the leading conception was sin.

The Gentiles sinned always and in all their ways, but the Jews, alas, were only too apt to fall into sin themselves.

When they did so, they were defeated in battle and had to weep by the waters of Babylon.

It is this pattern which has inspired moralists ever since. The virtuous man has been conceived as one who, though continually surrounded by temptation, though passionately prompted to sin, nevertheless, by almost superhuman strength of will, succeeds in walking along the straight and narrow path, looking meanwhile disdainfully to the right and left at those inferior beings who have loitered to pluck flowers along the way.

In this conception, virtue is difficult, negative, and arid.

It is constrictive and suspicious of happiness.

It is persuaded that our natural impulses are bad and that society can only be held together by means of rigid prohibitions.

I do not wish to pretend that society can hold together if people murder and steal.

What I do say is, that the kind of man whom I should wish to see in the world is one who will have no impulse to murder, and who will abstain from murder not because it is prohibited but because his thoughts and feelings carry him away from impulses of destruction. (NHCW 8–9)

What mistake does conventional morality make? [1918]

Conventional morality leads us to expect unselfishness in decent people. This is an error.

Man is an animal bent on securing food and propagating the species. One way of succeeding in these objects is to persuade others that one is after *their* welfare—but to be really after any welfare but one's own and one's children's is unnatural. It occurs like sadism and sodomy, but is equally against nature.

A good social system is not to be secured by making people unselfish, but by making their own vital impulses fit in with other people's. This is feasible.

Our present system [Capitalism] makes self-preservation only possible at the expense of others. The system is at fault; but it is a weakness to be disgusted with people because they aim at self-preservation. One's idealism needs to be too robust for such weaknesses. It doesn't do to forget or deny the animal in man. The God in man will not be visible, as a rule, while the animal is thwarted.

Those who have produced stoic philosophies have all had enough to eat and drink.

The sum total of the matter is that one's idealism must be *robust* and must fit in with the facts of nature, and that which is horrible in the actual world is mainly due to a bad system. (A2 120)

Is there something better than traditional morality?

I should wish to persuade those to whom traditional morals have gone dead, and who yet feel the need of some serious purpose over and above momentary pleasure, that there is a way of thinking and feeling which is not difficult for those who have not been trained in its opposite, and which is not one of self-restraint, negation, and condemnation.

The good life, as I conceive it, is a happy life.

I do not mean that if you are good you will be happy; I mean that if you are happy you will be good.

Unhappiness is deeply implanted in the souls of most of us. How many people we all know who go through life apparently gay, and who yet are perpetually in search of intoxication whether of the Bacchic kind or some other.

The happy man does not desire intoxication. Nor does he envy his neighbor and therefore hate him.

He can live the life of impulse like a child, because happiness makes his impulses fruitful and not destructive.

There are many men and women who imagine themselves emancipated from the shackles of ancient codes but who, in fact, are emancipated only in the upper layers of their minds.

Below these layers lies the sense of guilt crouching like a wild beast waiting for moments of weakness or inattention, and growling venomous angers which rise to the surface in strange distorted forms.

Such people have the worst of both worlds.

The feeling of guilt makes real happiness impossible for them, but the conscious rejection of old codes of behavior makes them act perpetually in ways that feed the maw of the ancient beast beneath.

A way of life cannot be successful as long as it is a mere intellectual conviction.

It must be deeply felt, deeply believed, dominant even in dreams.

I do not think that the best kind of life is possible in our day for those who, below the level of consciousness, are still obsessed by the load of sin.

It is obvious that there are things that had better not be done, but I do not think the best way to avoid the doing of such things is to label them sin and represent them as almost irresistably attractive.

And so I should wish to offer to the world something scarcely to be called an ethic, at any rate in the old acceptance of that word, but something which will nonetheless, save men from moral perplexity and from remorse and from condemnation of others.

What I should put in the place of an ethic in the old sense is encouragement and opportunity for all the impulses that are creative and expansive.

I should do everything possible to liberate men from fear, not only conscious fears, but the old imprisoned primeval terrors that we brought with us out of the jungle.

I should make it clear, not merely as an intellectual proposition, but as something that the heart spontaneously believes, that it is not by making others suffer that we shall achieve our own happiness, but that happiness and the means to happiness depend upon harmony with other men.

When all this is not only understood but deeply felt, it will be easy to live in a way that brings happiness equally to ourselves and to others. (NHCW 10)

Wouldn't it be a mess if everyone had his own private system of morality?

It would be if that were so but in fact they're not so private as all that, because they get embodied in the criminal law and in public approval and disapproval.

People don't like to incur public disapproval and in that way the accepted code of morality becomes a very potent thing. (SHM 53)

Are intelligence and morality compatible?

The solution of the dilemma between freedom and discipline must obviously be sought in a compromise.

We cannot admire a social system which allows no scope for individual achievement, and we cannot approve one in which excessive individualism makes the social system unstable.

Some would argue that there is a fundamental opposition between intelligence and morality, that only stupidity and superstition makes men good, and that an intellectually emancipated man is bound to be completely selfish.

This, however, is an obscurantist theory, which takes a wrong view both of morality and of intelligence.

Where genuine and superstitious morality have been hopelessly confused in the teaching of the young, it may be difficult for them to disentangle the two.

If you have been taught that it is as wicked to swear as it is to steal, you may, when you decide that swearing is permissible, conclude that there is no harm in stealing, but if so that only shows that you are not intelligent and that you were taught a foolish morality.

Genuine morality cannot be such as intelligence would undermine, nor does intelligence necessarily promote selfishness.

It only does so when unselfishness has been inculcated for the wrong reasons, and then only so long as its purview is limited.

In this respect science is a useful element in culture, for it has a stability which intelligence does not shake, and it generates an impersonal habit of mind that makes it natural to accept a social rather than a purely individual ethic.

But history is perhaps an even better antidote to anarchic individualism as well as to a lifeless traditionalism. (UH 52)

What is taboo morality?

I mean the sort of morality that consists in giving a set of rules mainly as to what things you must not do, without giving any reasons for those rules.

Sometimes reasons cannot be found, other times they can, but in any case, the rules are considered absolute and these things you must not do.

Of course a great deal of taboo morality is entirely compatible with what one might call rational morality, for instance, that you shouldn't steal or that you shouldn't murder. Those are precepts which are entirely in accord with reason, but they are set forth as taboos; they have consequences that they ought not to have.

For instance, in the case of murder, it is considered that it forbids euthanasia, which I think a rational person would be in favor of. (SHM 51)

What harm do moral taboos do?

They are usually ancient and come down from a different sort of society from that in which we live, where really a different ethic was appropriate, and very often they are not appropriate to modern times.

I think that applies in particular to artificial insemination, which is a thing that the moralists of the past hadn't thought of.

Take the question of birth control. There is a very powerful taboo by certain sections of the community which is calculated to do enormous harm.

It is calculated to promote poverty and war and to make the solution of many social problems impossible. (SHM 57)

What are two types of moral guidelines?

Popular morality—including that of the churches, though not that of the great mystics—lays down rules of conduct rather than ends of life.

The morality that ought to exist lays down ends of life rather than rules of conduct.

Christ says: "Thou shalt love thy neighbor as thyself"; this lays down one of the ends of life.

The Decalogue says, "Remember that thou keep holy the Sabbath Day"; this lays down a rule of action.

The belief in the importance of rules of conduct is superstitious; what is important is to care for good ends.

A good man is a man who cares for the happiness of his relations and friends, and, if possible, that of mankind in general, or, again, a man who cares for art and science.

Whether such a man obeys the rules laid down by the Jews thousands of years ago is quite unimportant. (BW 348)

Lord Russell, what do you mean by personal morality?

No man is wholly free, and no man is wholly a slave.

To the extent to which a man has freedom, he needs a personal morality to guide his conduct.

There are some who would say that a man need only obey the accepted moral code of his community.

But I do not think any student of anthropology would be content with this answer.

Such practices as cannibalism, human sacrifice, and head hunting have died out as a result of moral protests against conventional moral opinion.

If a man seriously desires to live the best life that is open to him, he must learn to be critical of the tribal customs and tribal beliefs that are generally accepted among his neighbors. (AI 68)

MYSTICISM

Do mystical insights have value?

Of the reality or unreality of the mystic's world I know nothing.

I have no wish to deny it, nor even to declare that the insight which reveals it is not a genuine insight.

What I do wish to maintain—and it is here that the scientific attitude becomes imperative—is that insight, untested and unsupported, is an insufficient guarantee of truth, in spite of the fact that much of the most important truth is first suggested by its means.

It is common to speak of an opposition between instinct and reason; in the eighteenth century, the opposition was drawn in favor of reason, but under the influence of Rousseau and the romantic movement, instinct was given the preference, first by those who rebelled against artificial forms of government and thought, and then, as the purely rationalistic defense of traditional theology became increasingly difficult, by all who felt in science a menace to creeds which they associated with a spiritual outlook on life and the world.

Bergson, under the name of "intuition," has raised instinct to the position of sole arbiter of metaphysical truth.

But in fact, the opposition of instinct and reason is mainly illusory.

Instinct, intuition, or insight is what first leads to the beliefs which subsequent reason confirms or confutes; but the confirmation, where it is possible, consists, in the last analysis, of agreement with other beliefs no less instinctive.

Reason is a harmonizing, controlling force rather than a creative one.

Even in the most purely logical realms, it is insight that first arrives at what is new. (SPBR 334)

NATIONALISM

Why do people want to be divided up into nation-states?

It's part of our emotional apparatus that we are liable to both love and hate, and we like to exercise them.

We love our compatriots and we hate foreigners.

Of course, we love our compatriots only when we're thinking of foreigners.

When we've forgotten foreigners, we don't love them so much. (SHM 85)

Is nationalism good or bad?

One would have to distinguish between cultural and political aspects of nationalism.

From the cultural point of view one of the rather sad things about the modern world is its extraordinary uniformity.

If you go to an expensive hotel, there's nothing whatever to show you which continent it's in or which part of the world; they are all exactly alike all over the whole world, and that gets a little dull and makes rich traveling really hardly worth doing.

If you want to see foreign countries, you have to travel poor.

There's a great deal to be said for nationalism, for keeping diversity— in literature, in art, in language, and in all kinds of cultural things.

But when it comes to politics, I think nationalism is unmitigated evil.

I don't think there's a single thing to be said in its favor. (SHM 83)

What are the main purposes of the nation-state?

The main purposes are what the state itself calls "defensive"—and what all other states call "aggression." It's the same phenomenon only it has different names from two sides.

In fact the state is primarily an organization for killing foreigners, that's its main purpose.

There are, of course, other things they do.

They do a certain amount of educating, but in the course of educating, they try very hard to make the young think it is a grand thing to kill foreigners. (SHM 83)

What is harmful about nationalism?

[It] inculcates the view that your own country is glorious and has always been right in everything, whereas other countries—well, as Mr. Podsnap says in Dickens, "Foreign nations, I am sorry to say, do as they do."

I don't think it's right to view foreign nations in that way.

I wrote a book in which I said, "There is, of course, one nation which has all the supreme virtues that every nation arrogates to itself. That one is the one to which my reader belongs."

And I got a letter from a Pole saying, "I'm so glad you recognize the superiority of Poland." (SHM 84)

How serious is the problem of nationalism?

I think nationalism, apart from the tension and danger of an East-West war, is the greatest danger that man is faced with at the present time [1959]. (SHM 89)

How can we keep nationalism from going too far?

You can never make sure [that it doesn't go too far].

But what you can say and what the world will have to say, if man is to survive, is that armies and navies and air forces should not be national but international.

Then it won't much matter if you think ill of some other country provided you're not in a position to kill them off. (SHM 85)

Don't people do splendid things for the glory of their nation?

I think there are plenty of ways of keeping that.

Take a thing like the Everest expedition; it's not only a country that does it, but almost always some institution or some collection of very rich men, or something of that sort, and you can do it for their glory just as well as for the glory of your country. (SHM 86)

In times of national danger, shouldn't we support our nation?

You've got to get into people's heads that while it's quite proper to resist aggression, it is not proper to commit aggression. (SHM 87)

Isn't nationalism a useful way of stimulating competition?

I don't mind at all having competition and emulation provided it doesn't involve killing.

I think that municipal rivalry is all right. If one city builds a very fine town hall, another thinks, "We must have a fine town hall." All that's to the good.

Manchester and Liverpool, I understand, don't love each other, but they haven't got private armies to go to war with each other. (SHM 86)

Why is nationalism more virulent today?

It's due to education.

Education has done an awful lot of harm.

I sometimes think it would have been better if people were still unable to read or write.

Because the great majority, when they learn to read and write, become open to propaganda, and in each country propaganda is controlled by the state and is what the state likes.

And what the state likes is to have you quite ready to commit murder when you're told to. (SHM 90)

How nationalistic are the countries of Africa and Asia?

I should think that both African and Asian nationalism are, at the moment, more fierce than any that exist among Europeans, because they've just awakened to it.

I think it is a very, very great danger. (SHM 89)

Recent Arab nationalism has produced self-confidence. Is that good or bad?

Insofar as it involves raising the self-respect of Arabs and making Arabs think they are capable of great achievements—in all that, it's good.

But insofar as it involves hatred of people who are not Arabs, for example the people of Israel, it can't be considered good. (SHM 87)

Should there be limits to national freedom?

It does not follow, although many people seem to think that it does, that a nation should be subject to no control whatever.

Insofar as nations form an international community, individual nations need the control of law just as individual persons do in a national community.

There is as much difference between imperialism and international control as there is between slavery and the control of the criminal law.

In the reaction against imperialism, nations which emancipate themselves from the control of a single imperialistic power are apt to make a claim for complete independence of all control, which can only be justified on principles which lead straight to anarchism.

It must be said that the great powers are about equally to blame.

They tend to favor an international authority only so long as they feel sure of dominating it, and they thus make it appear as merely a disguised prolongation of the old imperialism. (FF 53)

NATURE

Is nature a friend of man, an enemy, or neither?

The philosophy of nature should not be unduly terrestrial; the earth is merely one of the smaller planets of one of the smaller stars of the Milky Way.

Vitalism as a philosophy, and evolutionism, show, in this respect, a lack of sense of proportion and logical relevance. They regard the facts of life, which are personally interesting to us, as having a cosmic significance, not a significance confined to the earth's surface.

Optimism and pessimism, as cosmic philosophies, show the same naive humanism; the great world, so far as we know it from the philosophy of nature, is neither good nor bad, and is not concerned to make us happy or unhappy.

All such philosophies spring from self-importance, and are best corrected by a little astronomy. (WIB 15)

What is "natural" or "unnatural"?

I think there is a mixture of truth and falsehood in the admiration of "nature," which it is important to disentangle.

To begin with, what is "natural"? Roughly speaking, anything to which the speaker was accustomed in childhood.

Lao-Tze objects to roads and carriages and boats, all of which were probably unknown in the village where he was born.

Rousseau has got used to these things, and does not regard them as against nature. But he would no doubt have thundered against railways, if he had lived to see them.

Clothes and cooking are too ancient to be denounced by most of the apostles of nature, though they all object to new fashions in either.

Birth control is thought wicked by people who tolerate celibacy, because the former is a new violation of nature and the latter an ancient one.

In all these ways those who preach "nature" are inconsistent, and one is tempted to regard them as mere conservatives. (WIB 80)

OPTIMISM

Is optimism always desirable?

Optimism is pleasant as long as it is credible, but when it is not, it is intensely irritating.

Especially irritating is the optimism about our own troubles which is displayed by those who do not have to share them.

Optimism about other people's troubles is a very risky business unless it goes with quite concrete proposals as to how to make the troubles disappear.

A medical man has the right to be optimistic about your illness if he can prescribe a treatment which will cure it, but a friend who merely says, "Oh, I expect you will soon feel better," is exasperating.

In every kind of trouble what is wanted is not emotional cheerfulness but constructive thinking. (MAO 73)

What can an optimist believe today about the future? [1948]

During the First World War it still seemed possible to hope—indeed most people did hope—that after the peace a better world would be created than that which preceded 1914.

Few had such a hope during the Second World War, and hardly any retained it after the fighting ceased.

The optimist now is the man who thinks it possible to hope that the world will not get worse. (RTF 6)

Lord Russell, are you optimistic about the future? [1956]

I grew up in the full flood of Victorian optimism, and although the easy cheerfulness of that time is no longer possible, something remains with me of the hopefulness that then was easy.

It demands a certain fortitude and a certain capacity to look beyond the moment to a more distant future.

But I remain convinced, whatever dark times may lie before us, that mankind will emerge, that the habit of mutual forbearance, which now seems lost, will be recovered, and that the reign of brutal violence will not last forever.

Mankind has to learn some new lessons of which the necessity is due to increase of skill without increase of wisdom.

Moral and intellectual requirements are inextricably intertwined.

Evil passions [like hatred] make men incapable of seeing the truth, and false beliefs [like fundamentalism] afford excuses for evil passions.

If the world is to emerge, it requires both clear thinking and kindly feeling.

It may be that neither will be learnt except through utmost disaster.

I hope this is not the case. I hope that something less painful can teach wisdom.

But by whatever arduous road, I am convinced that the new wisdom which the new world requires will be learnt sooner or later, and that the best part of human history lies in the future, not in the past. (PFM 17)

Lord Russell, considering the sorry state of the world, why do you feel optimistic about the future? [1952]

I am convinced that intelligence, patience, and eloquence can, sooner or later, lead the human race out of its self-imposed tortures provided it does not exterminate itself meanwhile.

On the basis of this belief, I have always had a certain degree of optimism, although, as I have grown older, the optimism has grown more sober and the happy issue more distant.

But I remain completely incapable of agreeing with those who accept fatalistically the view that man is born to trouble.

The causes of unhappiness in the past and in the present are not difficult to ascertain.

There have been poverty, pestilence, and famine, which were due to man's inadequate mastery of nature.

There have been wars, oppressions, and tortures, which have been due to men's hostility to their fellow men.

And there have been morbid miseries fostered by gloomy creeds, which have led men into profound inner discords that made all outward prosperity of no avail.

All these are unnecessary. In regard to all of them, means are known by which they can be overcome.

In the modern world, if communities are unhappy, it is because they choose to be so.

Or, to speak more precisely, because they have ignorances, habits, beliefs, and passions, which are dearer to them than happiness or even life.

I find many men in our dangerous age who seem to be in love with misery and death, and who grow angry when hopes are suggested to them.

They think that hope is irrational and that, in sitting down to lazy despair, they are merely facing facts.

I cannot agree with these men.

To preserve hope in our world makes calls upon our intelligence and our energy.

In those who despair it is very frequently the energy that is lacking. (PFM 54)

How is Shakespeare's King Lear *not completely pessimistic?*

In *King Lear,* even in the blackest and most despairing passages there is a redeeming sublimity.

One feels in reading that, though life may be bad and the world full of unmerited suffering, yet there is in man a capacity of greatness and occasional splendor which makes ultimate and complete despair impossible. (FF 31)

OUTLOOK

How do you view the world situation today, Lord Russell? [1951]

It must be said that the purely intellectual problems presented by the world of our day [1951] are exceedingly difficult.

There is not only the great problem: can we defend our Western world without actual war?

There are also problems in Asia and problems in Africa and problems in tropical America which cannot be solved within the framework of the traditional political ideas.

There are those, it is true, who are quite certain that they can solve these problems by ancient methods.

Consider MacArthur and his Republican supporters.

So limited is his intelligence and his imagination that he is never puzzled for one moment.

All we have to do is to go back to the days of the Opium War.

After we have killed a sufficient number of millions of Chinese, the survivors among them will perceive our moral superiority and hail MacArthur as a savior. But let us not be one-sided.

Stalin, I should say, is equally simple-minded and equally out of date.

He, too, believes that if his armies could occupy Britain and reduce us all to the economic level of Soviet peasants and the political level of convicts, we should hail him as a great deliverer and bless the day when we were freed from the shackles of democracy.

One of the painful things about our time is that those who feel certainty are stupid, and those with any imagination and understanding are filled with doubt and indecision.

I do not think this is necessary.

I think there is a view of man and his destiny and his present troubles which can give certainty and hope together with the completest understanding of the moods, the despairs, and the maddening doubts that beset modern men. (Italics added) (NHCW 14)

PANACEAS

Lord Russell, are there programs that can solve the world's problems?

I have never been able to believe wholeheartedly in any simple nostrum by which all ills are to be cured.

On the contrary, I have come to think that one of the main causes of trouble in the world is dogmatic and fanatical belief in some doctrine for which there is no adequate evidence.

Nationalism, Fascism, Communism, and now anti-Communism have all produced their crop of bigoted zealots ready to work untold horror in the interests of some narrow creed.

All such fanaticisms have in greater or less degree the defect which I found in the Moscow Marxists, namely, that their dynamic power is largely due to hate. (PFM 38)

PERSECUTION

Why were Protestants persecuted in the sixteenth century?

I have no wish to enter upon a theological argument, but anyone who cares to examine the theological innovations introduced by the Protestants in the sixteenth century will find that practically every one of them was such as to diminish the income of the clergy, and I think it would be contrary to all we know about human nature to suppose that this had nothing to do with the opposition offered by the Catholic Church to the heretics.

The clergy caused many thousands to be burnt at the stake, believing, no doubt, that their motive was wholly laudable.

In this they resembled Stalin and the British landowners who passed the Enclosure Acts, but in all cases alike, the fury which gave momentum to the movement had a very egotistical source, though one which perhaps remained subconscious. (FF 89)

What has often been the excuse for persecution?

Within a national state, there are certain matters which should be left free from government control.

It is now generally recognized that religion is one of these matters.

In the sixteenth and seventeenth centuries, this was not recognized, and violent persecutions were carried out to ensure theological uniformity.

In the modern world, it is not theology, but politics, that rouses the persecuting spirit.

In Russia this spirit is in absolute control.

In America it is much stronger than it ought to be.

The excuse is, of coure, that political dissidents are a danger to the State, but this excuse also existed in the sixteenth and seventeenth centuries.

Queen Elizabeth persecuted the Jesuits, but Jesuits maintained that she was not the lawful Sovereign, and acted as fifth columnists for the Spaniards.

There is the same excuse in the present day for objecting to Communists in non-Communist countries.

But in the one case as in the other, people are subversive because of persecution as well as being persecuted because of the subversiveness. Any lessening of one lessens the other.

No English Jesuit of the present day wants the new Queen Elizabeth dethroned for the benefit of some Jacobite heir.

And this is no doubt partly because Jesuits are no longer persecuted. (FF 101)

PERSUASION

How does advertising persuade?

It is pleasant to believe in so-and-so's pills, since it gives you hope of better health; it is possible to believe in them, if you find their excellence very frequently and emphatically asserted.

Nonrational propaganda like the rational sort must appeal to existing desires, but it substitutes iteration for appeal to fact.

The opposition between a rational and an irrational appeal is, in practice, less clear-cut than in the above analysis. Usually there is *some* rational evidence, though not enough to be conclusive; the irrationality consists in attaching too much weight to it. (P 144)

How do religions persuade?

The process, reduced to its bare formula, is this: if a certain proposition is true, I shall be able to realize my desires; therefore I wish this proposition to be true; therefore, unless I have exceptional intellectual self-control, I believe it to be true.

Orthodoxy, and a virtuous life, I am told, will enable me to go to heaven when I die; there is pleasure in believing this, and therefore I shall probably believe it if it is forcibly presented to me.

The cause of belief, here, is not, as in science, the evidence of fact, but the pleasant feelings derived from belief, together with sufficient vigor of assertion in the environment to make the belief seem not incredible. (P 144)

PHILOSOPHY

What is philosophy?

That's a very controversial question.

I think no two philosophers will give the same answer.

My own view would be that philosophy consists of speculations about matters where exact knowledge is not yet possible. (SHM 9)

It is not definite knowledge, for that is science.

Nor is it groundless credulity, such as that of savages.

It is something between these two extremes: perhaps it might be called "The art of rational conjecture."

According to this definition, philosophy tells us how to proceed when we want to find out what may be true, or is *most likely* to be true, where it is impossible to know with certainty what *is* true.

The art of rational conjecture is very useful in two different ways.

First: often the most difficult step in the discovery of what *is* true is thinking of a hypothesis which *may* be true; when once the hypothesis has been thought of, it can be tested, but it may require a man of genius to think of it.

Second: we often have to act in spite of uncertainty, because delay would be dangerous or fatal; in such a case, it is useful to possess an art by which we can judge what is probable. This art, so far as very general hypotheses are concerned, is philosophy.

Particular questions, such as "Will it rain tomorrow?" do not belong to philosophy; philosophy is concerned with general questions, such as: "Is the world governed by mechanical laws, or has it a cosmic purpose, or has it both characteristics at once?"

Philosophy examines whether anything can be said on such general questions. (AP 1)

What's the difference between science and philosophy?

Roughly, science is what we know and philosophy is what we don't know. (SHM 9)

What kinds of topics does philosophy deal with?

Almost all the questions of most interest to speculative minds are such as science cannot answer, and the confident answers of theologians no longer seem so convincing as they did in former centuries.

Is the world divided into mind and matter, and, if so, what is mind and what is matter? Is mind subject to matter, or is it possessed of independent powers?

Has the universe any unity or purpose? Is it evolving toward some goal?

Are there really laws of nature, or do we believe in them only because of our innate love of order?

Is man what he seems to the astronomer, a tiny lump of impure carbon and water impotently crawling on a small and unimportant planet? Or is he what he appears to Hamlet? Is he perhaps both at once?

Is there a way of living that is noble and another that is base, or are all ways of living merely futile?

If there is a way of living that is noble, in what does it consist, and how shall we achieve it?

Must the good be eternal in order to deserve to be valued, or is it worth seeking even if the universe is inexorably moving towards death?

Is there such a thing as wisdom, or is what seems such merely the ultimate refinement of folly?

To such questions no answer can be found in the laboratory. Theologians have professed to give answers, all too definite; but their very definiteness causes modern minds to view them with suspicion.

The studying of these questions, if not the answering of them, is the business of philosophy. (HWP xiii)

What are three main types of philosophy currently?

Philosophy, from the earliest times, has made greater claims, and achieved fewer results, than any other branch of learning.

Ever since Thales said that all is water, philosophers have been ready with glib assertions about the sum-total of things; and equally glib denials have come from other philosophers ever since Thales was contradicted by Anaximander.

I believe that the time has now arrived when this unsatisfactory state of things can be brought to an end. I shall try, chiefly, by taking certain special problems as examples, to indicate wherein the claims of philosophers have been excessive and why their achievements have not been greater.

Among present-day philosophies, we may distinguish three principal types, often combined in varying proportions by a single philosopher, but in essence and tendency distinct.

The first of these, which I shall call the classical tradition, descends in the main from Kant and Hegel; it represents the attempt to adapt to present needs the methods and results of the great constructive philosophers from Plato downwards.

The second type, which may be called evolutionism, derived its prominence from Darwin, and must be reckoned as having had Herbert Spencer for its first philosophical representative, but in recent times it has become, chiefly through William James and M. Bergson, far bolder and more searching in its innovations than it was in the hands of Herbert Spencer.

The third type, which may be called "logical atomism" for want of a better name, has gradually crept into philosophy through the critical scrutiny of mathematics.

This type of philosophy, which is the one that I wish to advocate, has not as yet many wholehearted adherents, but the "new realism" which owes its inception to Harvard is very largely impregnated with its spirit.

It represents, I believe, the same kind of advance as was introduced into physics by Galileo: the substitution of piecemeal, detailed, and verifiable results for large untested generalities recommended only by a certain appeal to imagination. (SPBR 312)

What good is philosophy? Why become a philosopher?

I think philosophy has two uses.

One is to keep alive speculation about things that are not yet amenable to scientific knowledge.

Scientific knowledge covers a very small part of the things that interest mankind.

I don't want people's imaginations to be limited and enclosed within what can now be known.

But there's another use, equally important, which is to show that there are things we thought we knew, and don't know. On the one hand, philosophy is to keep us thinking about things that we may come to know, and on the other hand to keep us modestly aware of how much that seems like knowledge isn't knowledge. (SHM 9)

Science tells us what we can know, but what we can know is little, and if we forget how much we cannot know, we become insensitive to many things of very great importance.

Theology, on the other hand, induces a dogmatic belief that we have knowledge where in fact we have ignorance, and by doing so generates a kind of impertinent insolence towards the universe.

Uncertainty, in the presence of vivid hopes and fears, is painful, but must be endured if we wish to live without the support of comforting fairy tales.

It is not good either to forget the questions that philosophy asks, or to persuade ourselves that we have found indubitable answers to them.

To teach how to live without certainty, and yet without being paralyzed by hesitation, is perhaps the chief thing that philosophy, in our age, can still do for those who study it. (HWP xiv)

If you wish to become a philosopher, you must try, as far as you can, to get rid of beliefs which depend solely upon the place and time of your education, and upon what your parents and schoolmasters told you.

No one can do this completely, and no one can be a perfect philosopher, but up to a point we can all achieve it if we wish to.

"But why should we wish to?" you may ask. There are several reasons.

One of them is that irrational opinions have a great deal to do with war and other forms of violent strife.

The only way in which a society can live for any length of time without violent strife is by establishing social justice. Justice between classes is difficult where there is a class that believes itself to have a right to more than a proportionate share of power or wealth.

Justice between nations is only possible through the power of neutrals, because each nation believes in its own superior excellence.

Justice between creeds is even more difficult, since each creed is convinced that it has a monopoly of the truth of the most important of all subjects.

It would be increasingly easier than it is to arrange disputes amicably if the philosophic outlook were more widespread.

A second reason for wishing to be philosophic is that mistaken beliefs do not, as a rule, enable you to realize good purposes.

In the Middle Ages, when there was an epidemic of plague, people crowded into churches to pray, thinking that their piety would move God to take pity on them; in fact, the crowds in ill-ventilated buildings provided ideal conditions for the spread of the infection.

If your means are to be adequate to your ends, you must have knowledge, not merely superstition or prejudice.

A third reason is that truth is better than falsehood.

There is something ignominious in going about sustained by comfortable lies.

The deceived husband is traditionally ludicrous, and there is something of the same laughable or pitiable quality about all happiness that depends upon being deceived or deluded. (AP 4)

What kind of knowledge is most important to a philosopher?

The knowledge that is needed above all, if you wish to become a philosopher, is knowledge of science—not in its minute detail, but in its general results, its history, and especially its method.

It is science that makes the difference between the modern world and the world before the seventeenth century.

It is science that has destroyed the belief in witchcraft, magic, and sorcery.

It is science that has made the old creeds and the old superstitions impossible for intelligent men to accept.

It is science that has made it laughable to suppose the earth the center of the universe and man the supreme purpose of the creation.

It is science that is showing the falsehood of the old dualisms of soul and body, mind and matter, which have their origin in religion.

It is science that is beginning to make us understand ourselves, and to enable us, up to a point, to see ourselves from without as curious mechanisms.

It is science that has taught us the way to substitute tentative truth for cocksure error.

The scientific spirit, the scientific method, the framework of the scientific world, must be absorbed by anyone who wishes to have a philosophic outlook belonging to our time, not a literary antiquarian philosophy fetched out of old books.

Assuredly, Plato was a man of great genius, and Aristotle was comprehensively encyclopedic; but in their modern disciples they can inspire only error.

An hour with Galileo or Newton will give you more help towards a sound philosophy than a year with Plato and Aristotle.

But if you go to a university, this will not be the opinion of your professors. (AP 9)

How should a philosopher proceed in thinking about a problem?

It is necessary to practice methodological doubt, like Descartes, in order to loosen the hold of mental habits; and it is necessary to cultivate logical imagination, in order to have a number of hypotheses at command, and not to be the slave of the one which common sense has rendered easy to imagine.

These two processes, of doubting the familiar, and imagining the unfamiliar, are correlative, and form the chief part of the mental training required for a philosopher. (KEW 184)

What is the right attitude to have in studying a philosopher?

The right attitude is neither reverence nor contempt, but first a kind of hypothetical sympathy, until it is possible to know what it feels like to believe in his theories, and only then, a revival of the critical attitude, which should resemble, as far as possible, the state of mind of a person abandoning opinions which he has hitherto held.

Contempt interferes with the first part of the process, and reverence with the second.

Two things are to be remembered: that a man whose opinions and theories are worth studying may be presumed to have had some intelligence, but that no man is likely to have arrived at complete and final truth on any subject whatever.

When an intelligent man expresses a view which seems to us obviously absurd, we should not attempt to prove that it is somehow true, but we should try to understand how it ever came to *seem* true.

This exercise of historical and psychological imagination at once enlarges the scope of our thinking, and helps us to realize how foolish many of our own cherished prejudices will seem to an age which has a different temper of mind. (HWP 39)

How must a philosopher train his emotions?

The training of the emotions is as important, in the making of a philosopher, as training of the intellect.

It is important to be able to view human beings as products of circumstances.

Given that certain sorts of people are more desirable than certain other sorts, it is a scientific question to discover how the more desirable sorts are to be made more common.

The orthodox view is that this is to be done by preaching, but experience hardly supports this theory.

All sorts of causes may lead a man to behave badly: faulty education, wrong diet, economic worries, and so on.

It is a waste of energy to be angry with a man who behaves badly: just as it is to be angry with a car that won't go.

The difference is that you can compel your car to go to a garage, but you cannot compel Hitler to go to a psychiatrist.

You can, however, do something about the young potential Hitlers who exist everywhere.

You will not do anything wise about these young people if you view them as "sinners."

It is important to learn not to be angry with opinions different from your own, but to set to work understanding how they come about.

If, after you have understood them, they still seem false, you can then combat them much more effectively than if you had continued to be merely horrified.

I am not suggesting that the philosopher should have no feelings; the man who has no feelings, if there be such a man, does nothing, and therefore achieves nothing.

No man can hope to be a good philosopher unless he has certain feelings which are not very common.

He must have an intense desire to understand the world, as far as that is possible; and for the sake of understanding, he must be willing to overcome those narrownesses of outlook that make a correct perception impossible.

He must learn to think and feel, not as a member of this or that group, but as just a human being.

If he could, he would divest himself of the limitations to which he is subject as a human being.

If he could perceive the world as a Martian or as an inhabitant of Sirius, he could see it as it seems to a creature that lives for a day and also as it would seem to one that lived for a million years, he would be a better philosopher.

But this he cannot do; he is tied to a human body with human organs of perception.

To what extent can this subjectivity be overcome?

Can we know anything at all about what the world *is,* as opposed to what it *seems?*

This is what the philosopher wishes to know, and it is to this end that he has to undergo such long training of impartiality. (Italics added) (AP 24)

What's wrong with the classical tradition in philosophy?

The original impulse out of which the classical tradition developed was the naive faith of the Greek philosophers in the omnipotence of reasoning.

The discovery of geometry had intoxicated them, and its *a priori* deductive method appeared capable of universal application.

They would prove, for instance, that all reality is one, that there is no such thing as change, that the world of sense is a world of mere illusion; and the strangeness of their results gave them no qualms because they believed in the correctness of their reasoning.

Thus it came to be thought that by mere thinking the most surprising and important truths concerning the whole of reality could be established with a certainty which no contrary observations could shake.

As the vital impulse of the early philosophers died away, its place was taken by authority and tradition, and reinforced in the Middle Ages, and almost to our own day, by systematic theology.

Modern philosophy, from Descartes onwards, though not bound by authority like that of the Middle Ages, still accepted more or less uncritically the Aristotelian logic.

Moreover, it still believed, except in Great Britain, that *a priori* reasoning could reveal otherwise undiscoverable secrets about the universe, and could prove reality to be quite different from what, to direct observation, it appears to be.

It is this belief, rather than any particular tenets resulting from it, that I regard as the distinguishing characteristic of the classical tradition, and as hitherto the main obstacle to a scientific attitude in philosophy. (SPBR 314)

To the early Greeks, to whom geometry was practically the only known science, it was possible to follow reasoning with assent even when it led to the strangest conclusions.

But to us, with our methods of experiment and observation, our knowledge of the long history of *a priori* errors refuted by empirical science, it has become natural to suspect a fallacy in any deduction of which the conclusion appears to contradict patent facts. (SPBR 318)

Why was classical philosophy gradually left behind?

The classical tradition in philosophy is the last surviving child of two very diverse parents: the Greek belief in reason, and the medieval belief in the tidiness of the universe.

To the schoolmen, who lived amid wars, massacres, and pestilences, nothing appeared so delightful as safety and order. In their idealizing dreams, it was safety and order that they sought: the universe of Thomas Aquinas or Dante is as small and neat as a Dutch interior.

To us, to whom safety has become monotony, to whom the primeval savageries of nature are so remote as to become a mere pleasing condiment to our ordered routine, the world of dreams is very different from what it was amid the wars of Guelf and Ghibelline.

Hence William James's protest against what he calls the "block universe" of the classical tradition; hence Nietzsche's worship of force; hence the verbal bloodthirstiness of many quiet literary men.

The barbaric substratum of human nature, unsatisfied in action, finds an outlet in imagination.

In philosophy, as elsewhere, this tendency is visible; and it is this, rather than formal argument, that has thrust aside the classical tradition for a philosophy which fancies itself more virile and more vital [namely, evolutionism]. (SPBR 321)

What four well-known philosophers have been philosophy's misfortune, according to Russell?

Allen Tate: In what respect does Hegel's despotism as thesis, aristocracy and democracy as antithesis, and monarchy as the synthesis of the two differ from the kind of compromise that Aristotle contemplated? I think it's the Aristotelian "commonwealth" that is a compromise between oligarchy and raw democracy. Now, doesn't Aristotle have some notion there of the Hegelian "synthesis"?

Huntington Cairns: It has always seemed to me that Hegel's theory was quite similar to some of Aristotle's thought.

Russell: I agree. I think it is very similar; but I do not think the better of it on that account.

Cairns: Are you implying that Aristotle is as wicked a man as Hegel?

Russell: Yes.

All together: Oh, are you?

Tate: Mr. Russell, before we began this conversation, you said that Plato was very wicked. You would have neither of them, then?

Russell: I think that philosophy has suffered four misfortunes in the world's history: Plato, Aristotle, Kant, and Hegel. If they were eliminated, philosophy would have done very well.

Cairns: Who would be left, Mr. Russell? We will exclude present company.

Russell: There would be very many people left. There would be Locke, Berkeley, Hume, Leibnitz, and Spinoza. (ITL 418)

What's wrong with "evolutionism" in philosophy?

Evolutionism, in one form or another, is the prevailing creed of our time.

It dominates our politics, our literature, and not least our philosophy.

Nietzsche, pragmatism, Bergson, are phases in its philosophic development, and their popularity far beyond the circles of professional philosophers shows its consonance with the spirit of the age.

It believes itself firmly based on science, a liberator of hopes, an inspirer of an invigorating faith in human power, a sure antidote to the ratiocinative authority of the Greeks and the dogmatic authority of medieval systems.

Against so fashionable and agreeable a creed it may seem useless to raise a protest; and with much of its spirit every modern man must be in sympathy.

But I think that, in the intoxication of a quick success, much that is important and vital to a true understanding of the universe has been forgotten.

Something of Hellenism must be combined with the new spirit before it can emerge from the ardor of youth into the wisdom of manhood.

And it is time to remember that biology is neither the only science, nor yet the model to which all other sciences must adapt themselves.

Evolutionism, as I shall try to show, is not truly scientific philosophy, either in its method or in the problems which it considers.

The true scientific philosophy is something more arduous and more aloof, appealing to less mundane hopes, and requiring a severer discipline for its successful practice. (SPBR 323)

Darwin's *Origin of Species* persuaded the world that the difference between different species of animals and plants is not the fixed immutable difference that it appears to be.

The doctrine of natural kinds, which had rendered classification easy and definite, which was enshrined in the Aristotelian tradition, and protected by the supposed necessity for orthodox dogma, was suddenly swept away forever out of the biological world.

The difference between man and the lower animals, which to our human conceit appears enormous, was shown to be a gradual achievement, involving intermediate beings who could not with certainty be placed either within or without the human family.

The sun and planets had already been shown by Laplace to be very probably derived from a primitive more or less undifferentiated nebula.

Thus the old fixed landmarks became wavering and indistinct, and all sharp outlines were blurred. Things and species lost their boundaries, and none could say where they began or where they ended.

But if human conceit was staggered for a moment by its kinship with the ape, it soon found a way to reassert itself, and that way is the "philosophy" of evolution.

A process which led from the amoeba to man appeared to the philosophers to be obviously a progress—though whether the amoeba would agree with this opinion is not known.

Hence the cycle of changes which science had shown to be the probable history of the past was welcomed as revealing a law of development towards good in the universe—an evolution or unfolding of an ideal slowly embodying itself in the actual.

But such a view, though it might satisfy Spencer and those we may call Hegelian evolutionists, could not be accepted as adequate by the more wholehearted votaries of change.

An ideal to which the world continuously approaches is, to these minds, too dead and static to be inspiring. Not only the aspirations, but the ideal, too, must change and develop with the course of evolution; there must be no fixed goal, but a continual fashioning of fresh needs by the impulse which is life and which alone gives unity to the process.

Ever since the seventeenth century, those whom William James described as the "tender-minded" have been engaged in a desperate struggle with the mechanical view of the course of nature which physical science seems to impose.

A great part of the attractiveness of the classical tradition was due to the partial escape from mechanism which it provided.

But now, with the influence of biology, the "tender-minded" believe that a more radical escape is possible, sweeping aside not merely the laws of physics, but the whole apparently immutable apparatus of logic, with its fixed concepts, its general principles, and its reasonings which seem able to compel even the most unwilling assent.

The older kind of teleology, therefore, which regarded the End as a fixed goal, already partly visible, toward which we were gradually approaching, is rejected by M. Bergson as not allowing enough for the absolute dominion of change. (SPBR 325)

PLATO

What are the chief issues with which Plato deals?

The most important matters in Plato's philosophy are:
    first, his Utopia, which was the earliest of a long series;
    second, his theory of ideas, which was a pioneer attempt to deal with the still unsolved problem of universals;
    third, his arguments in favor of immortality;
    fourth, his cosmogony;
    fifth, his conception of knowledge as reminiscence rather than perception. (HWP 104)

How did Plato stack the deck?

Plato is always concerned to advocate views that will make people what he thinks virtuous; he is hardly ever intellectually honest, because he allows himself to judge doctrines by their social consequences.

Even about this, he is not honest; he pretends to follow the argument and to be judging by purely intellectual standards, when in fact he is twisting the discussion so as to lead to a virtuous result.

He introduced this vice into philosophy, where it has persisted ever since.

It was largely hostility to the Sophists that gave this character to his dialogues.

One of the defects of all philosophers since Plato is that their inquiries into ethics proceed on the assumption that they already know the conclusions to be reached. (HWP 78)

What were the sources of Plato's opinions?

The purely philosophical influences on Plato were such as to predispose him in favor of Sparta.

These influences, speaking broadly, were Pythagoras, Parmenides, Heraclitus, and Socrates.

From Pythagoras, Plato derived the Orphic elements in his philosophy, the religious trend, the belief in immortality, the otherworldliness, the priestly tone, and all that is involved in the simile of the cave; also his respect for mathematics, and his intimate intermingling of intellect and mysticism.

From Parmenides he derived the belief that reality is eternal and timeless, and that, on logical grounds, all change must be illusory.

From Heraclitus he derived the negative doctrine that there is nothing permanent in the sensible world.

This, combined with the doctrine of Parmenides, led to the conclusion that knowledge is not to be derived from the senses, but is only to be achieved by the intellect.

This, in turn, fitted in well with Pythagoreanism.

From Socrates he probably learnt his preoccupation with ethical problems, and his tendency to seek teleological rather than mechanical explanations of the world.

"The Good" dominated his thought more than that of the pre-Socratics, and it is difficult not to attribute this fact to the influence of Socrates. (HWP 105)

How did the various influences on Plato move him toward authoritarianism in politics?

In the *first* place: Goodnesss and Reality, being timeless, the best state will be the one which most nearly copies the heavenly model, by having a minimum of change and a maximum of static perfection, and its rulers should be those who best understand the eternal Good.

In the *second* place: Plato, like all mystics, has, in his beliefs, a core of certainty which is essentially incommunicable except by way of life.

The Pythagoreans had endeavored to set up a rule of the initiate, and this is, at bottom, what Plato desires.

If a man is to be a good statesman, he must know the Good; this he can only do by a combination of intellectual and moral discipline.

If those who have not gone through this discipline are allowed to share in the government, they will inevitably corrupt it.

In the *third* place: much education is needed to make a good ruler on Plato's principles.

He was sufficiently Pythagorean to think that without mathematics no true wisdom is possible.

This view implies an oligarchy.

In the *fourth* place: Plato, in common with most Greek philosophers, took the view that leisure is essential to wisdom, which will therefore not be found among those who have to work for their living, but only among those who have independent means, or who are relieved by the state from anxieties as to their subsistence. This point of view is essentially aristocratic. (Italics added) (HWP 106)

Why did Sparta appeal to Plato as a model for his Republic?

Plato was born in 428-7 B.C. in the early years of the Peloponnesian War. He was a well-to-do aristocrat.

He was a young man when Athens was defeated, and he could

attribute the defeat to democracy, which his social position and his family connections were likely to make him despise.

He was a pupil of Socrates, for whom he had a profound affection and respect; and Socrates was put to death by the democracy.

It is not, therefore, surprising that he should turn to Sparta for an adumbration of his ideal commonwealth. (HWP 105)

What would life be like in Plato's Republic?

As for economics: Plato proposes a thoroughgoing communism for the guardians.

The guardians are to have small houses and simple food; they are to live as in a camp, dining together in companies; they are to have no private property beyond what is absolutely necessary.

Gold and silver are to be forbidden.

Though not rich, there is no reason why they should not be happy; but the purpose of the city is the good of the whole, not the happiness of one class.

Both wealth and poverty are harmful, and in Plato's city neither will exist.

Friends should have all things in common, including women and children.

Girls are to have exactly the same education as boys, learning music, gymnastics, and the art of war along with the boys.

Women are to have complete equality with men in all respects.

The legislator, having selected the guardians, some men and some women, will ordain that they shall all share common houses and common meals.

Marriage, as we know it, will be radically transformed. "These women shall be, without exception, the common wives of these men, and no one shall have a wife of his own."

All children will be taken away from their parents at birth, and great care will be taken that no parents shall know who are their children, and no children shall know who are their parents.

Mothers are to be between twenty and forty, fathers between twenty-five and fifty-five.

Outside these ages, intercourse is to be free, but abortion or infanticide is to be compulsory.

In the "marriages" arranged by the State, the people concerned have no voice; they are to be actuated by the thought of their duty to the State, not by any of those common emotions that the banished poets used to celebrate.

Since no one knows who his parents are, he is to call everyone "father" whose age is such that he might be his father, and similarly as regards "mother" and "brother" and "sister."

I come last to the theological aspect of the system.

I am not thinking of the accepted Greek gods, but of certain myths which the government is to inculcate.

Lying, Plato says explicitly, is to be a prerogative of the government, just as giving medicine is of physicians.

The government is to deceive people in pretending to arrange marriages by lot, but this is not a religious matter.

There is to be "one royal lie" which, Plato hopes, may deceive the rulers, but will at any rate deceive the rest of the city.

This "lie" is set forth in considerable detail. The most important part of it is the dogma that God has created men of three kinds, the best made of gold, the second of silver, and the comon herd of brass and iron. Those made of gold are fit to be guardians; those made of silver should be soldiers; the others should do the manual work. It is thought hardly possible to make the present generation believe this myth, but the next and all subsequent generations can be so educated as not to doubt it.

Plato was right in thinking that this myth could be generated in two generations. The Japanese have been taught that the Mikado is descended from the sun-goddess, and that Japan was created earlier than the rest of the world. (HWP 111–13)

How are citizens to be segregated, and the young treated, in Plato's Republic?

Plato begins by deciding that the citizens are to be divided into three classes: the common people, the soldiers, and the guardians.

The last, alone, are to have political power.

There are to be much fewer of them than of the other two classes.

In the first instance, it seems, they are to be chosen by the legislator; after that, they will usually succeed by heredity, but in exceptional cases a promising child may be promoted from one of the inferior classes, while among the children of guardians a child or young man who is unsatisfactory may be degraded.

The main problem, as Plato perceives it, is to ensure that the guardians shall carry out the intentions of the legislator.

Culture is to be devoted to making men *gentlemen,* in the sense which, largely owing to Plato, is familiar in England.

The Athens of his day was, in one respect, analagous to England in the nineteenth century: there was in each an aristocracy enjoying wealth and social prestige, but having no monopoly of political power; and in each the aristocracy had to secure as much power as it could by means of impressive behavior.

In Plato's Utopia, however, the aristocracy rules unchecked.

Gravity, decorum, and courage seem to be the qualities mainly to be cultivated in education.

There is to be rigid censorship, from very early years, over the literature to which the young have access and the music they are allowed to hear.

Mothers and nurses are to tell their children only authorized stories.

Homer and Hesiod are not to be allowed, for a number of reasons.

First, they represent the gods as behaving badly on occasion, which is unedifying; the young must be taught that evils never come from the gods, for God is not the author of all things, but only of good things.

Second, there are things in Homer and Hesiod which are calculated to make their readers fear death, whereas everything ought to be done in education to make young people willing to die in battle.

Our boys must be taught to consider slavery worse than death, and therefore they must have no stories of good men weeping and wailing, even for the death of friends. [And much more.]

Up to a certain age, the young are to see no ugliness or vice.

But at a suitable moment, they must be exposed to "enchantments," both in the shape of terrors that must not terrify, and of bad pleasures that must not seduce the will.

Only after they have withstood these tests will they be judged fit to be guardians. (HWP 109)

What would Plato's Republic achieve, if established?

The answer is rather humdrum.

It will achieve success in wars against roughly equal populations, and it will secure a livelihood for a certain small number of people.

It will almost certainly produce no art or science, because of its rigidity; in this respect, as in others, it will be like Sparta.

In spite of all the fine talk, skill in war and enough to eat is all that will be achieved.

Plato had lived through famine and defeat in Athens; perhaps, subconsciously, he thought the avoidance of these evils the best that statesmanship could accomplish. (HWP 115)

Plato's Republic, unlike modern Utopias, was perhaps intended to be actually founded.

This was not so fantastic or impossible as it might naturally seem to us.

Many of its provisions, including some that we should have thought quite impracticable, were actually realized at Sparta. The rule of philosophers had been attempted by Pythagoras, and in Plato's time, Archytas the Pythagorean was politically influential in Taras when Plato visited Sicily and southern Italy.

It was a common practice for cities to employ a sage to draw up their laws.

Solon had done this for Athens, and Protagoras for Thurii. Colonies, in those days, were completely free from control by their parent cities, and it would have been quite feasible for a band of Platonists to establish the Republic on the shores of Spain.

Unfortunately chance led Plato to Syracuse, a great commercial city engaged in desperate wars with Carthage; in such an atmosphere, no philosopher could have achieved much.

In the next generation, the rise of Macedonia had made all small states antiquated, and had brought about the futility of all political experiments in miniature. (HWP 118)

To ask Plato a modern question, Is there such a thing as "wisdom"?

"Wisdom," in the sense supposed, would not be any kind of specialized skill, such as is possessed by the shoemaker or the physician or the military tactician.

It must be something more generalized than this, since its possession is supposed to make a man capable of governing wisely.

I think Plato would have said that it consists in knowledge of the good, and would have supplemented this definition with the Socratic doctrine that no man sins knowingly, from which it follows that whoever knows what is good does what is right.

To us such a view seems remote from reality.

We should more naturally say that there are divergent interests, and that the statesman should arrive at the best available compromise.

The members of a class or a nation may have a common interest, but it will usually conflict with the interests of other classes or other nations.

There are, no doubt, some interests of mankind as a whole, but they do not suffice to determine political action.

Perhaps they will do so at some future date, but certainly not so long as there are many sovereign states.

And even then the most difficult part of the pursuit of the general interest would consist in arriving at compromises among mutually hostile special interests. (HWP 106)

Why did Russell call Plato one of philosophy's misfortunes?

Plato possessed the art to dress up illiberal suggestions in such a way that they deceived future ages, which admired the *Republic* without ever becoming aware of what was involved in its proposals.

It has always been correct to praise Plato, but not to understand him.

This is the common fate of great men.

My object is the opposite.

I wish to understand him, but to treat him with as little reverence as if he were a contemporary English or American advocate of totalitarianism. (HWP 105)

POLICE

How may the police be a threat to democracy?

There is one matter in which many democracies have been unsuccessful, and that is the control of the police.

Given a police force which is corrupt and unscrupulous, and judges who are not anxious to discover its crimes, it is possible for ordinary citizens to find themselves at the mercy of a powerful organization which, just because it is supposed to enforce the law, has exceptional facilities for acting illegally.

I think this is a danger which is much too little realized in many countries.

Happily it is realized in England, and most English people regard the policeman as a friend, but in many countries he is viewed with terror, as a man who may, at any moment, bring grave trouble upon any person whom he happens to dislike or whom the police, as a whole, consider politically objectionable.

When the Communists were acquiring control of what are now satellite states, they always aimed, first of all, at control of the police.

If they acquired that, they could accuse their enemies of plots or other crimes and terrify everybody into subservience. (FF 85)

How could police power be curbed?

I should like to see everywhere two police forces, one to prove guilt, the other to prove innocence.

Suppose you were unjustly accused of murder.

The taxpayer pays all the expense of proving that you did the murder, and you, out of your own pocket, have to pay the expense of proving that you didn't, and that seems hardly fair. (SHM 63)

POLITICS

What personal motives are important in politics?

Four in particular, which we can label acquisitiveness, rivalry, vanity, and love of power.

Acquisitiveness—the wish to possess as much as possible of goods, or the title to goods—is a motive which, I suppose has its origin in a combination of fear with the desire for necessaries.

I once befriended two girls from Estonia, who had narrowly escaped death from starvation in a famine. They lived in my family, and of course had plenty to eat. But they spent all their leisure visiting neighboring farms and stealing potatoes, which they hoarded.

Rockefeller, who in his infancy had experienced great poverty, spent his adult life in a similar manner.

Rivalry is a much stronger motive. Over and over again in Mohammedan history, dynasties have come to grief because the sons of a sultan by different mothers could not agree, and in the resulting civil war, universal ruin resulted.

The same sort of thing happens in modern Europe.

When the British government very unwisely allowed the Kaiser to be present at a naval review at Spithead, the thought which arose in his mind was not the one which we had intended. What he thought was, "I must have a navy as good as Grandmama's."

And from this thought have sprung all our subsequent troubles.

Vanity is a motive of immense potency.

Anyone who has much to do with children knows how they are constantly performing some antic, and saying, "Look at me." "Look at me" is one of the most fundamental desires of the human heart.

It can take innumerable forms, from buffoonery to the pursuit of posthumous fame.

There was a Renaissance Italian princeling who was asked by the priest on his deathbed if he had anything to repent of.

"Yes," he said, "There is one thing. On one occasion I had a visit from the Emperor and the Pope simultaneously. I took them to the top of my tower to see the view, and I neglected the opportunity to throw them both down, which would have given me immortal fame."

History does not relate whether the priest gave him absolution.

But great as is the influence of the motives we have been considering, there is one which outweighs them all. I mean the love of power.

Love of power is closely akin to vanity but it is not by any means the same thing.

What vanity needs for its satisfaction is glory, and it is easy to have glory without power.

The people who enjoy the greatest glory in the United States are film stars, but they can be put in their place by the Committee for Un-American Activities, which enjoys no glory whatever.

In England the king has more glory than the Prime Minister, but the Prime Minister has more power than the king.

Many people prefer glory to power, but on the whole these people have less effect on the course of events than those who prefer power to glory.

Power, like vanity, is insatiable. Nothing short of omnipotence could satisfy it completely.

And as it is especially the vice of energetic men, the causal efficacy of love of power is out of all proportion to its frequency.

It is, indeed, by far the strongest motive in the lives of important men.

Since power over human beings is shown in making them do what they would rather not do, the man who is actuated by love of power is more apt to inflict pain than to permit pleasure.

If you ask your boss for leave of absence from the office on some legitimate occasion, his love of power will derive more satisfaction from a refusal than from a consent. (HSEP 144)

What qualities are needed to succeed in politics?

The qualities which make a successful politician in a democracy vary according to the character of the times; they are not the same in quiet times as they are during war or revolution.

In quiet times a man may succeed by giving the impression of solidity and sound judgment, but in times of excitement something more is needed.

At such times, it is necessary to be an impressive speaker—not necessarily eloquent in the conventional sense, for Robespierre and Lenin were not eloquent, but determined, passionate, and bold.

The passion may be cold and controlled, but must exist and be felt.

In excited times, a politician needs no power of reasoning, no apprehension of impersonal facts, and no shred of wisdom. What he must have is the capacity of persuading the multitude that what they passionately desire is attainable, and that he, through his ruthless determination, is the man to attain it.

The most successful democratic politicians are those who succeed in abolishing democracy and becoming dictators.

This, of course, is only possible in certain circumstances; no one could have achieved it in nineteenth-century England.

But when it is possible, it requires only a high degree of the same qualities as are required by democratic politicians in general, at any rate, in excited times.

Lenin, Mussolini, and Hitler owed their rise to democracy. (Italics added) (P 47)

Why does success in politics depend on love of power?

Unless he [the statesman or politician] has also a considerable love of power, he will fail to sustain the labors necessary for success in a political enterprise.

I have known many high-minded men in public affairs, but unless they had an appreciable dose of personal ambition, they seldom had the energy to accomplish the good at which they aimed.

On a certain crucial occasion Abraham Lincoln made a speech to two recalcitrant senators, beginning and ending with the words, "I am the President of the United States, clothed with great power."

It can hardly be questioned that he found some pleasure in asserting this fact.

Throughout all politics, both for good and for evil, the two chief forces are the economic motive and the love of power. (MM 202)

Why are politicians held in low esteem?

It is an odd fact that, in a democracy, where the eminent politicians are chosen by the people, there is almost everywhere a general agreement that politicians are a poor lot, so much so that the very word "politician" has acquired a flavor of contempt.

The chief reason for this state of affairs, I should say, is to be found in the rigidity of party discipline.

A party has, at any given moment, a set of opinions and policies which must be adhered to by all active members, however little they may agree at heart.

Orthodoxy is more valued than either honesty or acumen, with the result that most young men who are not mediocre find the whole business intolerable and abandon it before they have had a chance to become leaders. (MAO 42)

POLYGAMY

Should polygamy be permitted?

It is generally assumed without question that the state has a right to punish certain kinds of sexual irregularity.

No one doubts that the Mormons sincerely believed polygamy to be a desirable practice, yet the United States required them to abandon its legal recognition, and probably any other Christian country would have done likewise.

Nevertheless, I do not think this prohibition was wise. Polygamy is legally permitted in many parts of the world, but is not much practiced except by chiefs and potentates.

If, as Europeans generally believe, it is an undesirable custom, it is probable that the Mormons would have soon abandoned it, except perhaps for a few men of exceptional position.

If, on the other hand, it had proved a successful experiment, the world would have acquired a piece of knowledge it is now unable to possess.

I think in all such cases, the law should only intervene when there is some injury inflicted without the consent of the injured person. (PI 67)

POPULATION

From whom did Malthus get the idea for his doctrine?

It is a curious fact that those who are led to advocate birth control through a study of Malthus's doctrines, although they are sometimes called neo-Malthusians, are really reverting to a doctrine which preceded Malthus, and suggested his doctrine to him.

The principle of population was really discovered not by Malthus but by Condorcet, who, however, avoided the pessimistic conclusions which gave Malthus so much pleasure, by supplementing the doctrine with the advocacy of birth control.

Malthus, as a clergyman, thought birth control wicked, and as a

Manchester economist, enjoyed the iron law of wages, which assumed that wage earners, though poor, would remain prolific.

It is a pity that it was these doctrines, and not those of Condorcet, which acquired wide publicity. (NHCW 46)

What are Malthus's ways of keeping populations down?

There are two ways of checking increase of populations: one is by increasing the death rate, the other by diminishing the birth rate.

Old-fashioned moralists tell us that the first is virtuous, the second wicked.

True, the first involves vast and terrible suffering, while the second involves no suffering at all.

But what of that?

We ought to think of the next world, not of this one.

Those who believe that a benevolent Creator insists upon either misery in this life or eternal torment in the next are welcome to their opinion, but I do not think it is one which ought to control practical statesmanship.

Malthus held that there were only three restraints to the growth of population: moral restraint, vice, and misery.

He had little hope of moral restraint, and as a clergyman he condemned vice; he therefore advocated misery—of course, only for the lower orders.

I hope the world has advanced beyond this point of view during the 150 years since Malthus wrote.

I hope that those who control the world's policy are now ready to admit that what is necessary in order to preserve mankind from wretchedness is not to be labeled "vice." (NHCW 39)

Has modern technique improved life in underdeveloped countries?

But although the Malthusian limit can always be pushed back by improving technique, there are always limits beyond which it cannot be pushed.

To take an extreme hypothesis: it would obviously be impossible for mankind to have an adequate supply of food if there were only just standing room for the human race.

And without imagining so extreme an hypothesis, there is, in any given society at any given time, a very considerable possibility that increase of population may outstrip improvement in technique, and therefore cause a general lowering in the standard of life.

This, in fact, is happening at the present time throughout very large parts of the world.

There seems to be little doubt that the inhabitants of the Indus valley were more prosperous and generally happier three thousand years ago than they are now.

In India generally there has been an increase in poverty among the peasants in recent times.

And what is true of India is true of Southeast Asia generally, of most parts of Africa, and of the tropical parts of Latin America.

In most of these regions, modern medicine has brought about a fall in the death rate, but not in the birth rate. It has thereby contributed to human misery. (NHCW 38)

What has higher farm output done for India and Pakistan?

Increase in agricultural productivity can be used in two ways, it can be used to increase the share of each, or it can be used to increase the number of those who share.

In general, except in Western countries in quite recent years, increase in the productivity of labor has been devoted mainly to increase of numbers.

If, like the behaviorists, we were to judge man's desires by what he does, we should infer that the thing he desires most ardently is an increase of the population of the world.

In early times, one person to two square miles was as much as the land would support, and that only when it had considerable natural fertility.

England at the present day supports a population of about 750 per square mile, that is to say, fifteen hundred times as many as it could support before human skills had been invented.

This, of course, depends mainly upon industry, not upon agriculture, but if we take India and Pakistan, which are mainly agricultural, we find a population of 174 per square mile.

These, as we know, are for the most part very near the lowest

level at which life can be supported, that is to say, the inhabitants of
India and Pakistan have chosen to employ the techniques of civilization
almost entirely for the purpose of increase of population, to the exclu-
sion of increase of happiness and culture. (NHCW 22)

What is the basic problem in Africa? [1951]

In Africa the same problems exist [as in Asia], though for the present
they are less menacing.

Everything done by European administrators to improve the lot
of Africans is, at present, totally and utterly futile because of the growth
of population.

The Africans, not unnaturally, though now mistakenly, attribute
their destitution to their exploitation by the white man.

If they achieve freedom suddenly before they have men trained
in administration and a habit of responsibility, such civilization as white
men have brought to Africa will quickly disappear.

It is no use for doctrinaire liberals to deny this; there is a standing
proof in the island of Haiti. (NHCW 7)

POWER

What is the basic concept in studying society?

I shall be concerned to prove that the fundamental concept in social
science is Power, in the same sense in which Energy is the fundamental
concept in physics.

Like energy, power has many forms, such as wealth, armament,
civil authority, influence on opinion.

No one of these can be regarded as subordinate to any other, and
there is no one form from which the others are derivative.

Wealth may result from military power or from influence over
opinion, just as either of these may result from wealth.

In our day, it is common to treat economic power as the source
from which all other kinds are derived; this, I shall contend, is just
as great an error as that of the purely military historians whom it has
caused to seem out of date.

There are those who regard propaganda power as the fundamental form of power.

This is by no means a new opinion; it is embodied in such traditional sayings as *magna est veritas et prevalibit* and "the blood of the martyrs is the seed of the Church."

It has about the same measure of truth and falsehood as the military view or the economic view.

Propaganda, if it can create an almost unanimous opinion, can generate an irresistible power; but those who have military or economic control can, if they choose, use it for the purpose of propaganda.

To revert to the analogy of physics: power, like energy, must be regarded as continually passing from any one of its forms into any other. (P 11)

What are the different kinds of power?

There are different ways of classifying power.

One of the most obvious is power over the body. This is the power of armies and the police force.

Then there is the power of reward and punishment, which is called eonomic power.

Finally, there is propaganda power, the power to persuade. (SHM 61)

What is the origin of the desire for power?

I should suppose that the original impulses came in times that were liable to occasional famine, and if you wanted to be sure that, if the food supply ran short, it wouldn't be you who would suffer.

It required that you have power. (SHM 61)

What is the attraction of having power?

Power enables us to realize more of our desires than would otherwise be possible, and since it secures deference from others, it is natural to desire power, except insofar as timidity interferes. (P 23)

Are there good as well as bad motives for wanting power?

Certainly.

Almost everybody who has had any important effect in the world has been actuated by some form of love of power, and that applies to saints as well as sinners. (SHM 61)

How may love of power be limited or disguised?

Those who most desire power are, broadly speaking, those most likely to acquire it.

The posts which confer power will, as a rule, be occupied by men who differ from the average in being exceptionally power-loving.

Love of power, though one of the strongest of human motives, is very unevenly distributed, and is limited by various other motives, such as love of ease, love of pleasure, and sometimes love of approval.

It is disguised, among the more timid, as an impulse of submission to leadership, which increases the scope of the power-impulses of bold men.

When men willingly follow a leader, they do so with a view to the acquisition of power by the group which he commands, and they feel that his triumphs are theirs.

Those whose love of power is not strong are unlikely to have much influence on the course of events. (P 12)

How do timid people acquire and enjoy power?

Among the timid, organization is promoted, not only by submission to a leader, but by the reassurance which is felt in being one of a crowd who all feel alike.

In an enthusiastic public meeting with whose purpose one is in sympathy, there is a sense of exaltation, combined with warmth and safety: the emotion which is shared becomes more and more intense until it crowds out all other feelings except an exultant sense of power produced by the multiplication of the *ego*.

Collective excitement is a delicious intoxication, in which sanity, humanity and even self-preservation are easily forgotten, in which atrocious massacres and heroic martyrdom are equally possible. (P 27)

How did "naked" power change the course of history?

Power not based on tradition or assent I call "naked" power.

Naked power is usually military, and may take the form either of internal tyranny or of foreign conquest.

Its importance, especially in the latter form, is very great indeed—greater, I think, than many modern "scientific" [Marxist] historians are willing to admit.

Alexander the Great and Julius Caesar altered the whole course of history by their battles.

But for the former, the Gospels would not have been written in Greek, and Christianity could not have been preached throughout the Roman Empire.

But for the latter, the French would not speak a language derived from Latin, and the Catholic Church could scarcely have existed. (P 39)

How are the powerful indifferent to evil?

Holders of power, always and everywhere, are indifferent to the good or evil of those who have no power, except insofar as they are restrained by fear.

This may sound too harsh a saying.

It may be said that decent people will not inflict torture on others beyond a point.

This may be *said,* but history shows that it is not true. The decent people in question succeed in not knowing, or pretending not to know, when torments are inflicted to make them happy.

Lord Melbourne, Queen Victoria's first Prime Minister, was just such a decent person. In private life he was charming. He was cultivated, well read, humane, and liberal.

He was also rich.

His money came to him from coal mines where children worked for long hours in darkness for a pittance. It was by the agony of these children that he was enabled to be so urbane.

Nor is his case in any way exceptional.

Analogous things affect even the origins of Communism. Marx lived on the charity of Engels, and Engels lived by exploiting the proletariat of Manchester during the hungry [eighteen] forties.

The polished young men in Plato's dialogues, whom English classicists have held up as models to the British upper-class youth, lived on slave labor and on the exploitation of the short-lived Athenian Empire.

Injustices by which we profit can always be justified by some kind of sophistry. (FF 87)

What tyranny does technology make possible?

The psychology of the oligarch who depends upon mechanical power is not, as yet, anywhere fully developed.

It is, however, an imminent possibility, and quantitatively, though not qualitatively, quite new.

It would now be feasible for a technically trained oligarchy, by controlling aeroplanes, navies, power stations, motor transport, and so on, to establish a dictatorship demanding almost no conciliation of subjects.

The empire of Laputa was maintained by its power of interposing itself between the sun and a rebellious province; something almost equally drastic would be possible for a union of scientific technologies.

They could starve a recalcitrant region, and deprive it of light and heat and electrical power after encouraging dependence on these sources of comfort; they could flood it with poison gas or bacteria.

Resistance would be utterly hopeless. (P 30)

How is science the modern devil?

In former days, men sold themselves to the Devil to acquire magical powers.

Nowadays they acquire these powers from science, and find themselves compelled to become devils.

There is no hope for the world unless power can be tamed, and brought into the service not of this or that group of fanatical tyrants, but of the whole human race, white and yellow and black, fascist and communist and democrat; for science has made it inevitable that all must live or all must die. (P 34)

Has the ability to curb the use of force gone far enough?

[No, but] it's not very easy to see what to do about it. In the modern world decisions have to be taken quickly.

You must leave the capacity for decision in the hands of a very few, so that protection from their power is not very easy. (P 63)

PRIDE

Is there a place for pride?

The men who think out administrative reforms and schemes of social amelioration are for the most part earnest men who are no longer young.

Too often they have forgotten that to most people, not only spontaneity but some kind of personal pride is necessary to happiness.

The pride of a great conqueror is not one that a well-regulated world can allow, but the pride of the artist, of the discoverer, of the man who has turned a wilderness into a garden or has brought happiness where, but for him, there would be misery—such pride is good, and our social system should make it possible, not only for the few, but for the many. (AI 77)

PROBLEMS

What are some world problems and their unrealistic solutions?

How long will it be before the accessible oil in the world is exhausted?

Will all the arable land in the world be turned into dust bowls as it has been in large parts of the United States?

Will the population increase to the point where men again, like their remote ancestors, have no leisure to think of anything but the food supply?

Such questions are not to be decided by general philosophical reflections.

Communists think that there will be plenty of oil if there are no capitalists.

Some religious people think that there will be plenty of food if we trust in Providence.

Such ideas are superficial even when they are called scientific, as they are by the Communists. (NHCW 28)

PROGRESS

What are the three great ages of progress?

There have been three great ages of progress: the first, when agriculture was discovered, when kings became powerful and states began to grow, when vast buildings were erected in honor of kings and gods, when the art of writing was invented, the Babylonians discovered the rudiments of mathematics, and the arts of peace and war passed out of the barbarian stage.

Next, after thousands of years of ossification, came the great age of Greece, from the time of Homer (whenever that was) to the death of Archimedes at the hands of a Roman soldier.

Then another long period of decay and darkness, followed by the incredibly rapid progress from the fifteenth century to the present day.

Throughout recorded history, progress has been the exception, not the rule; but when it has come, it has been swift and decisive. (UH 13)

What makes for progress in the world?

The desire to understand the world and the desire to reform it are the two great engines of progress in the world, without which human society would stand still or retrogress. (MM 203)

What encourages progress? What hinders it?

The important and effective attitudes to the world may be broadly divided into the religious and the scientific.

The scientific attitude is tentative and piecemeal, believing what it finds evidence for, and no more.

Since Galileo, the scientific attitude has proved itself increasingly capable of ascertaining important facts and laws, which are acknowledged by all competent people regardless of temperament or self-interest or political pressure.

Almost all the progress in the world from the earliest times is attributable to science and the scientific temper; almost all the major ills are attributable to religion. (PTB 55)

What is the effect of happiness on progress?

It may be that too complete a happiness may cause the impulses to knowledge and reform to fade.

When Cobden wished to enlist John Bright* in the free trade campaign, he based a personal appeal upon the sorrow that Bright was experiencing owing to his wife's recent death. It may be that without this sorrow Bright would have had less sympathy with the sorrow of others.

And many a man has been driven to abstract pursuits by despair of the actual world.

To a man of sufficient energy, pain may be a valuable stimulus, and I do not deny that if we were all perfectly happy, we should not exert ourselves to become happier.

But I cannot admit that it is any part of the duty of human beings to provide others with pain on the off-chance that it might prove fruitful. (MM 203)

What role does the individual play in promoting progress?

There has been in recent times a dangerous tendency, not unconnected with totalitarianism, to think only in terms of whole communities, and to ignore the contributions of individuals.

The need of individual genius is shown by the fact that the Mayans and the Incas, though in some ways highly civilized, never hit upon this simple invention [of the wheel].

The difference between our world and the world before the industrial revolution is due to the discoveries and inventions of a small number

---

*RICHARD COBEN (1804–1865) and JOHN BRIGHT (1811–1889). (Ed.)

of men; if by some misfortune, a few thousand men of exceptional ability had perished in infancy, the technique of production would now be very little different from what it was in the eighteenth century.

Individuals can achieve great things, and the teacher of history ought to make this clear to his pupils. For without hope nothing of importance is accomplished. (UH 13)

PROOF

What is the best attitude toward things that cannot be proved?

Veracity, or love of truth, is defined by John Locke as "not entertaining any proposition with greater assurance than the proofs it is built upon will warrant."

This definition is admirable in regard to all those matters as to which proof may reasonably be demanded.

But since proofs need premise, it is impossible to prove anything unless some things are accepted without proof.

We must therefore ask ourselves: What sort of thing is it reasonable to believe without proof?

I should reply: The facts of sense experience and the principles of mathematics and logic—including the inductive logic employed in science.

These are things which we can hardly bring ourselves to doubt, and as to which there is a large measure of agreement among mankind.

But in matters as to which men disagree, or as to which our own convictions are wavering, we should look for proofs, or, if proofs cannot be found, we should be content to confess ignorance. (from *The Listener,* May 29, 1947) (RGR 88)

PROPAGANDA

What is essential if propaganda is to succeed?

Propaganda must appeal to desire, and this may be confirmed by the failure of State propaganda when opposed to national feeling as in large parts of Austria-Hungary before the War [World War I], in Ireland until 1922, and in India down to the present time [1938].

Propaganda is only successful when it is in harmony with something in the patient: his desire for an immortal soul, for health, for the greatness of his nation, or what not.

Where there is no such fundamental reason for acquiescence, the assertions of authority are viewed with cynical skepticism. (P 145)

How do holders of power use repetition to influence belief?

It is through the potency of iteration that the holders of power acquire their capacity of influencing belief.

Official propaganda has old and new forms.

The Church has a technique which is in many ways admirable, but was developed before the days of printing, and is therefore less effective than it used to be.

The State has employed certain methods for many centuries: the King's head on coins, coronations and jubilees; the spectacular aspects of the army and navy, and so on.

But these are far less potent than the more modern methods: education, the press, the cinema, the radio, etc.

These are employed to the utmost in totalitarian states, but it is too soon to judge of their success. (P 145)

Who are the chief purveyors of propaganda in democratic countries?

Systemic propaganda, on a large scale, is at present, in democratic countries, divided [among] the churches, business advertisers, political parties, the plutocracy, and the State.

In the main, all these forces work on the same side, with the exception of political parties in opposition, and even they, if they have any hope of office, are unlikely to oppose the fundamentals of State propaganda. (P 146)

How does propaganda fare in totalitarian countries?

In the totalitarian countries, the State is virtually the sole propagandist.

But in spite of all the power of modern propaganda I do not believe that the official view would be widely accepted in the event of defeat in war.

It is easy to overestimate the power of official propaganda, especially when there is no competition.

Insofar as it devotes itself to causing belief in false propositions of which time will prove the falsity, it is in as bad a position as the Aristotelians in their opposition to Galileo.

Given two opposing groups of States, each of which endeavors to instill the certainty of victory in war, one side, if not both, must experience a dramatic refutation of official statements.

When all opposing propaganda is forbidden, rulers are likely to think that they can cause anything to be believed, and so to become overweening and careless.

Lies need competition if they are to retain their vigor.

In the long run, those who possess the power are likely to become too flagrantly indifferent to the interests of the common man, as the Popes were in the time of Luther.

Sooner or later, some new Luther will challenge the authority of the State, and, like his predecessor, be so quickly successful that it will be impossible to suppress him.

This will happen because the rulers believe that it cannot happen.

But whether the change will be for the better it is impossible to foresee. (Italics added) (P 146)

Does propaganda power need curbing?

Certainly, propaganda power needs enormous curbing.

I understand that the opinions of the average Russian as to what takes place in Western countries are very far from the truth, and that is due to the propaganda control over education which takes place in Communist countries.

There is a slightly less tight control in non-Communist countries, but still a very great control aiming not to make people think truly, but to make them think what their government thinks. (P 67)

PROVERBS

Do proverbs embody great wisdom?

The supposed wisdom of proverbs is mainly imaginary. As a rule, proverbs go in pairs which say opposite things.

The opposite of "More haste, less speed" is "A stitch in time saves nine."

The opposite of "Take care of the pence and the pounds will take care of themselves" is "Penny wise, pound foolish."

The opposite of "Two heads are better than one" is "Too many cooks spoil the broth."

The great advantage of a proverb in argument is that it is supposed to be incontrovertible, as embodying the quintessential sagacity of our ancestors.

But once you have realized that proverbs go in pairs, you can never again be downed by a proverb; you merely quote the opposite. (MAO 136)

PSYCHOLOGY

What makes people tick?

The impulses that lead to the complex desires of adult life can be arranged under a few simple heads.

Power, sex, and parenthood appear to me to be the source of most of the things that people do, apart from what is necessary for self-preservation.

Of these three, power begins first and ends last.

The child, since he has very little power, is dominated by the desire to have more. Indeed, a large proportion of his activities spring from this desire.

His other dominant desire is vanity—the wish to be praised and the fear of being blamed or left out. It is vanity that makes him a social being and gives him the virtues necessary for life in a community.

Vanity is a motive closely intertwined with sex, though in theory separable from it.

But power has, so far as I can see, very little connection with sex, and it is love of power, at least as much as vanity, that makes a child work at his lessons and develop his muscles.

Curiosity and the pursuit of knowledge should, I think, be regarded as a branch of the love of power.

If knowledge is power, then love of knowledge is love of power. (MM 201)

What makes man gregarious—instinct or self-interest?

Man is sometimes classed as a gregarious animal, but he is not quite similar psychologically to other gregarious animals.

His gregariousness, when it goes beyond a very limited degree, is a product rather of self-interest than of instinct.

Ants and bees instinctively serve the purposes of their group; they have no need of morals and decalogues, and apparently never feel any impulse to sin.

Gregarious mammals are not so completely dominated by the herd as ants and bees are, but have less tendency to individualism than human beings have.

In human beings there is a constant conflict between the individual and the herd, a conflict which as a rule is subjective, and waged in the mind of the individual, but occasionally breaks out into open disagreement.

Every man feels himself at once an individual and a member of a group, and it is because both these feelings are so deeply engrained in his nature that he has found it necessary to make moral codes and prohibitions and a vast apparatus of praise and blame.

Almost everything that goes wrong in the relations of man with man, goes wrong because the self-impulses outweigh the herd-impulses in cases where self-interest, or at any rate, the self-interest of the herd, would demand the opposite. (NHCW 53)

What is behaviorism?

There was one region [of psychology] where there was a very considerable body of precise experimental knowledge.

It was the region of Pavlov's observations on conditioned reflexes in dogs.

These experiments led to a philosophy called Behaviorism which had a considerable vogue.

The gist of this philosophy is that in psychology we are to rely wholly upon external observations and never to accept data for which the evidence is entirely derived from introspection.

As a philosophy, I never felt any inclination to accept this view, but, as a method to be pursued as far as possible, I thought it valuable.

I determined in advance that I would push it as far as possible while remaining persuaded that it had very definite limits. (MPD 129)

PYTHAGORAS

How did Pythagoras change philosophy for the worse?

Greek philosophy did not live up to its brilliant beginning: there was a serpent in the philosophic paradise, and his name was Pythagoras.

The Orphic religion, which had revivalist features, had captivated many previously rationalistic Greeks, and a form of Orphism was introduced by Pythagoras into philosophy, which ceased to be an honest attempt to understand the world, and became a search for salvation through intoxication.

Orphism was an offshoot of the worship of Bacchus, but sought to substitute a spiritual intoxication for the frankly alcoholic intoxication of the original cult.

From that day to this, there has been thought to be something divine about muddleheadedness, provided it had the quality of spiritual intoxication: a wholly sober view of the world had been thought to show a limited and pedestrian mind. From Pythagoras this outlook descended to Plato, from Plato to Christian theologians, from them, in a new form, to Rousseau and the romantics and the myriad purveyors of nonsense who flourish wherever men and women are tired of the truth.

There is, however, in our day, a powerful antidote to nonsense, which hardly existed in earlier times—I mean science.

Science cannot be ignored or rejected because it is bound up with modern technique; it is essential alike to prosperity in peace and to victory in war.

This is, perhaps, from an intellectual point of view, the most hopeful feature of our age, and one which makes it most likely that we shall escape complete submersion in some new or old superstition. (UH 42)

RACISM

How to improve the white man's attitude toward nonwhites?

To this day [1944] it is hardly possible to imagine anything more civilized than a cultivated Chinese.

All this should be more widely known, and a similar work should be done in diffusing appreciation of what has been achieved in India, in Persia, and by the Arabs in their great days.

By this means, the somewhat condescending attitude of white men towards Asiatics might be transformed into the respect which is felt towards those whom we acknowledge as equals. (DMMM 77)

RATIONALITY

What makes an opinion a rational opinion?

Rationality in opinion: I should define it merely as the habit of taking account of all relevant evidence in arriving at a belief.

Where certainty is unattainable, a rational man will give most weight to the most probable opinion, while retaining others which have an appreciable probability, in his mind, as hypotheses which subsequent evidence may show to be preferable.

This, of course, assumes that it is possible in many cases to ascertain facts and probabilities by an objective method—i.e., a method which will lead any two careful people to the same result. (SE 46)

REASON

Is reason alone sufficient as a guide to action?

No sensible man, however agnostic, has "faith in reason alone."

Reason is concerned with matters of fact, some observed, some inferred.

The question whether there is a future life and the question whether there is a God concern matters of fact, and the agnostic will hold that they should be investigated in the same ways as the question, "Will there be an eclipse of the moon tomorrow?"

But matters of fact alone are not sufficient to determine action, since they do not tell us what ends we ought to pursue.

In the realm of ends, we need something other than reason.

The agnostic will find his ends in his own heart and not in an external command.

Let us take an illustration.

Suppose you wish to travel by train from New York to Chicago; you will use your reason to discover when the trains run, and a person who thought there was some faculty of insight or intuition enabling him to dispense with the timetable would be thought rather silly.

But no timetable will tell him that it is wise to travel to Chicago.

No doubt, in deciding that it is wise, he will have to take account of further matters of fact; but behind all the matters of fact, there will be the ends he thinks fitting to pursue, and these, for an agnostic as for other men, belong to a realm which is not that of reason, though it should be in no degree contrary to it.

The realm I mean is that of emotion and feeling and desire. (from *Look* magazine, 1953) (RGR 89)

What is a sound opinion?

The question is how to arrive at your opinions and not what your opinions are.

The thing in which we believe is the supremacy of reason.

If reason should lead you to orthodox conclusions, well and good; you are still a Rationalist.

To my mind the essential thing is that one should base one's arguments upon the kind of grounds that are accepted in science, and that one should not regard anything one accepts as quite certain, but only as probable in a greater or a less degree.

Not to be absolutely certain is, I think, one of the essential things in rationality. (RGR 84)

How does belief through reason differ from belief through faith?

The important thing is not what you believe but how you believe it [i.e., how you arrive at your belief].

There was a time when it was rational to believe that the earth is flat. . . .

But the people who, in our day, persist in believing that the earth is flat, have to close their minds against reason and to open them to every kind of absurdity in addition to the one from which they start.

If you think your belief is based upon reason, you will support it by argument rather than by persecution, and will abandon it if the argument goes against you.

But if your belief is based on faith, you will realize that argument is useless, and will therefore resort to force either in the form of persecution or by stunting or distorting the minds of the young in what is called "education."

This last is peculiarly dastardly since it takes advantage of the defenselessness of immature minds. (from *The Rationalist Annual*) (RGR 287)

What proves that Reason has played a part in human affairs?

It is customary nowadays to decry Reason as a force in human affairs, yet the rise of science is an overwhelming argument on the other side.

The men of science proved to intelligent laymen that a certain kind of intellectual outlook ministers to military prowess and to wealth; these ends were so ardently desired that the new intellectual outlook overcame that of the Middle Ages, in spite of the force of tradition and the revenues of the Church and the sentiments associated with Catholic theology.

The world ceased to believe that Joshua caused the sun to stand still, because Copernican astronomy was useful in navigation; it abandoned Aristotle's physics, because Galileo's theory of falling bodies made it possible to calculate the trajectory of a cannonball; it rejected the story of the flood, because geology is useful in mining; and so on.

It is now generally recognized that science is indispensable both in war and in peacetime industry, and that, without science, a nation can be neither rich nor powerful.

All this effect on opinion has been achieved by science merely through appeal to fact: what science had to say in the way of general theories might be questionable, but its results in the way of technique were patent to all.

Science gave the white man the mastery of the world, which he has begun to lose only since the Japanese acquired his technique. (P 142)

When can Reason succeed, and when is it bound to fail?

As to the power of Reason in general: in the case of science, Reason prevailed over prejudice because it provided means of realizing *existing* purposes and because the proof that it did so was overwhelming.

Those who maintain that Reason has no power in human affairs overlook these two conditions.

If, in the name of Reason, you summon a man to alter his fundamental purposes—to pursue, say, the general happiness rather than his own power—you will fail, and you will deserve to fail, since Reason alone cannot determine the ends of life. And you will fail equally if you attack deep-seated prejudices while your argument is still open to question, or is so difficult that only men of science can see its force.

But if you can prove, by evidence which is convincing to every sane man who takes the trouble to examine it, that you possess a means of facilitating the satisfaction of existing desires, you may hope, with a certain degree of confidence, that men will ultimately believe what you say.

This, of course, involves the proviso that the existing desires which you can satisfy are those of men who have power or are capable of acquiring it. (P 143)

RELIGION

How would you define religion, Lord Russell?

By religion I mean a set of beliefs held as dogmas, dominating the conduct of life, going beyond or contrary to evidence, and inculcated by methods which are emotional or authoritarian, not intellectual. (PTB 55)

What has made man demand religion over the centuries?

Mainly fear. Man feels himself rather powerless.

There are three things that cause him fear.

One is what nature can do to him. It can strike him by lightning or swallow him up in an earthquake.

And one is what other men can do—they can kill him in war.

And the third, which has a great deal to do with religion, is what his own violent passions may lead him to do—things which he knows in a calm moment he would regret having done.

For that reason, most people have a great deal of fear in their lives, and religion helps them to be not so frightened by these fears. (SHM 21)

Religion is based, I think, primarily and mainly on fear.

It is partly the terror of the unknown, and partly the wish to feel that you have a kind of elder brother who will stand by you in all your troubles and disputes.

Fear is the basis of the whole thing—fear of the mysterious, fear of defeat, fear of death.

Fear is the parent of cruelty, and therefore it is no wonder if cruelty and religion go hand in hand. (DMMM 73)

Fear is the basis of religious dogma, as of so much else in human life.

Fear of human beings, individually or collectively, dominates much of our social life, but it is fear of nature that gives rise to religion.

[There are] things that can be affected by our desires and things which cannot be so affected.

If the world is controlled by God, and God can be moved by prayer, we acquire a share in omnipotence.

In former days, miracles happened in answer to prayer; they still do in the Catholic Church, but Protestants have lost this power. (WIB 11)

Why is religion so attractive to so many?

Belief in God serves to humanize the world of nature, and to make men feel that physical forces [of nature] are their allies.

In like manner immortality removes the terror from death. People who believe that when they die they will inherit eternal bliss may be expected to view death without horror.

It does soothe men's fears somewhat even when it cannot allay them wholly. (WIB 12)

Will religion continue to maintain its hold on man?

It depends on whether people solve their social problems or not.

If there go on being great wars and great depressions and many people leading very unhappy lives, probably religion will go on, because I've observed that the belief in the goodness of God is inversely proportional to the evidence.

When there's no evidence for it at all, people believe it, and when things are going well, and you might believe it, they don't.

You can get illustrations of that in the past.

In the eighteenth century when things were quiet, a great many educated people were freethinkers.

Then came the French Revolution and certain English aristocrats came to the conclusion that freethought led to the guillotine, and they dropped it, and they all became deeply religious and you got Victorianism.

And the same thing happened with the Russian Revolution.

It terrified people, and they thought that unless they believed in God their property would be confiscated, so they believed in Him.

I think you'll find these social upheavals are very good for religion. (SHM 25)

Doesn't man seek something greater than himself to work for?

There are plenty of things bigger than oneself.

First of all, there's your family; then there's your nation; then there's mankind in general.

These are all bigger than oneself, and are quite sufficient to occupy any genuine feelings of benevolence that a man may have. (SHM 25)

Can religion and science be reconciled?

The answer turns upon what is meant by "religion."

It it means merely a system of ethics, it can be reconciled with science.

If it means a system of dogma, regarded as unquestionably true, it is incompatible with the scientific spirit, which refuses to accept matters of fact without evidence, and also holds that complete certainty is hardly ever attainable. (from *Look* magazine, 1953) (RGR 81)

How does religion make its appeal?

I come now to another form of unforceful persuasion, namely that of the founders of religions.

Here the process, reduced to its bare formula, is this: if a certain proposition is true, I shall be able to realize my desires, therefore I wish this proposition to be true; therefore, unless I have exceptional intellectual self-control, I believe it to be true.

Orthodoxy and a virtuous life, I am told, will enable me to go to heaven when I die; there is pleasure in believing this, and therefore I shall probably believe it if it is forcibly presented to me.

The cause of belief here is not, as in science, the evidence of fact, but the pleasant feelings derived from belief, together with sufficient vigor of assertion in the environment to make belief seem not incredible.

The power of advertisement comes under the same head.

It is pleasant to believe in so-and-so's pills, since it gives you hope of better health; it is possible to believe in them, if you find their excellence very frequently and emphatically asserted.

Nonrational propaganda like the rational sort must appeal to existing desires, but it substitutes iteration for the appeal to fact. (P 143)

Have the effects of religion been good or bad, overall?

I think most of its effects in history have been harmful.

Religion caused the Egyptian priests to fix the calendar, and to note the occurrences of eclipses so well that in time they were able to predict them.

Those were beneficial effects of religion; but I think a great majority have been bad, because it was held important that people should believe something for which there did not exist good evidence, and that falsified everybody's thinking, falsified systems of education, and set up complete moral heresy, namely, that it is right to believe certain things, and wrong to believe certain others, apart from the question of whether the things in question are true or false.

I think religion has done a great deal of harm, largely by sanctifying conservatism and adhesion to ancient habits, and still more by sanctifying intolerance and hatred. (SHM 20)

Is religion doing any harm today?

At this present day, religion, as embodied in the Churches, discourages honest thinking, in the main, and gives importance to things that are not very important.

Its sense of importance seems to be quite wrong.

[In ancient times,] when the Roman Empire was falling, the Fathers of the Church didn't bother much with the fall of the Roman Empire.

What they bothered about was how to preserve virginity. That was what they thought important.

In the present day, when the human race is falling, I find that eminent divines think it's much more important to prevent artificial insemination than it is to prevent the kind of world war that will exterminate the whole lot of us.

That seems to me to show a lack of sense of proportion. (SHM 22)

REVOLTS

What happens after oppressive regimes are overthrown?

Mazzini's* history was very typical: he inspired the enthusiasm which created united Italy; but Cavour harnessed this enthusiasm to the House of Savoy, and the result was profoundly disgusting to the man who had done so much to bring it about.

There was nothing peculiar to Italy in this series of events.

In one country after another, the old regime was overthrown, and the momentum which produced the overthrow was generated and at first led by romantic idealists.

Everywhere the regime which emerged from successful revolution was disillusioning to the idealists.

But their hopes did not wholly die; they only traveled on to some new land where present oppression was certain and future glory still seemed possible.

When I was young, it was the Russian revolutionaries, above all, who were the inheritors of the tradition of romantic revolt.

Czarist Russia was viewed with shuddering horror by Liberals throughout the world.

The very word "Siberia" froze their blood.

Ever since the Decembrists in 1825, heroic Russians had struggled to overthrow the regime.

No Liberal doubted that they would succeed some day and that the result would be a splendid growth of freedom in regions where the human spirit had hitherto been enslaved.

I shared these hopes, and I found in Turgenev's books imaginative portraits of the men who were to create the new world. (FF 18)

---

*GIUSEPPE MAZZINI (1805–1872). Italian patriot, who was prominent in the "young Italy" movement that aimed to liberate Italy from foreign and domestic tyranny. (Ed.)

ROMANTICISM

What are the characteristics of Romanticism?

It is not the psychology of the romantics that is at fault; it is their standard of values.

They admire strong passions, of no matter what kind, and whatever may be their social consequences.

Romantic love, especially when unfortunate, is strong enough to win their approval, but most of the strongest passions are destructive—hate and resentment and jealousy, remorse and despair, outraged pride and the fury of the unjustly oppressed, martial ardor and contempt for slaves and cowards.

Hence the type of man encouraged by romanticism, especially of the Byronic variety, is violent and anti-social, an anarchic rebel or a conquering tyrant.

This outlook makes an appeal for which the reasons lie very deep in human nature.

By self-interest Man has become gregarious, but in instinct he has remained to a great extent solitary; hence the need of religion and morality to reinforce self-interest.

But the habit of foregoing present satisfactions for the sake of future advantages is irksome, and when passions are roused, the prudent restraints of social behavior become difficult to endure.

Those who, at such times, throw them off, acquire a new energy and sense of power from the cessation of inner conflict, and, though they may come to disaster in the end, enjoy meanwhile a sense of god-like exaltation which, though known to the great mystics, can never be experienced by a merely pedestrian virtue.

The solitary part of their nature reasserts itself, but if the intellect survives, the reassertion must clothe itself in myth.

The mystic becomes one with God, and in the contemplation of the Infinite feels himself absolved from duty to his neighbor.

The anarchic rebel does even better: he feels himself not one with God, but God.

Truth and duty, which represent our subjection to matter and to our neighbors, exist no longer for the man who has become God; for others, truth is what *he* posits, duty what *he* commands.

If we could all live solitary and without labor, we could all enjoy the ecstasy of independence; since we cannot, its delights are only available to madmen and dictators. (HWP 681)

What have been the political consequences of Romanticism?

The romantic form [of revolt] is to be seen in Byron in an unphilosophical dress, but in Schopenhauer and Nietzsche it has learnt the language of philosophy.

It tends to emphasize the will at the expense of the intellect, to be impatient of chains of reasoning, and to glorify violence of certain kinds.

In practical politics it is important as an ally of nationalism.

In tendency, if not always in fact, it is definitely hostile to what is commonly called reason, and tends to be anti-scientific.

Some of its more extreme forms are to be found among Russian anarchists, but in Russia it was the rationalist form that finally prevailed.

It was Germany, always more susceptible to romanticism than any other country, that provided a governmental outlet for the anti-rational philosophy of naked will. (HWP 724)

When do men write romantic poetry?

On the whole, the characteristic love poetry of the Renaissance is cheerful and straightforward.

"Do not mock me in thy bed
While these cold nights freeze me dead,"

says an Elizabethan poet. This sentiment, it must be admitted, is straightforward and uninhibited, and by no means Platonic. The Renaissance had, however, learnt from the Platonic love of the Middle Ages to employ poetry as a means of courtship.

It is curious that before the Middle Ages, though there had been a good deal of poetry concerned with love, there was very little that was directly a part of courtship.

One gathers that men had so little difficulty in securing the women they desired that it hardly ever became necessary to woo them with music and poetry.

From the point of view of the arts, it is certainly regrettable when women are too accessible; what is most to be desired is that they should be difficult but not impossible of access. This situation has existed more or less since the Renaissance. The difficulties have been partly external and partly internal, the latter being derived from scruples due to conventional moral teaching.

Romantic love reached its apogee in the Romantic movement, and one may perhaps take Shelley as its chief apostle. Shelley when he fell in love was filled with exquisite emotions and imaginative thoughts of a kind lending themselves to expression in poetry; naturally enough he considered that the emotion that produced these results was wholly good, and he saw no reason why love should ever be restrained.

His argument, however, rested on bad psychology.

It was the obstacles to his desires that led him to write poetry. If the noble and unfortunated Lady Emilia Viviani had not been carried off to a convent, he would not have found it necessary to write "Epipsychidion"; if Jane Williams had not been a fairly virtuous wife, he would never have written "The Recollection." The social barriers against which he inveighed were an essential part of the stimulus to his best activities.

Romantic love as it existed in Shelley depends upon a state of unstable equilibrium, where the conventional barriers still exist but are not quite insuperable; if the barriers are rigid, or if they do not exist, romantic love is not likely to flourish.

In a state of complete freedom, a man capable of great love poetry is likely to have so much success through his charm that he will seldom have need of his best imaginative efforts in order to achieve a conquest.

Thus love poetry depends upon a certain delicate balance between convention and freedom, and is not likely to exist in its best form where this balance is upset in either direction. (MM 48)

What is the essence of romantic love?

To say that romantic love was unkown before the Middle Ages would not be correct, but it was only in the Middle Ages that it became a commonly recognized form of passion.

The essential of romantic love is that it regards the beloved object as very difficult to possess and as very precious. It makes, therefore, great efforts of many kinds to win the love of the beloved object, by poetry, by song, by feats of arms, or by whatever other method may be thought most pleasing to the lady.

The belief in the immense value of the lady is a psychological effect of the difficulty of obtaining her, and I think it may be laid down that when a man has no difficulty in obtaining a woman, his feeling toward her does not take the form of romantic love.

Romantic love, as it appears in the Middle Ages, was not directed at first towards women with whom the lover could have either legitimate or illegitimate sexual relations; it was directed towards women of the highest respectability, who were separated from their romantic lovers by insuperable barriers of morality and convention.

So thoroughly had the Church performed its task of making men feel sex inherently impure, that it had become impossible to feel any poetic sentiment towards a lady unless she was regarded as unattainable. Accordingly love, if it was to have any beauty, had to be Platonic.

It is very difficult for the modern to feel in imagination the psychology of the poet lovers in the Middle Ages. They profess ardent devotion without any desire for intimacy, and this seems to a modern so curious that he is apt to regard their love as no more than a literary convention. Doubtless on occasion it was no more than this, and doubtless its literary expression was dominated by conventions.

But the love of Dante for Beatrice, as expressed in *Vita Nuova,* is certainly not merely conventional; I should say, on the contrary, that it is an emotion more passionate than any known to most moderns.

The noble spirits of the Middle Ages thought ill of this terrestrial life; our human instincts were to them the products of corruption and original sin; they hated the body and its lusts; pure joy was to them only possible in ecstatic contemplation of a kind which seemed to them free from all sexual alloy.

In the sphere of love this outlook could not but produce the kind of attitude which we find in Dante. A man who deeply loved and respected a woman would find it impossible to associate with her the idea of sexual intercourse, since all sexual intercourse would be to him more or less impure; his love would therefore take poetic and imaginative forms, and would naturally become filled with symbolism.

The effect of all this upon literature was admirable, as may be seen in the gradual development of love poetry, from its beginning in the court of the Emperor Frederick II to its flowering in the Renaissance. (MM 45)

ROUSSEAU

How to view Rousseau's arguments that life is better in the next world?

The rejection of reason in favor of the heart was not, to my mind, an advance.

In fact, no one thought of this device so long as reason appeared to be on the side of religious belief.

In Rousseau's environment, reason, as represented by Voltaire, was opposed to religion, therefore away with reason!

There is no law of nature guaranteeing that mankind should be happy.

Everybody can see that this is true of our life here on earth, but by a curious twist, our very sufferings in this life are made into an argument for a better life hereafter.

We should not employ such an argument in any other connection.

If you had bought ten dozen eggs from a man, and the first dozen were all rotten, you would not infer that the remaining nine dozen must be of surpassing excellence; yet this is the kind of reasoning that "the heart" encourages as a consolation for our sufferings here below. (HWP 694)

What was Rousseau's idea of a proper democracy?

Rousseau, who professes to be a believer in democracy, considers that this word is only rightly applicable to the ancient form in which every citizen votes on every legislative act.

When the power is delegated to elected representatives, Rousseau calls the system "Elective Aristocracy."

He admits what is obvious, that it is impossible to have democracy in the ancient sense in such countries as France or England.

Such a system, he says, is too perfect for our imperfect world, except in his own city of Geneva.

There alone it is possible to have the sort of government that he thinks really good.

In view of this conclusion, it is odd that his books caused such a commotion. (FF 82)

RUSSELL

Lord Russell, why did you take to philosophy?

In almost all philosophy doubt has been the goad and certainty has been the goal.

There has been doubt about the senses, doubt about science, and doubt about theology.

In some philosophers, one of these has been more prominent, in others another.

Philosophers have also differed widely as to the answers they have suggested to these doubts and even as to whether any answers are possible.

All the traditional motives combined to lead me to philosophy, but there were two that specially influenced me.

The one which operated first and continued longest was the desire to find some knowledge that could be accepted as certainly true.

The other motive was the desire to find some satisfaction for religious impulses. (PFM 18)

Lord Russell, have you found it rewarding to be a philosopher?

I have always thought of myself as primarily an abstract philosopher.

I have tried to extend the exact and demonstrative methods of mathematics and science into regions traditionally given over to vague speculation.

I like precision. I like sharp outlines. I hate misty vagueness.

For some reason which I do not profess to understand, this has caused large sections of the public to think of me as a cold person destitute of passion.

It seems to be supposed that whoever feels any passion must enjoy self-deception and choose to live in a fool's paradise on the ground that no other sort of paradise is attainable. I cannot sympathize with this point of view.

The more I am interested in anything, the more I wish to know the truth about it, however unpleasant the truth may be.

When I first became interested in philosophy, I hoped that I should find in it some satisfaction for my thwarted desire for a religion.

For a time I found a sort of cold comfort in Plato's eternal world of ideas, but in the end I thought this was nonsense and I have found in philosophy no satisfaction whatever for the impulse toward religious belief.

In this sense I have found philosophy disappointing, but as a clarifier I have found it quite the opposite.

Many things which, when I was young, were matters of taste or conjecture have become exact and scientific.

In this I rejoice and in so far as I have been able to contribute to the result, I feel that my work in philosophy has been worth doing. (PFM 16)

Lord Russell, why have you changed your opinions in philosophy?

I am not myself in any degree ashamed of having changed my opinions.

What physicist who was already active in 1900 would dream of boasting that his opinions had not changed during the last half century?

In science men change their opinions when new knowledge becomes available, but philosophy in the minds of many is assimilated rather to theology than to science.

A theologian proclaims eternal truths, the creeds remain unchanged since the Council of Nicaea.

Where nobody knows anything, there is no point in changing your mind. (DMMM, preface)

Lord Russell, since you do not believe in God, to whom or to what do you give your allegiance?

The universe is vast, and men are but tiny specks on an insignificant planet.

But the more we realize our minuteness and our impotence in the face of cosmic forces, the more astonishing becomes what human beings have achieved.

It is to the possible achievements of Man that our ultimate loyalty is due, and in that thought the brief troubles of our unquiet epoch become endurable.

Much wisdom remains to be learned, and if it is only to be learned through adversity, we must endeavor to endure adversity with what fortitude we can command.

But if we can acquire wisdom soon enough, adversity may not be necessary, and the future of Man may be happier than any part of his past. (Italics added) (RSN52 5)

Lord Russell, what have been the major forces in your life?

Three passions, simple but overwhelmingly strong, have governed my life: the longing for love, the search for knowledge, and unbearable pity for the suffering of mankind. These passions, like great winds, have blown me hither and thither, in a wayward course, over a deep ocean of anguish, reaching to the very verge of despair.

I have sought love, first because it brings ecstasy—ecstasy so great that I would often have sacrificed all the rest of life for a few hours of this joy. I have sought it, next, because it relieves loneliness—that terrible loneliness in which one shivering consciousness looks over the rim of the world into the cold unfathomable lifeless abyss. I have sought it, finally, because in the union of love I have seen, in mystic miniature, the prefiguring vision of the heaven that saints and poets have imagined. This is what I sought, and though it might seem too good for human life, this is what—at last—I have found.

With equal passion I have sought knowledge. I have wished to understand the hearts of men. I have wished to know why the stars shine. And I have tried to apprehend the Pythagorean power by which number holds sway above the flux. A little of this, but not much, I have achieved.

Love and knowledge, so far as they were possible, led upward toward the heavens. But always pity brought me back to earth. Echoes of cries of pain reverberate in my heart. Children in famine, victims tortured by oppressors, helpless old people a hated burden to their sons, and the whole world of loneliness, poverty, and pain make a mockery of what human life should be. I long to alleviate the evil, but I cannot, and I too suffer.

This has been my life. I have found it worth living, and would gladly live it again if the chance were offered me. (A1 3)

Lord Russell, have you missed anything by not being religious?

I don't feel I've missed anything through not believing in religion.

I think, on the contrary, that the religious people have missed a very great deal.

They've missed the kind of pride that stands upright and looks at the world, and says, "Well, you can kill me, but anyway, here I am. I stand firm."

And they miss that. And I think that's a very very valuable thing that a person should have.

I shouldn't like at all to go through life in a sort of creepy-crawly way, full of terror, and being bolstered up all the time as if I were a fainting lady being kept from sprawling on the ground . . . because no human being whom I can respect needs the consolation of things that are untrue.

He can face the truth. (SP)

Lord Russell, have you always believed what you now believe, and if not, what has changed . . . and what has not changed?

My inner life [has been] a perpetual battle.

I set out with a more or less religious belief in a Platonic world, in which mathematics shone with a beauty like that of the last Cantos of the Paradiso.

I came to the conclusion that the eternal world is trivial, and that mathematics is only the art of saying the same thing in different words.

I set out with a belief that love, free and courageous, could conquer the world without fighting.

I ended by supporting a bitter and terrible war.

In these respects there was failure.

But beneath all this load of failure I am still conscious of something that I feel to be victory.

I may have conceived theoretical truth wrongly, but I was not wrong in thinking that there is such a thing and that it deserves our allegiance.

I may have thought the road to a world of free and happy human beings shorter than it is proving to be, but I was not wrong in thinking that such a world is possible, and that it is worthwhile to live with a view to bringing it nearer.

I have lived in the pursuit of a vision, both personal and social.

Personal: to care for what is noble, for what is beautiful, for what is gentle; to allow moments of insight to give wisdom at more mundane times.

Social: to see in imagination the society that is to be created, where individuals grow freely, and where hate and greed and envy die because there is nothing to nourish them.

These things I believe, and the world, for all its horrors, has left me unshaken. (PFM 56)

Lord Russell, what things have given you the greatest personal pleasure?

That's rather a difficult question, isn't it?

Passionate private relations perhaps would come first of all.

I get immense pleasure from natural beauty.

And intellectual pleasure, understanding something that had been puzzling, and the moment comes when you understand it, that is a very delightful moment. (CBC)

Lord Russell, have you ever belonged to a political party?

Throughout my life I have longed to feel that oneness with large bodies of human beings that is experienced by the members of enthusiastic crowds.

The longing has often been strong enough to lead me into self-deception.

I have imagined myself in turn a Liberal, a Socialist, or a Pacifist, but I have never been any of these things in any profound sense.

Always the skeptical intellect, when I have most wished it silent, has whispered doubts to me, has cut me off from the facile enthusiasm of others, and has transported me into a desolate solitude.

During the First War, I worked with Quakers, nonresisters and Socialists. While I was willing to accept unpopularity and the inconvenience of belonging to unpopular opinion, I would tell the Quakers that l thought many wars in history had been justified, and the Socialists that I dreaded the tyranny of the State.

They would look askance at me, and while continuing to accept my help would feel that I was not one of them.

Underlying all occupations and pleasures, I felt from early youth the pain of solitude.

This feeling of isolation, however, has grown much less since 1939, for during the last fifteen years I have been broadly in agreement with most of my compatriots on important issues. (PFM 38)

Lord Russell, why do you prefer democracy?

For my part, I retain the tastes and prejudices of an old-fashioned liberal.

I like democracy. I like individual liberty, and I like culture.

I do not like to see ignorant or despotic officials interfering needlessly with private lives; I do not like to see creative thought crushed by the tyranny of stupid majorities.

I do not like persecution, whether by majorities or minorities.

I am suspicious of government and distrustful of politicians; but insofar as there must be government, I prefer that it should be democratic. (DMMM 45)

Lord Russell, what was your attitude toward the Russian Revolution?

When the Russian Revolution first broke out I welcomed it as did almost everybody else, including the British Embassy in Petrograd (as it then was).

It was difficult at a distance to follow the confused events of 1918 and 1919 and I did not know what to think of the Bolsheviks.

But in 1920 I went to Russia, had long talks with Lenin and other prominent men, and saw as much as I could of what was going on.

I came to the conclusion that everything that was being done and everything that was being intended was totally contrary to what any person of a liberal outlook would desire.

I thought the regime already hateful and certain to become more so.

I found the source of the evil in a contempt for liberty and democracy which was a natural outcome of fanaticism.

It was thought by radicals in those days that one ought to support the Russian Revolution whatever it might be doing, since it was opposed by reactionaries, and criticism of it played into their hands.

I felt the force of this argument and was for some time in doubt as to what I ought to do.

But in the end I decided in favor of what seemed to me to be the truth.

I stated publicly that I thought the Bolshevik regime abominable, and I have never seen any reason to change this opinion.

In this I differed from almost all the friends that I had acquired since 1914.

Most people still hated me for having opposed the war, and the minority, who did not hate me on this ground, denounced me for not praising the Bolsheviks.

My visit to Russia in 1920 was a turning point in my life. During the time that I was there I felt a gradually increasing horror which became an almost intolerable oppression. The country seemed to be one vast prison in which the jailers were cruel bigots.

When I found my friends applauding these men as liberators and regarding the regime that they were creating as a paradise, I wondered in a bewildered manner whether it was my friends or I that were mad.

As a matter of historical dynamics it seemed obvious that revolutionary ardor must develop into imperialism as it had done in the French Revolution.

When I finally decided to say what I thought of the Bolsheviks, my former political friends, including very many who have since come to my opinion, denounced me as a lackey of the *bourgeoisie.*

But reactionaries did not notice what I said and continued to describe me in print as a "lily-livered Bolshie swine."

And so I succeeded in getting the worst of both worlds. (PFM 13)

Lord Russell, what do you feel you can do about the world situation?

When I come to what I myself can do or ought to do about the world situation, I find myself in two minds.

A perpetual argument goes on within me between two different points of view which I will call that of the Devil's Advocate and that of the Earnest Publicist.

My family during four centuries was important in the public life of England, and I was brought up to feel a responsibility which demanded that I should express my opinion on political questions.

This feeling is more deeply implanted in me than reason would warrant, and the voice of the Devil's Advocate is, at least in part, the voice of reason.

"Can't you see," says this cynical character, "that what happens in the world does not depend upon you?

"Whether the populations of the world are to live or die rests with the decisions of Krushchev, Mao Tse-tung, and Mr. John Foster Dulles, not with ordinary mortals like ourselves?

"If they say 'Die,' we shall die. If they say 'Live,' we shall live.

"They do not read your books, and would think them very silly if they did.

"You forget that you are not living in 1688 when your family and a few others gave the king notice and hired another. It is only a failure to move with the times that makes you bother your head with public affairs."

Perhaps the Devil's Advocate is right—but perhaps he is wrong.

Perhaps dictators are not so all-powerful as they seem; perhaps public opinion can still sway them, at any rate in some degree; and perhaps books can help create public opinion.

And so I persist, regardless of his taunts.

There are limits to his severities. "Well, at any rate," he says, "writing books is an innocent occupation and it keeps you out of mischief."

And so I go on writing books, though whether any good will come of doing so, I do not know. (PFM 48)

Lord Russell, how do you feel when your views are misrepresented?

There has been a tendency to think that everything that Xenophon says [about Socrates] must be true, because he had not the wits to think of anything untrue.

This is a very invalid line of argument.

A stupid man's report of what a clever man says is never accurate, because he unconsciously translates what he hears into something he can understand.

I would rather be reported by my bitterest enemy among philosophers than by a friend innocent of philosophy. (HWP 83)

SCIENCE

What is the essence of scientific method?

The essential matter is an intimate association of hypothesis and observation.

The Greeks were fruitful in hypothesis but deficient in observation.

Aristotle, for example, thought that women have fewer teeth than men, which he could not have thought if he had had a proper respect for observation.

Francis Bacon, on the other hand, overestimated the mere collecting of facts, supposing that this, if carried far enough, would of itself give rise to fruitful hypotheses.

But there are so many facts, and so many ways of arranging facts, that no one can collect facts usefully except under the stimulus of some hypothesis to which they are relevant.

Throughout any scientific investigation, even from the very beginning, generalizing hypotheses must exist in the mind of the investigator to determine the direction of his observations.

The hypotheses must, however, continually change and develop as new facts prove the old hypotheses to be inadequate. (RSN34 7)

What are the two different elements in science?

There are two very different elements in science: scientific knowledge and scientific technique.

Those whom I am calling technocrats are interested solely in scientific technique, and the more extreme among them deny that there is such a thing as scientific knowledge.

Scientific theorists, on the other hand, are concerned to discover natural laws, and leave to others the discovery of practical ways in which such laws can be useful.

In a word, the technocrat wishes to change nature, while the theorist wishes to understand it.

There is practically no one left in the world who will maintain that the point of view of the theorist alone is adequate, but there are many who think that the point of view of the technocrat suffices.

Or if at moments they feel it somewhat arid, they supplement it, not by any doubt that can be entertained by a scientific inquirer, but by an unscientific form of arrogance, namely the belief that, without the patience and without the submission involved in observing nature, we can arrive by a form of self-assertion at kinds of knowledge which science is incapable of supplying.

This again is megalomania.

Man is neither impotent nor omnipotent; he has powers and his powers are surprisingly great, but they are not infinite and they are not so great as he might wish. (NHCW 27)

What is the most difficult step in scientific investigation?

It is commonly said that the framing of hypotheses is the most difficult, and perhaps this is true of men who have undergone a thorough education in science.

But viewed historically, it would seem that respect for fact is more difficult for the human mind than the invention of remarkable theories.

It is still believed by a large percentage of the inhabitants of this country [U.K.] that people born in May are specially liable to corns, that the moon affects the weather, and that it is dangerous to see the new moon through glass.

None of those who hold these theories think it necessary to verify them.

Aristotle's physics, as interpreted by medieval commentators, supplied a number of admirable theories, which covered the ground more adequately than Galileo could do.

There was nothing against the theories except that they were not in accordance with the facts, but this objection struck Galileo's Aristotelian adversaries as frivolous.

And when he discovered Jupiter's moons, their existence was denied, on the ground that the number of the heavenly bodies must be seven.

I think therefore that in the beginning, the respect for fact demanded by science is more difficult even than the framing of what may prove good hypotheses.

And the hypotheses that prove good are very seldom such as commend themselves to our initial prejudices. (RSN34 7)

Are there failures to recognize the limits of science?

The old humility of the shepherds who felt themselves subject to the influences of the Pleiades is no longer appropriate in the scientific world.

But there is a danger lest it should be replaced by a species of arrogance toward nature, which can lead to great disasters.

Man, however scientific he may be, is not omnipotent.

He is hedged in by natural limits.

By means of his knowledge and technique, he can diminish the narrowness of these limits, but he can never remove them wholly.

Some astronomers try to cheer us up in moments of depression by assuring us that one fine day the sun will explode, and in the twinkling of an eye, we shall all be turned into gas.

I do not know whether this is going to happen, nor when it will happen if it does happen, but I think it is safe to say that if it does, it will be a matter outside human control, and that even the best astronomers will be unable to prevent it.

This is an extreme example and one which it is useless to think about, because there is no way in which human behavior can be adapted to it.

It does, however, serve one purpose, which is to remind us that we are not gods. You may exclaim indignantly, "but I never thought we were!" No doubt, dear reader, you are not one of those who suffer from the most extreme follies of our age, for if you were, you would not be one of my readers.

But if you consider the Politburo or the American technocrats you will see that there are those who escape atheism by impiously imagining themselves on the throne of the Almighty.

Such men have forgotten that while we can coax physical nature into satisfying many of our wishes, we cannot exercise authority over it or make it change its ways one jot.

The Russian Government appears to think that Soviet decrees can change the laws of genetics; the Vatican apparently believes that ecclesiastical decrees could secure adequate nourishment for us all, even if there were only standing room on the planet.

Such opinions, to my mind, represent a form of insane megalomania entirely alien to the scientific spirit. (NHCW 26)

Will progress in science continue to depend on remarkable men?

Now that scientific method has been developed, a great deal can be achieved without the genius that was necessary in the pioneers.

Any man possessed of patience and fair abilities and the necessary equipment can, nowadays, be pretty sure to find out *something,* and it may happen to be something of great importance.

I do not think that Mendel's work required any extraordinary gifts, and yet the Mendelian theory of heredity is transforming scientific agriculture, and probably will in time considerably alter the congenital character of human beings.

The more science advances, the easier it becomes to make new discoveries. That is why the rapidity of scientific progress has been continually increasing since the seventeenth century. (RSN34 7)

What ancient errors are the parents of today's sciences?

Most sciences, at their inception, have been connected with some form of false belief, which gave them a fictitious value.

Astronomy was connected with astrology, chemistry with alchemy.

Mathematics was associated with a more refined type of error.

Mathematical knowledge appeared to be certain, and applicable to the real world; moreover, it was obtained by mere thinking, without the need of observation.

Consequently, it was thought to supply an ideal, from which everyday empirical knowledge fell short.

It was supposed, on the basis of mathematics, that thought is superior to sense, intuition to observation.

If the world of sense does not fit mathematics, so much the worse for the world of sense.

In various ways, methods of approaching nearer to the mathematician's ideal were sought, and the resulting suggestions were the source of much that was mistaken in metaphysics and theory of knowledge. (HWP 34)

How did science seek to achieve a permanent substructure?

Science, like philosophy, has sought to escape from the doctrine of perpetual flux by finding some permanent substratum amid changing phenomena.

Chemistry seemed to satisfy this desire.

It was found that fire, which appears to destroy, only transmutes: elements are recombined, but each atom that existed before combustion still exists when the process is completed. Accordingly, it was supposed that atoms are indestructible, and that all change in the physical world consists merely in rearrangement of persistent elements.

This view prevailed until the discovery of radioactivity, when it was found that atoms could disintegrate.

Nothing daunted, the physicists invented new and smaller units, called electrons and protons, out of which atoms were composed; and these units were supposed, for a few years, to have the indestructibility formerly attributed to atoms.

Unfortunately, it seemed that protons and electrons could meet and explode, forming, not new matter, but a wave of energy spreading through the universe with the velocity of light.

Energy had to replace matter as what is permanent.

But energy, unlike matter, is not a refinement of the commonsense notion of a "thing"; it is merely a characteristic of physical processes.

It might be fancifully identified with the Heraclitean Fire, but it is the burning, not what burns.

"What burns" has disappeared from modern physics. (HWP 46)

What have been the effects of science, good and bad?

Science as technique was building up in practical men a quite different outlook from any that was to be found among theoretical philosophers.

Technique conferred a sense of power; man is now much less at the mercy of his environment than he was in former times. But the power conferred by technique is social, not individual; an average individual wrecked on a desert island could have achieved more in the seventeenth century than he could now.

Scientific technique requires the cooperation of a large number of individuals organized under a single direction.

Its tendency, therefore, is against anarchism and even individualism, since it demands a well-knit social structure.

Unlike religion, it is ethically neutral: it assures men that they can perform wonders, but does not tell them what wonders to perform. In this way it is incomplete.

In practice, the purposes to which scientific skill will be devoted depend largely on chance.

The men at the head of the vast organizations which it necessitates can, within limits, turn it this way or that as they please.

The power impulse thus has a scope which it never had before.

The philosophies that have been inspired by scientific *technique* are power philosophies, and tend to regard everything nonhuman as mere raw material.

Ends are no longer considered; only the skillfulness of the process is valued.

This also is a form of madness. It is, in our day, the most dangerous form, and the one against which a sane philosophy should provide an antidote.

The ancient world found an end to anarchy in the Roman Empire, but the Roman Empire was a brute fact, not an idea.

The Catholic world sought an end to anarchy in the Church, which was an idea, but was never adequately embodied in fact.

Neither the ancient solution nor the medieval solution was satisfactory—the one because it could not be idealized, the other because it could not be actualized.

The modern world, at present, seems to be moving towards a solution like that of antiquity: a social order imposed by force, representing the will of the powerful rather than the hopes of common men.

The problem of a durable and satisfactory social order can only be solved by combining the solidity of the Roman Empire with the idealism of Saint Augustine's City of God.

To achieve this a new philosophy will be needed. (HWP 494)

Has the freedom that science has given us been a boon?

The liberation from bondage to nature has left men, in theory, free to choose their own ends to a degree that was never possible at any earlier time.

I say "in theory," because impulses incorporated into human nature by long ages of training and natural selection remain to determine human action independently of present physical needs.

What a nation can spare from increasing its own numbers, it devotes only in part to its own welfare.

To a very great extent it devotes its energies to killing other people or preparing to kill them, or paying those who have helped to kill them in the past.

In the United States, about one-fifth of the total production of the country is being spent in rearmament.

The freedom from bondage to nature, therefore, is by no means wholly a boon.

It is only a boon in so far as the resulting liberty of choice leads to an increase of those activities which are of use to mankind as a whole.

But in so far as it merely liberates combative impulses, it does no good at all but quite the opposite.

Some people tell fine stories about the use of atomic energy in industry, and the economies which will result.

Such economies, if the world remains what it is now, will do nothing but harm, since they will set free a greater part of human energy for the purpose of mutual destruction.

This example illustrates the way in which our new mastery of nature brings new responsibilities and new duties.

If men prove incapable of this adaptation, the whole movement of science and scientific technique will have proved a misfortune, and perhaps will have taken man along a blind alley.

While we were slaves to nature, we could allow ourselves a slave mentality, and leave to nature decisions which now must be ours.

This is difficult, since great parts of traditional religion and morality were inspired by man's bondage to nature, and the ways of thought and feeling that we acquire from our culture and from our early upbringing are hard to overcome, even when circumstances imperatively demand a different outlook. (NHCW 23)

How does Gulliver's Travels *foreshadow scientific horrors?*

Gulliver's Travels has had the curious fate of being regarded as one for the amusement of children, although it is the most biting and devastating and completely black of all the satires ever penned by embittered men.

The account of Laputa is an early example of science fiction; not, by any means, the first, since it had been anticipated, for example, by Francis Godwin and Cyrano de Bergerac.

But it is, I think, the first to represent a scientific community in the manner familiarized for our generation by Huxley's *Brave New World.*

Other writers, until nearly our own day, had thought of science optimistically as a liberator.

Swift was, I believe, the first to think of it as affording a means to ruthless tyranny.

I imbibed this point of view at the age of fifteen, and it left my imagination well prepared for the shock of nuclear bombs.

I realized then, and have remembered ever since, that science in itself is ethically neutral.

It confers power, but for evil just as much as for good.

It is to feeling not knowlege that we must appeal if science is to be beneficent.

Laputa showed me the possibility of scientific horrors and made me realize that, however scientific, they remain horrors.

Abominations are abominations even if the utmost skill is required to contrive them. (FF 32)

Science has done much for man, but where has it fallen short?

Our nomad ancestors, while they watched their flocks by night, observed the stars in their inexorable courses, and believed themselves subject to the influences of celestial bodies.

Wind and storm, drought and heat, comets and meteors, and plagues filled their lives with awe, and they hoped to escape by means of humility.

Modern man does not combat plagues by humility; he has found that they are to be combatted by scientific knowledge.

Scientific knowledge, in fact, gives the means (when there are means) of combatting any extrahuman enemy, but it does not give the means of combatting the human enemy without, or the part of the individual soul which leads it towards death rather than towards life.

The problems of man's contest with nature, in so far as they are soluble, can be solved by physical science, but they are not the only problems with which man is faced.

For his other problems, other methods are necessary. (NHCW 24)

In what area has resistance to science been strongest?

The prejudice against scientific investigation of facts has been strongest where human beings are concerned.

Throughout the Middle Ages anatomy was hampered by a rooted objection to dissection of corpses.

In China, not many years ago, a French surgeon, who had been invited to found a medical school, demanded corpses for dissection.

He was told that to cut up corpses would be an impiety, but that he could operate instead on living criminals. (RSN34 7)

In what parts of the world did science originate?

Science is a product of Europe. The only exception of importance that I can think of is the Babylonian discovery that eclipses could be predicted.

A very few nations—Italy, France, the Low Countries, Britain, and Germany—contributed quite 90 percent of the great discoveries. Poland contributed Copernicus, Russia contributed Mendeleeff, but on the whole, the share of Eastern Europe has not been a large one.

Within Western Europe, as may be seen from a map showing the birthplaces of eminent men of science, there has been a correlation with commerce and industry. But commerce does not necessarily lead to science. It did not do so among the Phoenicians and Carthaginians, and the Arabs, though they studied science of a sort, made no discoveries in any way comparable to those of Western Europe since 1600.

I do not think that seventeenth-century science can be regarded as an inevitable outcome of social and economic conditions; the existence of individuals possessed of very rare abilities was also necessary. Why they should have been born there and then cannot be explained in scientific terms by means of our present knowledge. It certainly does not have a racial explanation, as may be seen from the fact that many of the best men of science have been Jews, who, though living in Western Europe, are not of course of West European stock. (RSN34 7)

SELF

What's wrong with taking care of our own?

If your hopes and wishes are confined to yourself, or your family, or your nation, or your class, or the adherents of your creed, you will find that all your affections and all your kindly feelings are paralleled by dislikes and hostile sentiments.

From such a duality in men's feelings spring almost all the major evils in human life—cruelties, oppressions, persecutions, and wars.

If our world is to escape the disasters which threaten it men must learn to be less circumscribed in their sympathies.

This has no doubt always been true in a measure but it is more true now than it ever was before.

Mankind, owing to science and scientific technique, are unified for evil but are not yet unified for good.

They have learnt the technique of world-wide mutual destruction but not the more desirable technique of world-wide cooperation.

The failure to learn this more desirable technique has its source in emotional limitations, and in indulgence in hatred and fear towards other groups. (PFM 169)

SEX

Do sexual matters call for a special kind of morality?

I should deal with sexual morality exactly as I should with everything else.

I should say that if what you're doing does no harm to anybody, there's no reason to condemn it.

And you shouldn't condemn it merely because some ancient taboo has said that this is wrong. (SHM 55)

What is a sensible sexual morality?

Sexual morality, freed of superstition, is a simple matter.

Fraud and deceit, assault, seduction of persons under age, are proper matters for the criminal law.

Relations between adults who are free agents are a private matter, and should not be interfered with either by the law or by public opinion, because no outsider can know whether they are good or bad.

When children are involved, the state becomes interested to the extent of seeing that they are properly educated and cared for, and it ought to ensure that the father does his duty by them in the way of maintenance.

But neither the state nor public opinion ought to insist on the parents living together if they are incompatible; the spectacle of parents' quarrels is far worse for children than the separation of the parents could possibly be. (BW 349)

How to deal with sexual obsession?

I am quite in agreement with the Church in thinking that obsession with sexual topics is an evil, but I am not in agreement with the Church as to the best methods of avoiding this evil.

It is notorious that St. Anthony was more obsessed by sex than the most extreme voluptuary who ever lived; I will not adduce more recent examples for fear of giving offense.

Sex is a natural need, like food and drink.

We blame the gormandizer and the dipsomaniac, because in the case of each, an interest which has a certain legitimate place in life has usurped too large a share of his thoughts and emotions.

But we do not blame a man for a normal and healthy enjoyment of a reasonable quantity of food.

Ascetics, it is true, have done so, and have considered that a man should cut down his nutriment to the lowest point compatible with survival, but this view is not now common, and may be ignored.

The Puritans, in their determination to avoid the pleasures of sex, became somewhat more conscious than people had been before of the pleasures of the table. As a seventeenth-century critic of Puritanism says:

Would you enjoy gay nights and pleasant dinners?
Then must you board with saints and bed with sinners.

It would seem, therefore, that the Puritans did not succeed in subduing the purely corporeal part of our human nature, since what they took away from sex they added to gluttony. (MM 195)

How did Catholicism and Protestantism differ in the way they dealt with the sin of fornication?

Catholicism has always had a certain degree of toleration for what it held to be sin.

The Church has recognized that ordinary human nature could not be expected to live up to its precepts, and has been prepared to give absolution for fornication provided the sinner acknowledged his fault and did penance.

This practical toleration was a method of increasing the power of the clergy, since they alone could pronounce absolution, and but for absolution fornication would entail eternal damnation.

The outlook of Protestantism has been somewhat different, in theory less severe, but in practice, in some ways more so.

Luther was much impressed by the text, "It is better to marry than to burn," and was also in love with a nun.

He inferred that in spite of vows of celibacy, he and the nun had a right to marry, since otherwise, given the strength of his passions, he would have been led into mortal sin.

Protestantism accordingly abandoned the praise of celibacy, which had been characteristic of the Catholic Church, and wherever it was vigorous it also abandoned the doctrine that marriage is a sacrament, and tolerated divorce in certain circumstances.

But Protestants were more shocked than Catholics by fornication, and altogether more rigid in their moral condemnations.

The Catholic Church expected a certain amount of sin, and arranged methods for dealing with it; the Protestants, on the contrary, abandoned the Catholic practice of confession and absolution, and left the sinner in a much more hopeless position than he occupies in the Catholic Church.

One sees this attitude in both its aspects in modern America, where divorce is exceedingly easy, but adultery is condemned with far more severity than in most Catholic countries. (MM 37)

SIN

Is there such a thing as sin?

I don't think sin is a useful conception.

I think sin is something that it is positively good to punish, such as murder, not only because you want to prevent murder, but because the murderer deserves to suffer. (SHM 53)

Is euthanasia a sin?

The whole conception of "Sin" is one which I find very puzzling, doubtless owing to my sinful nature.

If "Sin" consisted in causing needless suffering, I could understand, but on the contrary, sin often consists in avoiding needless suffering.

Some years ago, in the English House of Lords, a bill was introduced to legalize euthanasia in cases of painful and incurable disease.

The patient's consent was to be necessary, as well as several medical certificates.

To me, in my simplicity, it would seem natural to require the patient's consent, but the late Archbishop of Canterbury, the English official expert on Sin, explained the erroneousness of such a view.

The patient's consent turned euthanasia into suicide, and suicide is sin.

Their Lordships listened to the voice of authority and rejected the bill. (UE 76)

Is calling something a sin sometimes an excuse for cruelty?

I think very largely. It's to enable you to inflict suffering without a bad conscience, and therefore it is a bad thing. (SHM 54)

SKEPTICISM

Can one be too skeptical?

When one admits that nothing is certain, one must, I think, also add that some things are much more nearly certain than others.

It is much more nearly certain that we are here assembled tonight than it is that this or that political party is in the right.

Certainly there are degrees of certainty, and one should be very careful to emphasize that fact, because otherwise one is landed in an utter skepticism, and complete skepticism would, of course, be totally barren and totally useless. (published by Haldeman-Julius, 1949) (RGR 85)

SOCIALISM

What changes should be made when an industry is nationalized?

In industry, it must not be thought that all problems are solved when there is nationalization.

A large industry—e.g., railways—should have a large measure of self-government; the relation of employees to the state in a nationalized industry should not be a mere reproduction of their former relation to private employers. (AI 67)

In what areas should socialism permit competition?

Everthing concerned with opinion, such as books, newspapers and political propaganda, must be left to genuine competition, and carefully safeguarded from government control, as well as from every other form of monopoly.

But the competition must be cultural and intellectual, not economic, and still less military or by means of the criminal law. (BW 357)

How well does socialism curb love of power?

The mere possession of power tends to produce a love of power, which is a very dangerous motive, because the only sure proof of power consists in preventing others from doing what they wish to.

The essential theory of democracy is the diffusion of power among the whole people, so that the evils produced by one man's possession of great power shall be obviated.

But the diffusion of power through democracy is only effective when the voters take an interest in the question involved.

When the question does not interest them, they do not attempt to control the administration, and all actual power passes into the hands of officials.

For this reason, the true ends of democracy are not achieved by state socialism or by any system which places great power in the hands of men subject to no popular control except that which is more or less indirectly exercised through parliament.

Any fresh survey of men's political actions shows that, in those who have enough energy to be politically effective, love of power is a stronger motive than economic self-interest.

Love of power actuated the great millionaires, who have far more money than they can spend, but continue to amass wealth merely in order to control more and more of the world's finances.

Love of power is obviously the ruling motive of many politicians.

It is also the chief cause of wars, which are admittedly almost always a bad speculation from the mere point of view of wealth.

For this reason, a new economic system which does not interfere with the concentration of power is not likely to effect any very great improvement in the world.

This is one of the chief reasons for regarding state socialism with suspicion. (PI 49)

SOCIOLOGY

What's good about the sociology approach to history?

There is a modern school of sociology, which professes to be more strictly scientific than any other, and which is, at least to some extent, an outcome of Marx's doctrines.

According to this school, sociology can only become truly scientific by observing men in the mass rather than as individuals, and by observing only their bodily behavior without any attempt at psychological interpretation.

Up to a point, there is much to be said for this school.

Undoubtedly pleasure in what is dramatic has caused both the readers and the writers of history to lay too much stress on individuals; undoubtedly, also, there is an element of risk in any psychological interpretation of physical behavior.

As the poet says,

> It was all very well to dissemble your love,
> But why did you kick me downstairs?

The school in question will note only the kicking, and will not inquire whether it was caused by dissembled love or by hatred.

At any rate we can agree so far, that it is a good thing to record the indubitable facts of overt behavior before embarking upon the doubtful sea of inward motivation.

A book such as *Middletown,* although its authors do not subscribe to the theory we are examining, is one which the advocates of the theory can approve, and which shows that much valuable work may be suggested by the theory.

Some 50 years ago, Charles Booth's *Life and Labour of the People in London* performed, on a much larger scale, the same sort of task for London. It was an immensely valuable book, which inspired reforms that greatly increased the well-being of the poorer sections of the population in London.

To the reformer, if he is to act wisely, such surveys of the average lives of men, women, and children are immeasurably useful. (UH 36)

What's not *good about the sociology approach to history?*

They [books like *Middletown* and *Life and Labour of the People in London*] are, however, a means, not an end in themselves; when regarded as an end, they are in danger of losing their usefulness.

To begin with, the objection to psychological interpretations is foolish.

Why do we object to poverty and illness? Because they cause suffering, which is a mental phenomenon.

To a purely external observation, poverty and illness should be just as satisfactory as prosperity and good health.

When the astronomer observes the stars, he does not have to consider whether their condition is "good" or "bad," because we do not believe that they can feel; but human beings are different, and a sociology which ignores their feelings is leaving out what is most essential.

We do not wish to reform the solar system, but we do wish to reform the social system, if we have any sympathy with suffering.

And only psychological considerations can show us what reforms are desirable.

From a purely scientific point of view, the theory seems to me mistaken in minimizing the effect of individuals.

It often happens that large opposing social forces are in approximate momentary equilibrium, and that a comparatively small force may decide which shall be victorious, just as a very small force on a watershed may decide whether water shall flow into the Atlantic or the Pacific.

The Russian Revolution would have been very different without Lenin, and it was a very small force that decided the Germans to permit his return to Russia.

The Duke of Wellington remarked about the Battle of Waterloo "It was a damned nice thing. I do believe if I had not been there we should not have won." Probably he was right.

Such instances show that the main course of great events may sometimes depend upon the actions of an individual.

This, of course, is regrettable from the point of view of those who are impatient to turn history into a science.

But in fact, while some aspects of history can be made more or less scientific, and while it is important to do this whenever it is possible, the material is too complex to be reduced to scientific laws at present, and probably for centuries to come.

There is too much that, to our ignorance, appears as chance, and too great a likelihood of the intrusion of incalculable forces.

There is nothing genuinely scientific in a premature attempt to *seem* scientific. (UH 37)

SOCRATES

Are there doubts about what happened at Socrates' trial?

It is very hard to judge how far Plato means to portray the historical Socrates, and how far he intends the person called "Socrates" in his dialogues to be merely the mouthpiece of his own opinions.

Plato, in addition to being a philosopher, is an imaginative writer of great genius and charm.

No one supposes, and he himself does not seriously pretend, that the conversations in his dialogues took place just as he records them.

Nevertheless, at any rate in the earlier dialogues, the conversation is completely natural and the characters quite convincing.

It is the excellence of Plato as a writer of fiction that throws doubt on him as a historian.

His Socrates is a consistent and extraordinarily interesting character, far beyond the power of most men to invent; but I think Plato *could* have invented him.

Whether he did so is of course another question.

The dialogue which is most generally regarded as historical is the *Apology*.

This professes to be the speech that Socrates made in his own defense at his trial—not, of course, a stenographic report, but what remained in Plato's memory some years after the event, put together and elaborated with literary art.

Plato was present at the trial, and it certainly seems fairly clear that what is set down is the *sort* of thing that Plato remembered Socrates as saying, and that the intention is, broadly speaking, historical.

This, with all its limitations, is enough to give a fairly definite picture of the character of Socrates.

The main facts of the trial are not open to doubt.

The prosecution was based upon the charge that "Socrates is an evildoer and a curious person, searching into things under the earth and above the heavens, and making the worse appear the better cause, and teaching all this to others."

The real ground of hostility to him was, almost certainly, that he was supposed to be connected with the aristocratic party; most of his pupils belonged to this faction, and some, in positions of power, had proved themselves very pernicious.

But this ground could not be made evident on account of the amnesty.

He was found guilty by the majority, and it was then open to him, by Athenian law, to propose some lesser penalty than death.

The judges had to choose, if they found the accused guilty, between the penalty demands by the prosecution and that suggested by the defense.

It was therefore in the interest of Socrates to suggest a substantial penalty, which the court might have accepted as adequate.

He, however, proposed a fine of thirty minae, for which some of his friends, (including Plato), were willing to go surety.

This was so small a punishment that the court was annoyed, and condemned him to death by a larger majority than that which had found him guilty.

Undoubtedly he foresaw this result.

It is clear that he had no wish to avoid the death penalty by concessions which might seem to acknowledge his guilt. (Italics added) (HWP 84)

SPARTA

What was life like in Sparta?

To understand Plato, and indeed many later philosophers, it is necessary to know something of Sparta.

Sparta had a double effect on Greek thought: through the reality, and through the myth.

Each is important.

The reality enabled the Spartans to defeat Athens in war; the myth influenced Plato's political theory, and that of countless subsequent writers.

The myth, fully developed, is to be found in Plutarch's *Life of Lycurgus*; the ideals that it favors have had a great part in framing the doctrines of Rousseau, Nietzsche, and National Socialism. The myth is of even more importance, basically, than the reality. [However] the reality was the source of the myth.

The Spartans, who were the ruling race, had conquered the country at the time of the Dorian invasion from the north, and had reduced the population that they found there to the condition of serfs.

All the land belonged to the Spartans, who, however, were forbidden by law and custom to cultivate it themselves, both on the ground that such labor was degrading, and in order that they might always be free for military service.

The sole business of a Spartan citizen was war, to which he was trained from birth.

Sickly children were exposed after inspection by the heads of the tribe; only those judged vigorous were allowed to be reared.

Up to the age of twenty, all the boys were trained in one big school; the purpose of the training was to make them hardy, indifferent to pain, and submissive to discipline.

There was no nonsense about cultural or scientific education; the sole aim was to produce good soldiers, wholly devoted to the state.

Every citizen belonged to a mess, and dined with the other members; he had to make a contribution in kind from the produce of his lot.

It was the theory of the state that no Spartan citizen should be destitute, and none should be rich.

Each was expected to live on the produce of his lot.

None was allowed to own gold or silver, and the money was made of iron.

Spartan simplicity became proverbial. (HWP 94)

What was the status of women in Sparta?

The position of women in Sparta was peculiar.

They were not secluded, like respectable women elsewhere in Greece.

Girls went through the same physical training as was given to boys; what is more remarkable, boys and girls did their gymnastics together, all being naked. It was desired "that the maidens should harden their bodies with exercise of running, wrestling. . . ."

Women were not allowed to exhibit any emotion not profitable to the State. They might display contempt for a coward, and would be praised if he were their son; but they might not show grief if their new-born child was condemned to death as a weakling, or if their sons were killed in battle. (HWP 96)

What did other Greeks think of Sparta?

Sparta aroused among other Greeks an admiration which is to us somewhat surprising.

Originally, it had been much less different from other Greek cities than it become later; in early days it produced poets and artists as good as those elsewhere.

But about the seventh century B.C., its constitution crystallized into the form we have been considering: everything was sacrificed to success in war, and Sparta ceased to have any part in what Greece contributed to the civilization of the world.

To us, the Spartan state appears as a model, in miniature, of the state that the Nazis would establish if victorious.

To the Greeks it seemed otherwise. As Bury says:

> A stranger from Athens or Miletus in the fifth century visiting the struggling villages which formed her unwalled unpretentious city must have had a feeling of being transported into an age long past, when men were braver, better and simpler, unspoiled by wealth, undisturbed by ideas.
>
> To a philosopher, like Plato, speculating in political science, the Spartan State seemed the nearest approach to the ideal.
>
> The ordinary Greek looked upon it as a structure of severe and simple beauty, a Dorian city stately as a Dorian temple, far nobler than his own abode, but not so comfortable to dwell in. *History of Greece,* Vol. I, p. 141

(HWP 97)

What did Plutarch think of Sparta's ruler, Lycurgus?

Lycurgus—so Plutarch says—having resolved to give laws to Sparta, traveled widely in order to study different institutions.

He liked the laws of Crete, which were "very straight and severe," but disliked those of Ionia, where there were "superfluities and vanities."

In Egypt he learned the advantage of separating the soldiers from the rest of the people, and afterwards, having returned from his travels, "brought the practice of it into Sparta, where setting the merchants, artificers, and laborers every one a part by themselves, he did establish a noble Commonwealth."

He made an equal division of lands among all the citizens of Sparta, in order to "banish out of the city all insolvency, envy, covetousness, and deliciousness, and also all riches and poverty."

He forbade gold and silver money, allowing only iron coinage. . . .

By this means he banished "all superfluous and unprofitable sciences," since there was not enough money to pay their practitioners, and by the same law he made all external commerce impossible.

Rhetoricians, panders, and jewellers, not liking the iron money, avoided Sparta.

He next ordained that all the citizens should eat together, and all should have the same food.

Lycurgus, like other reformers, thought the education of children "the chiefest and greatest matter that a reformer of laws should establish"; and like all who aim chiefly at military power, he was anxious to keep up the birth rate. The "plays, sports and dances the maids did naked before young men were provocations to draw and allure the young men to marry. . . ." The habit of treating a marriage, for the first few years, as if it were a clandestine affair, "continued in both parties a still burning love, and a new desire of the one to the other"—such, at least, is the opinion of Plutarch.

He goes on to explain that a man was not thought ill of if, being old and having a young wife, he allowed a younger man to have children by her. "It was lawful also for an honest man that loved another man's wife . . . to interest her husband to suffer him to lie with her, and that he may plough in that lusty ground, and cast abroad the seed of well-favored children." There was to be no foolish jealousy. . . .

When a child was born, the father brought him before the elders of his family to be examined: if he was healthy, he was given back to the father to be reared; if not, he was thrown into a deep pit of water. (HWP 101)

At the age of seven, boys were taken away from home and put in a boarding school.

"Touching learning, they had as much as served their turn: for the rest of their time they spent in learning how to obey, to do away with pain, to endure labor, to overcome still in fight." (HWP 103)

They were taught to steal, and were punished if caught—not for stealing, but for stupidity.

Homosexual love, both male and female, was a recognized custom in Sparta, and had an acknowledged part in the education of adolescent boys.

A boy's lover suffered credit or discredit by the boy's actions.

Plutarch states that once, when a boy cried out because he was hurt in fighting, his lover was fined for the boy's cowardice.

There was little liberty at any stage in the life of a Spartan. . . .

> It was not lawful for any man to live as he listed.
>
> They were all of this mind, that they were not born to serve themselves, but to serve their country.
>
> One of the best and happiest things which Lycurgus ever brought into his city was the great rest and leisure which he made his citizens to have, only forbidding them that they should not profess any vile or base occupation; and they needed not also to be careful to get great riches, in a place where goods were nothing profitable, nor esteemed.

(HWP 103)

Spartans were not allowed to travel, nor were foreigners admitted to Sparta, except on business; for it was feared that alien customs would corrupt Lacedaemonian virtue.

Plutarch relates the law that allowed Spartans to kill helots [serfs] whenever they felt so disposed, but refuses to believe that anything so abominable can have been due to Lycurgus, "because I imagine his nature was gentle and merciful, by the clemency and justice we see he used in all his other doings."

Except in this matter, Plutarch has nothing but praise for the constitution of Sparta. (HWP 104)

What did Aristotle think of Sparta? Did his view prevail?

One reason for the admiration felt for Sparta by other Greeks was its stability.

All other Greek cities had revolutions, but the Spartan constitution remained unchanged for centuries, except for a gradual increase of the powers of the ephors [the chief magistrates, five in number], which occurred by legal means, without violence.

Aristotle, who lived after the downfall of Sparta, gives a very hostile acount of its constitution.

What he says is so different from what other people say that it is difficult to believe he is speaking of the same place, e.g., "The legislator wanted to make the whole state hardy and temperate, and he has carried out his intention in the case of men, but he has neglected the women, who live in every sort of intemperance and luxury.

"The consequence is that in such a state, wealth is too highly valued, especially if the citizens fall under the dominion of their wives, after the manner of most warlike races.

"Even in regard to courage, which is of no use in daily life, and is needed only in war, the influence of the Lacedaemonian women has been most mischievous. . . ."

Aristotle criticizes every point in the Spartan constitution.

He says that the ephors are often very poor, and therefore easy to bribe; [and] have too much license, and live in a manner contrary to the spirit of the constitution, while the strictness in relation to ordinary citizens is so intolerable that they take refuge in the secret illegal indulgence of sensual pleasures.

Aristotle wrote when Sparta was decadent. His tone is so dry and realistic that it is difficult to disbelieve him, and it is in line with all modern experience of the results of excessive severity in the laws.

But it was not Aristotle's Sparta that persisted in men's imaginations; it was the mythical Sparta of Plutarch and the philosophical idealization of Sparta in Plato's Republic. *Century after century, young men read these works, and were fired with the ambition to become Lycurguses or philosopher-kings.*

The resulting union of idealism and love of power has led men astray over and over again, and is still doing so in the present day. (Italics added) (HWP 98)

What has been the effect of Plutarch's view of Sparta?

The myth of Sparta, for medieval and modern readers, was mainly fixed by Plutarch.

When he wrote, Sparta belonged to the romantic past; its great period was as far removed from his time as Columbus is from ours.

What he says must be treated with great caution by the historian of institutions, but by the historian of myth it is of the utmost importance.

Greece has influenced the world, always, through its effect on men's imaginations, ideals, and hopes, not directly through political power.

Rome made roads which largely still survive, and laws which are the source of many modern legal codes, but it was the armies of Rome that made these things important.

The Greeks, though admirable fighters, made no conquests, because they expended their military fury mainly on each other. It was left to the semibarbarian Alexander to spread Hellenism throughout the Near East, and to make Greek the literary language in Egypt and Syria and the inland parts of Asia Minor.

The Greeks could never have accomplished this task, not for lack of military force, but owing to their incapacity for political cohesion.

The political vehicles of Hellenism have always been non-Hellenic; but it was the Greek genius that so inspired alien nations as to cause them to spread the culture of those whom they had conquered.

What is important to the historian of the world is not the petty wars between Greek cities, or the sordid squabbles for party ascendancy, but the memories retained by mankind when the brief episode was ended.

These memories, as they gradually faded, left in men's minds images. . . .

Of these, Plato was the most important in early Christianity, Aristotle in the medieval Church; but when, after the Renaissance, men began to value political freedom, it was above all to Plutarch that they turned.

He influenced profoundly the English and French liberals of the eighteenth century, and the founders of the United States; he influenced the Romantic movement in Germany, and has continued, mainly by indirect channels, to influence German thought down to the present day.

In some ways his influence was good, in some ways bad; as regards Lycurgus and Sparta, it was bad. (HWP 100)

TOLERANCE

How to define tolerance?

Toleration of opinion, if it's really full-blown, consists in not punishing any kind of opinion as long as it doesn't issue in some kind of criminal act.

The first really tolerant state was Holland.

All the leading intellects of the seventeenth century at some period of their lives had to take refuge in Holland, and if there hadn't been Holland, they'd have been wiped out.

The English were no bettter than other people at that time.

There was a parliamentary investigation which decided that Hobbes was very, very wicked, and it was decreed that no work by Hobbes was to be published in England.

And it wasn't, for a long, long time. (SHM 121)

What is the true test of tolerance?

The true test of a lover of freedom comes only in relation to things that he dislikes.

To tolerate what you like is easy.

It is toleration of what you dislike that characterizes the liberal attitude. (FF 58)

Are there—or should there be—limits to tolerance?

Tolerance, like all other virtues, has its limits.

I should not wish to see it carried to the point of thinking that any one system is as good as another.

But looking further afield to a time when fanaticism has grown less, and when cooperation among nations has become more possible than it is at present, it becomes obvious that the anarchic liberty at present claimed by national states is as much to be condemned as the anarchic liberty claimed by burglars and murderers.

There are liberties which, if tolerated, diminish the total amount of liberty in the world.

If there were no law against murder, we should all have to go armed and avoid solitude and be perpetually on the watch.

Many liberties which we now take for granted would disappear.

It is, therefore, in the interests of liberty to curtail the liberty of would-be murderers.

The argument is exactly the same in the case of the liberty of states. But in this case, it is very much more difficult to enforce the necessary restrictions.

Nevertheless, if a civilized way of life is to continue, it will be necessary to arrive at a method of preventing aggressive war.

I do not know of any way of securing this result except by the creation of an international government with a monopoly of all the major weapons of war.

Such a government, if it existed, should have only such powers as are necessary for the prevention of war, and should leave separate nations free except as regards armaments.

If such a government existed, it would be possible to inaugurate such a system of education as I spoke of a moment ago.

Such a system, instead of teaching nationalism, would teach consciousness of what men in different nations have in common and of what they can achieve by working together instead of working against each other.

Gradually, under the influence of such a system of education, bigotry and intolerance would diminish and social liberty would gain as much as political liberty. (FF 71)

What can be done when a large group holds unpopular opinions?

Where any large group is basically out of sympathy with the rest of the citizens of the State, democracy is apt to become unworkable, except by a use of force, which will produce great discontent in the subordinate group, and a harsh temper in the dominant group.

When the dissident minority is geographically concentrated, the matter can be dealt with by devolution, but when it is distributed throughout the population, there is much greater difficulty.

This is the situation of Jews in a country where popular sentiment is strongly anti-Semitic.

It is the situation of Mohmmedans in India; and Hindus in Pakistan.

It is the situation of Negroes in America. In all such cases the difficulty cannot be solved by *geographical* devolution.

Democracy in such cases can only be successful if there is a diffused sentiment of tolerance. (FF 93)

How does the desire for conformity cause intolerant attitudes?

There appears to be in human nature an impulse to demand conformity even when it serves no social purpose.

This is especially notable in schoolboys.

In a school where nobody wears a hat, a boy will be kicked if he does not go bare-headed.

Not one boy in a thousand would think that an eccentric in the matter of hats is harmless.

Civilized people gradually grow out of this blind impulse towards enforced uniformity, but many never become civilized, and retain through life the crude, persecuting instincts of the schoolboy.

If there is to be political liberty, this feeling must not be embodied in legislation.

It was only this feeling which caused hostility to the Mormons.

It was not a belief in the conventional moral code, since no one objected to polygamy in Asia and Africa. (FF 58)

TRADE

Why did interdependence create hostility instead of friendship?

A butcher needs bread and a baker needs meat. There is, therefore, every reason why the butcher and the baker should love one another, since each is useful to the other.

But if the butcher is one sovereign State and the baker is another, if the number of loaves the butcher can exchange for his joints depends upon his skill with the revolver, it is possible that the baker may cease to regard him with ardent affection.

This is precisely the situation in international trade at the present day; and if it did not occur, we should say that mankind could not be capable of anything so ridiculous.

Economic interdependence is very much greater than at any former time, but owing partly to the fact that our economic system has developed from one of private profit, and partly to separate national sovereignties, interdependence, instead of producing friendliness, tends to be a cause of hostility.

As economics everywhere has come to be more and more intimately connected with the State, it has become more and more subordinate to politics.

Marx held that politics is determined by economics, but that was because he was still under the influence of eighteenth-century rationalism, and imagined that what people most desire is to grow rich.

Experience since his time has shown that there is something which people desire even more strongly, and that is to keep others poor.

This is a matter in which military power necessarily plays a great part as soon as trade has come to be mainly between nations rather than between individuals.

That is why politics has more and more come to predominate over economics. (NHCW 89)

TRADITION

What attitude have the great innovators taken toward tradition?

Both religious and secular innovators—at any rate, those who have had most lasting success—have appealed, as far as they could, to tradition, and have done whatever lay in their power to minimize the elements of novelty in their systems.

The usual plan is to invent a more or less fictitious past and pretend to be restoring its institutions.

In 2 Kings xxvi we are told how the priests "found" the Book of the Law, and the King caused a "return" to observance of its precepts.

The New Testament appealed to the authority of the Prophets; the Anabaptists appealed to the New Testment; the English Puritans, in secular matters, appealed to the supposed institutions of England before the Conquest.

The Japanese, in A.D. 645, "restored" the power of the Mikado; in 1868, they "restored" the constitutions of A.D. 645.

A whole series of rebels, throughout the Middle Ages and down to 18 Brumaire, "restored" the republican institutions of Rome.

Napoleon "restored" the empire of Charlemagne, but this was felt to be a trifle too theatrical, and failed to impress even that rhetorically minded age.

These are only a few illustrations, selected at random, of the respect which even the greatest innovators have shown for the power of tradition. (P 56)

Tradition made the Renaissance Church powerful . . . but what caused its decline?

By far the greatest strength of the Church was the moral respect which it inspired.

It inherited, as a kind of moral capital, the glory of the persecutions in ancient times.

Its victories were associated with the enforcement of celibacy, and the mediaeval mind found celibacy very impressive.

Very many ecclesiastics, including not a few Popes, suffered great hardship rather than yield on a point of principle.

It was clear to ordinary men that, in a world of uncontrolled rapacity, licentiousness, and self-seeking, eminent dignitaries of the Church not infrequently lived for impersonal aims, to which they willingly subordinated their private fortune.

In successive centuries, men of impressive holiness—Hildebrand, St. Bernard, St. Francis—dazzled public opinion, and prevented the moral discredit that would otherwise have come from the misdeeds of others.

But to an organization which has ideal ends, and therefore an excuse for love of power, a reputation for superior virtue is dangerous, and is sure, in the long run, to produce a superiority only in unscrupulous ruthlessness.

The Church preached contempt for the things of this world, and in doing so acquired dominion over monarchs.

The Friars took a vow of poverty, which so impressed the world that it increased the already enormous wealth of the Church.

St. Francis, by preaching brotherly love, generated the enthusiasm required for the victorious prosecution of a long and atrocious war.

In the end the Renaissance Church lost all the moral purpose to which it owed its wealth and power, and the shock of the Reformation was necessary to produce regeneration.

All this is inevitable whenever superior virtue is used as a means of winning tyrannical power for an organization.

Except when due to foreign conquest, the collapse of traditional power is always the result of its abuse by men who believe, as Machiavelli believed, that its hold on men's minds is too firm to be shaken even by the grossest crimes. (Italics added) (P 74)

What's good, and what's bad, about tradition?

Human beings, ever since their fathers invented language, have allowed themselves to be dominated by tradition.

This has been at once the main cause of progress and the main obstacle to progress.

Consider it first as a cause of progress:

Where should we be if each generation had to invent reading, writing, and arithmetic for itself?

How should we get on if art and crafts were not handed on?

Even in the most progressive age, much the greater part of our activity is, and must be, based upon tradition.

We may rebel against our parents' narrow-mindedness, but we can only rise above them by standing on their shoulders.

But although respect for tradition and obedience to custom are necessary up to a point, most societies have carried them much too far, and some have brought themselves to destruction by this sole defect.

Human beings change their ways much more quickly than animals do; civilized men change their ways more quickly than uncivilized men, and modern civilized men change their ways more quickly than civilized men of former ages.

Civilized societies during the last hundred and fifty years have radically transformed their physical environment, the methods by which they secure a livelihood, and the apparatus of comfort over and above the minimum necessary for survival.

The prime cause of these changes has been a vast increase of knowledge and skill.

In an age of machines and skilled scientific production, we retain the feelings and many of the beliefs that were appropriate to the ages of scarcity and primitive agiculture.

Political ideas are exactly what they were in the eighteenth century. In the eighteenth century they worked, after a fashion; now they are heading straight to disaster.

In the old days, many things that are now possible could not be achieved by any known means.

Extreme poverty for the great majority was unavoidable.

Population perpetually pressed upon the limits of subsistence, except when it was catastrophically diminished by famine or pestilence.

Wars created aristocracies of conquerors, who lived without compunction upon the labor of the vanquished.

It was not until the French Revolution that this system began to be superseded by one involving less general misery.

Now, in certain important Western countries extreme poverty has almost disappeared, famine is unknown, large-scale pestilences have yielded to medical science, and a low birth rate has made it possible to preserve a high level of prosperity when it has been reached.

All this is new in human history. (NHCW 147)

TRUTH

What is the great value of veracity?

Veracity, which I regard as second only to kindly feeling, consists broadly in believing according to evidence and not because a belief is comfortable or a source of pleasure.

In the absence of veracity, kindly feeling will often be defeated by self-deception.

It used to be common for the rich to maintain either that it is pleasant to be poor or that poverty is the result of shiftlessness.

Some healthy people maintain that all illness is self-indulgence.

I have heard fox hunters argue that the fox likes to be hunted.

It is easy for those who have exceptional power to persuade themselves that the system by which they profit gives more happiness to the underdog than he would enjoy under a more just system.

And even when no obvious bias is involved, it is only by means of veracity that we can acquire the scientific knowledge required to bring out our common purposes.

Consider how many cherished prejudices had to be abandoned in the development of modern medicine and hygiene.

To take a different kind of illustration, how many wars would have been prevented if the side which was ultimately defeated had formed a just estimate of its prospects instead of one based on conceit and wish-fulfillment. (from *The Listener,* May 29, 1947) (RGR 88)

VALUES

What things are to be valued for themselves?

What are the things that I ultimately value? What would make me judge one sort of society more desirable than another sort? What sort of ends should I most wish to see realized in the world?

Different people will answer these questions differently, and I do not know of any argument by which I could persuade a man who gave an answer different from my own.

I must therefore be content merely to state the answer which appeals to me, in the hope that the reader may feel likewise.

The main things which seem to me important on their own account, and not merely as means to other things, are: knowledge, art, instinctive happiness, and relations of friendship or affection.

When I speak of knowledge, I do not mean all knowledge; there is much in the way of dry lists of facts that are merely useful, and still more that have no appreciable value of any kind.

But the understanding of nature, incomplete as it is, which is to be derived from science, I hold to be a thing which is good and delightful on its own account.

The same may be said, I think, of some biographies and parts of history.

To enlarge on this topic would, however, take me too far from my theme.

When I speak of art as one of the things that have value on their own account, I do not mean only the deliberate productions of trained artists, though of course these, at their best, deserve the highest place.

I mean also the almost unconscious effort after beauty which one finds among Russian peasants and Chinese coolies, the sort of impulse that creates folk songs, that existed among ourselves before the time of the Puritans, and survives in cottage gardens.

Instinctive happiness, or joy of life, is one of the most important widespread popular goods that we have lost through industrialism and the high pressure at which most of us live. (SPBR 196)

WAR

What keeps man from being at his best?

Is it not odd that people can in the same breath praise *The Free Man's Worship* and find fault with my views on the war [World War I]?

The Free Man's Worship is merely the expression of the pacifist outlook when it was new to me. So many people enjoy rhetorical expressions of fine feelings, but hate to see people perform the actions that must go with the feelings if they are genuine.

How could anyone, approving *The Free Man's Worship,* expect me to join in the trivial self-righteous moral condemnation of the Germans? All moral condemnation is utterly against the whole view of life that was then new to me but is now more and more a part of my being.

I am naturally pugnacious, and am only restrained (when I am restrained) by a realization of the tragedy of human existence, and the absurdity of spending our little moment in strife and heat.

That I, a funny little gesticulating animal on two legs, should stand beneath the stars and declaim in a passion about my rights—it seems so laughable, so out of proportion.

Much better, like Archimedes, to be killed because of absorption in eternal things.

And when once men get away from their rights, from the struggle to take up more room in the world than is their due, there is such a capacity of greatness in them.

All the loneliness and pain and the eternal pathetic hope—the power of love and the appreciation of beauty—the concentration of many ages and spaces in the mirror of a single mind—these are not things one would wish to destroy wantonly for any of the national ambitions that politicians praise.

There is a possibility in human minds of something mysterious as the night wind, deep as the sea, calm as the stars, and strong as death, a mystic contemplation, the "intellectual love of God."

Those who have known it cannot *believe* in wars any longer, or in any kind of hot struggle.

If I could give to others what has come to me in this way, I could make them too feel the futility of fighting. But I do not know how to communicate it; when I speak, they stare, applaud, or smile, but do not understand. (A2 118)

Why do we still have wars?

We hear much about the Western way of life and the need of defending it against the Eastern menace [Soviet Russia].

But few in the West are clear as to the essentials of the Western way of life, or as to what makes it worth defending.

What the West has discovered (though as yet the realization is incomplete) is a method by which practically everybody can have as much of material goods as is conducive to happiness, without excessive hours of labor, and with that degree of mental culture that is needed to make leisure delightful.

This is rendered possible by the fact that one man's work can now produce much more than is required for one man's subsistence.

But as yet this system has only a precarious life.

It is threatened from without by those whom envy renders destructive, and it is threatened from within by those who are still under the domination of beliefs and passions appropriate to a bygone age.

The kernel of these beliefs and passions is the STRUGGLE FOR EXISTENCE. Where this struggle is now still necessary, it is necessary because men are misguided, not because nature is niggardly.

In former times, if two men each wished to live on the produce of a piece of land which only yielded enough for one, they must either both starve or fight till one was killed.

In practice, it was not single men who fought, but groups of men, called successively tribes, nations, coalitions, or United Nations.

In spite of Christianity, when enjoined peace before the necessary industrial technique had been invented, sheer necessity drove men into conflict.

As it was the victors who left descendents, it was the mentality of victors that was handed down.

What the next generation imbibed from their parents was the righteousness of timely aggression.

And so war came to be surrounded with a halo of virtue.

On Sundays men pretended to believe that the meek shall inherit the earth, but on weekdays they effectively believed the exact opposite.

The Christian virtues, up to a point, could be tolerated within the tribe, but in dealings with those outside it, what was prized was courage, ruthlessness and ferocity disguised under the name of patriotism. (NHCW 149)

Are those who start wars good at predicting who will win them?

It may be said, only those who decide policy and military operations need to have correct views: it is desirable that the populace should feel sure of victory, and the government, the military chiefs, and their technical staffs need to know the facts; among all others, blind confidence and blind obedience are what is most to be desired.

If human affairs were as calculable as chess, and politicians and generals as clever as good chess players, there might be some truth in this view.

The advantages of successful war are doubtful, but the disadvantages of unsuccessful war are certain.

If therefore the supermen at the head of affairs could foresee who was going to win, there would be no wars.

But in fact there are wars, and in every war the government on one side, if not on both, must have miscalculated its chances.

For this there are many reasons: of pride and vanity, of ignorance, and of contagious excitement. (P 155)

Does the side with the greater economic power necessarily win the war?

It is sometimes said that victory in war is always due to superior economic resources, but history shows that this is by no means invariably the case.

The Romans, at the beginning of the Punic Wars, had much smaller resources than the Carthaginians, and yet they were victorious.

When the Roman Empire fell, it was overrun by German and Arab invaders who had nothing on their side except valor and greed.

The decadence of Spain in the late sixteenth and seventeenth centuries must be attributed almost entirely to stupidity and fanaticism, not to lack of resources.

In the present war [World War II], in spite of superior resources, the United Nations have lost France, the Malay Peninsula, Burma, the Philippines, the Dutch East Indies, Rumanian oil and Ukranian wheat; no doubt they will recover them, but their loss shows what can be done by nations which devote all their energies to war.

All that can be said is that, given equal skill and equal resolution, the side which has superior economic resources will win in the long run. (UH 28)

Is modern warfare more deadly? [1951]

It is a mistake to think that modern war is more destructive of life than the simpler wars of former times.

The actual casualties of past wars were often quite as high a percentage of the forces engaged as they are now; and apart from casualties in battle, the deaths from disease were usually enormous.

Over and over again in ancient and medieval times, you find whole armies practically exterminated by the plague.

The atom bomb is, of course, more spectacular, but the actual mortality rate among combatant populations, even where the atom bomb is employed, is not as great as in many former wars.

The population of Japan increased by about five million during the Second World War, whereas it is estimated that during the Thirty Years' War the population of Germany was halved.

Broadly speaking, it is not in general the case that as weapons become technically more efficient, the mortality in war is increased.

There is, however, in the use of the atom bomb and the hydrogen bomb a new danger, a danger which is not only new in kind but greater in degree than any that has existed in previous wars.

We do not quite know what may be the effects of letting loose great floods of radioactivity.

There are those—among them Einstein—who think that the result may be the extinction of all life on our planet.

Short of that, it may easily happen that large fertile regions become infertile and uninhabitable, and that the populations of considerable areas are wiped out.

I do not say that this will happen if atomic energy is employed in war; no one knows yet whether it will happen or not. But there is a risk that it may happen, *and if it does, repentance will come too late.* (Italics added) (NHCW 90)

What were the consequences of the First World War?

We owe to the first war and its aftermath Russian Communism, Italian Fascism, and German Nazism.

We owe to the first war the creation of a chaotic unstable world where there is every reason to fear that the Second World War was not the last, where there is the vast horror of Russian Communism to be combatted, where Germany, France, and what used to be the Austro-Hungarian Empire have all fallen lower in the scale of civilization, where there is every prospect of chaos in Asia and Africa, where the prospect of vast and horrible carnage inspires daily and hourly dread.

All these evils have sprung with the inevitability of Greek tragedy out of the First World War.

Consider what would have happened if Britain had remained neutral in that war.

The war would have been short.

It would have ended in victory for Germany. America would not have been dragged in.

Britain would have remained strong and prosperous.

Germany would not have been driven into Nazism, Russia, though it would have had a revolution, would in all likelihood have not had the Communist Revolution, since it could not, in a short war, have been reduced to the condition of utter chaos which prevailed in 1917.

The Kaiser's Germany, although war propaganda on our side represented it as atrocious, was in fact only swashbuckling and a little absurd.

I had lived in the Kaiser's Germany and I knew that progressive forces in that country were very strong and had every prospect of ultimate success.

There was more freedom in the Kaiser's Germany than there is now [1956] in any country outside Britain and Scandinavia.

We were told at the time that it was a war for freedom, a war for democracy, and a war against militarism.

As a result of that war freedom has vastly diminished and militarism has vastly increased.

As for democracy, its future is still in doubt.

I cannot think that the world would now be in anything like the bad state in which it is if English neutrality in the first war had allowed a quick victory to Germany.

On these grounds I have never thought that I was mistaken in the line that I took at the time.

I do not regret having attempted throughout the war years to persuade people that the Germans were less wicked than official propaganda represented them as being, for a great deal of the subsequent evil resulted from the severity of the Treaty of Versailles and this severity would not have been possible but for the moral horror with which Germany was viewed.

All this dreadful sequence is an outcome of the mistakes of 1914 and would not have occurred if those mistakes had been avoided. (Italics added) (PFM 11)

What was the real cause of Joan of Arc's triumph in battle?

Most people imagine that Joan of Arc had a great deal to do with the recovery of France after the defeats inflicted by the English under Henry V.

I had thought so myself until I discovered that the real cause of French success was the growing importance of artillery.

The English had depended on their archers, who were capable of defeating the French knights; but against cannon they were powerless.

Throughout western Europe, during the 60 years or so following Joan of Arc, the new form of warfare enabled kings to subdue the turbulent barons who had caused centuries of anarchy.

Despotic government and civil order were both brought into western Europe by gunpowder.

Will both be brought to the world as a whole by the aeroplane? Or will it bring only one of the two, and if so which? (UH 27)

What innovation in war came in with the French Revolution?

The French Revolution introduced a new kind of war, one in which the whole nation participated enthusiastically because it believed that it had something of value to defend.

War had been an affair of kings or small aristocracies; the armies were composed of mercenaries, and the general population looked on with indifference.

If Louis XIV conquered some part of Germany, that was unpleasant for a few princes and their hangers-on, but it made very little difference to most people.

But when all the reactionaries of Europe set to work in concert to destory revolutionary France and restore the Bourbons, every peasant who had been freed from feudal burdens and had acquired some portion of his seigneur's land, felt he had something to fight for.

And all the scientific intellect of France set to work to devise new methods of making more effective explosives, or otherwise helping the war effort.

The result astonished the world, and French successes were welcomed by large sections of Germany and Italy.

After Napoleon's tyranny had turned former friends of France into enemies, Germany, in the War of 1813, fought a similar popular war, and this time with more lasting success.

From that time until the present day, governments have increasingly realized the necessity of making wars popular, and have used the potent weapon of popular education to that end. (UH 27)

What is the connection between our machine age and war?

Machines deprive us of two things which are certainly important ingredients of human happiness, namely, spontaneity and variety.

Machines have their own pace, and their own insistent demands: a man who has an expensive plant must keep it working. The great trouble with the machine, from the point of view of the emotions, is its *regularity.*

And, of course, conversely, the great objection to the emotions, from the point of view of the machine, is their *irregularity.*

As the machine dominates the thoughts of people who consider themselves "serious," the highest praise they can give to a man is to suggest that he has the qualities of a machine—that he is reliable, punctual, exact, etc.

Against this point of view Bergson's philosophy was a protest—not, to my mind, wholly sound from an intellectual point of view, but inspired by a wholesome dread of seeing men turned more and more into machines.

In life, as opposed to thought, the rebellion of our instincts against enslavement to mechanism has hitherto taken a most unfortunate direction.

The impulse to war has always existed since men took to living in societies, but it did not, in the past, have the same intensity or virulence as it has in our day.

In the eighteenth century, England and France had innumerable wars, and contended for the hegemony of the world; but they liked and respected each other the whole time.

Officer prisoners joined in the social life of their captors, and were honored guests at their dinner parties.

The greater ferocity of modern war is attributable to machines.

They starve the anarchic, spontaneous side of human nature, which works underground, producing an obscure discontent, to which the thought of war appeals as affording possible relief.

It is a mistake to attribute a vast upheaval like the late war merely to the machinations of politicians.

In England, Germany, and the United States (in 1917), no government could have withstood the popular demand for war.

A popular demand of this sort must have an instinctive basis, and for my part, I believe that the modern increase in warlike instinct is attributable to the dissatisfaction (mostly unconscious) caused by the regularity, monotony, and tameness of modern life. (SE 87)

WEST

Why prefer life in the West to life in Russia? [1953]

I do not wish to be led by love of symmetry into an appearance of neutrality between Russia and the West.

The West has more than Russia of everything that I think valuable, and, first and foremost, it has more liberty.

But I think it of the highest importance, if liberty is to survive in the West, that we should be conscious of its value, conscious of its intellectual conditions, and conscious of the danger that in a desperate contest, it may be lost.

I cannot admit that, in pointing out unnecessary infringements of liberty in the West, one is showing disloyalty. On the contrary, those who have kept alive a knowledge of what it is that makes us prefer Western systems to that of Russia are doing something absolutely necessary to the victory of what they value.

What the West professes to stand for fundamentally is the belief that governments exist for the sake of individuals, not individuals for the sake of governments.

It is this principle that is at stake. (FF 76)

What must the West preserve for the sake of the future?

The Western nations are, for the present, the custodians of both democracy and liberty.

In neither respect are they perfect, but they are better than any other nations, and it is only by developing what is best in them that mankind can advance.

I think we of the West are sometimes insufficiently conscious of what it is that we have to preserve for the human race.

It is not only what we owe to the Graeco-Roman heritage and to Christianity, it is perhaps even more what we have achieved during the last four centuries: the substitution of science for superstition: of a technique capable of abolishing poverty throughout the world, of medical knowledge which, in the West, has put an end to those great plagues that used to devastate whole populations; and, more than any of these, although as yet imperfectly, that respect for the initiative and freedom of individuals whose work is creative and not destructive.

Mankind advanced slowly in the past largely because all those who suggested advance were persecuted.

In modern Western nations this is much less true, and the advance during the last four centuries has been more rapid than at any other period in human history. (FF 108)

Should the West be proud of so-called Western Values?

Some opponents of communism are attempting to produce an ideology for the Atlantic Powers, and for this purpose they have invented what they call "Western Values."

These are supposed to consist of toleration, respect for individual liberty, and brotherly love.

I am afraid this view is grossly unhistorical.

If we compare Europe with other continents, it is marked out as the persecuting continent.

Persecution only ceased after long and bitter experience of its futility; it continued as long as either Protestants or Catholics had any hope of exterminating the opposite party.

The European record in this respect is far blacker than that of the Mohammedans, the Indians, or the Chinese.

No, if the West can claim superiority in anything, it is not in moral values but in science and scientific technique. (NHCW 114)

WISDOM

What is "wisdom"?

I will do my best to convey what I think the word is capable of meaning.

It is a word concerned partly with knowledge and partly with feeling.

It should denote a certain intimate union of knowledge with apprehension of human destiny and the purposes of life.

It requires a certain breadth of vision, which is hardly possible without considerable knowledge.

But it demands, also, a breadth of feeling, a certain kind of universality of sympathy.

I think that higher education should do what is possible towards promoting not only knowledge but wisdom.

I do not think that this is easy; and I do not think that the aim should be too conscious, for, if it is, it becomes stereotyped and priggish.

It should be something existing almost unconsciously in the teacher and conveyed almost unintentionally to the pupil.

I agree with Plato in thinking that this is the greatest thing that education can do. (FF 169)

WIT

How would you describe Hell, Lord Russell?

Hell is a place where the police are German . . . the motorists French . . . and the cooks English. (RSN19 3)

Why have you never written anything on esthetics, Lord Russell?

Because I don't know anything about it . . . although that is not a very good excuse, for my friends tell me it has not deterred me from writing on other subjects. (RSN27 9)

What fields have interested you most during your lifetime, Lord Russell?

When I was young, I liked mathematics.
　　When this became too difficult, I took to philosophy, and when philosophy became too difficult, I took to politics. (RSN7 6)

Why did Russell eat in a certain cafeteria at Harvard?

"Near Harvard Yard I used to eat in a cafeteria where the food was cheap but not very good," says William Jovanovich. "I would sit at a long public table where on many occasions there also sat the philosopher, Bertrand Russell. One day I did not contain my curiosity.
　　" 'Mr. Russell,' I said, 'I know why I eat here. It is because I am poor. But why do you eat here?'
　　" 'Because,' he said, 'I am never interrupted.' " (from *The American Scholar*, vol. 36, no. 1) (RSN12 7)

WITTGENSTEIN

Lord Russell, what is your assessment of Wittgenstein?

There are two great men in history whom he somewhat resembles. One was Pascal, the other was Tolstoy. Pascal was a mathematician of genius, but abandoned mathematics for piety. Tolstoy sacrificed his genius as a writer to a kind of bogus humility which made him prefer peasants to educated men and *Uncle Tom's Cabin* to all other works of fiction.

Wittgenstein, who could play with metaphysical intricacies as cleverly as Pascal with hexagons or Tolstoy with emperors, threw away this talent and debased himself before common sense as Tolstoy debased himself before the peasants—in each case from an impulse of pride. I admired Wittgenstein's *Tractatus* but not his later work, which seemed to me to involve an abnegation of his own best talent very similar to those of Pascal and Tolstoy.

His followers, without (so far as I can discover) undergoing the mental torments which make him and Pascal and Tolstoy pardonable in spite of their treachery to their own greatness, have produced a number of works which, I am told, have merit, and in these works they have set forth a number of arguments against my views and methods. I have been unable, in spite of serious efforts, to see any validity in their criticisms of me. (MPD 214–15)

I have not found in Wittgenstein's *Philosophical Investigations* anything that seemed to me interesting and I do not understand why a whole school finds important wisdom in its pages. Psychologically this is surprising.

The earlier Wittgenstein, whom I knew intimately, was a man addicted to passionately intense thinking, profoundly aware of difficult problems of which I, like him, felt the importance, and possessed (or at least so I thought) of true philosophical genius.

The later Wittgenstein, on the contrary, seems to have grown tired of serious thinking and to have invented a doctrine which would make such an activity unnecessary. I do not for one moment believe that a doctrine which has these lazy consequences is true. I realize that I have an overpoweringly strong bias against it, for, if it is true, philosophy is, at best, a slight help to lexicographers, and at worst, an idle tea table amusement. (MPD 216–17)

In common with all philosophers before WII [Wittgenstein's *Philosophical Investigations*], my fundamental aim has been to understand the world as well as may be, and to separate what may count as knowledge from what must be rejected as unfounded opinion.

But for WII I should not have thought it worth while to state this aim, which I should have supposed could be taken for granted. But we are now told that it is not the world that we are to try to understand but only sentences, and it is assumed that all sentences can count as true except those uttered by philosophers. This, however, is perhaps an overstatement.

Adherents of WII are fond of pointing out as if it were a discovery, that sentences may be interrogative, imperative, or optative as well as indicative. This, however, does not take us beyond the realm of sentences.

There is a curious suggestion, already to be found among some Logical Positivists, that the world of language can be quite divorced from the world of fact. If you mention that a spoken sentence is a physical occurrence consisting of certain movements of matter and that a written sentence consists of marks of one color on a background of another color, you will be thought vulgar. You are supposed to forget that the things people say have nonlinguistic causes and nonlinguistic effects and that language is just as much a bodily activity as walking or eating. (MPD 217)

There had been two views about empirical statements: one that they were justified by some relation to facts; the other that they were justified by conformity to syntactical rules. But the adherents of WII do not bother with any kind of justification, and thus secure for language an untrammelled freedom which it has never hitherto enjoyed.

The desire to understand the world is, they think, an outdated folly. This is my most fundamental point of disagreement with them. (MPD 218–19)

WOMEN

Have women achieved freedom from male dominance?

The revolt of women against the domination of men is a movement which in its purely political sense, is practically completed, but in its wide aspects is still in its infancy.

Gradually its remoter effects will work themselves out.

The emotions which women are supposed to feel are still, as yet, a reflection of the interests and sentiments of men. (DMMM 275)

What methods were used to make sure that women remained virtuous, and how have things changed?

In early days, and in the East down to our own time, the virtue of women was secured by segregating them.

No attempt was made to give them inward self-control, but every-thing was done to take away all opportunity for sin.

In the West this method was never adopted wholeheartedly, but respectable women were educated from their earliest years so as to have a horror of sexual intercourse outside marriage. As the methods of this education became more and more perfected, the outward barriers were more and more removed.

Those who did most to remove the outward barriers were con-vinced that the inward barriers would be sufficient. It was thought, for example, that the chaperon was unnecessary, since a nice girl who had been well brought up would never yield to the advances of young men whatever opportunities of yielding might be allowed her.

It was generally held by respectable women when I was young that sexual intercourse was displeasing to the great majority of women, and was only endured within marriage from a sense of duty; holding this view, they were not unwilling to risk a greater degree of freedom for their daughters than had seemed wise in more realistic ages.

The results have perhaps been somewhat different from what was anticipated, and the difference has existed equally as regards wives and as regards unmarried women.

The women of the Victorian age were, and a great many women still are, in a mental prison. This prison was not obvious to consciousness, since it consisted of subconscious inhibitions. The decay of inhibitions, which has taken place among the young of our own time, has led to the reappearance in consciousness of instinctive desires which had been buried beneath mountains of prudery.

This is having a very revolutionary effect upon sexual morality, not only in one country or in one class, but in all civilized countries and in all classes. (MM 55)

WORLD GOVERNMENT

Why should we bother thinking about world government?

It may be thought needlessly Utopian to consider world government, since it remains totally impossible so long as the East-West tension continues.

It is, however, an urgent problem since, unless it is solved within the next generation, it is unlikely that the human race will survive.

A statement of this sort is found annoying, because people do not like changing their mental habits, and hating certain foreign nations is one of the most deeply ingrained of these habits.

It does not, of course, present itself in this way to their minds.

What presents itself consciously is a quick conviction that any unusual thought is absurd.

The conviction is so quick and firm that they never look to see whether it has a rational basis.

I think, however, that anybody who can resist this unreasoning impulse must perceive that the survival of the human race depends upon the abolition of war, and that war can only be abolished by the establishment of a world government. (FF 99)

What powers would a world government need?

Primarily those involving peace and war.

It would need a monopoly of all the more important weapons of war.

It would need the right to revise treaties between nations, and to refuse to recognize any treaty to which it would not give assent.

It would need a firm determination to make war upon any nation which rebelled against its authority or committed a hostile aggression against any other nation.

But it would not need to control nations as regards their internal economic development, as regards their education or their religious institutions, or any of the matters that could rightly be regarded as internal.

What, in fact, it should take away from a nation is what has long ago been taken away from an individual—namely, the right to kill.

Individual citizens, unless they are gangsters, do not feel their liberty unduly hampered by the fact that they cannot shoot their neighbor whenever he plays the piano too loudly.

Individual nations ought to learn that a similar limitation upon their liberty is equally unobjectionable.

They ought to be content with liberty to control their own affairs, and not demand the opportunity to shoot foreigners whenever the whim takes them.

It is this opportunity of which a world government would have to deprive them.

But it need not deprive them of any liberty that a decent person could desire. (Italics added) (FF 100)

What are the prospects for world government in the near future?

Attempts to form new groups by purely voluntary cooperation usually fail, because whatever government is constituted for such groups does not command traditional respect, and is not likely to be allowed enough power to enforce respect.

The most important application of this principle in the present day is to world government.

For the prevention of war, the existence of a single government for the whole planet is indispensable.

But a federal government formed by mutual agreement, as the League of Nations and the United Nations were formed, is sure to be weak, because the constituent nations will feel as the barons felt in the Middle Ages, that anarchy is better than loss of independence.

And just as the substitution of orderly government for anarchy in the Middle Ages depended on the victory of the royal power, so the substitution of order for anarchy in international affairs, if it comes about, will come about through the superior power of some one nation or group of nations.

And only after such a single government has been constituted will it be possible for the evolution towards a democratic form of international Government to begin.

This view, which I have held for the last thirty years, encounters vehement opposition from all people of liberal outlook, and also from all nationalists of whatever nation.

I agree, of course, that it would be far better to have an international government constituted by agreement, but I am quite convinced that the love of national independence is too strong for such a government to have effective power.

When a single Government for the world, embodying the military supremacy of some nation or group of nations, has been in power for a century or so, it will begin to command that degree of respect that will make it possible to base its power upon law and sentiment rather than on force, and when that happens, the international Government can become democratic.

I do not say this is a pleasant prospect; what I do say is that men's anarchic impulses are so strong as to be incapable of yielding in the first place to anything but superior force.

This would not be the case if men were more rational, or less filled with hatred and fear.

But so long as the present type of national sentiment persists, any attempt to establish a really vigorous international Government would be encountered by an irresistible propaganda: "Would you rather live as slaves than die as free men?" the champions of national independence would ask.

In every nation in which there was good hope of not dying, but living, as free men, this rhetorical question would be answered by a general shout in favor of dying for freedom.

I do not say that there is no hope of a better method of ending the international anarchy; what I do say is that there is no hope of this unless and until individuals are much changed from what they are now.

It will be necessary that individuals shall have less feeling of hostility and fear towards other individuals, more hope of security as regards their own lives, and a far more vivid realization that, in the world which modern technique has created, the need for worldwide cooperation is absolute, if mankind is to survive.

Can a leopard change his spots? I believe that he can but if not, terrible calamities must befall him. (Italics added) (NHCW 72)

WRITING

What are some good rules for writers?

There are some simple maxims which I think might be commended to writers of expository prose.

First: never use a long word if a short word will do.

Second: if you want to make a statement with a great many qualifications, put some of the qualifications in separate sentences.

Third: do not let the beginning of your sentence lead the reader to an expectation which is contradicted by the end. (PFM 196)

Sources and Acknowledgments

At the end of every quotation there is a code and a page number. This will enable the reader to locate the source of the quotation. Here is an example: FF 101. FF is the code; it stands for the book, *Fact and Fiction*. The source of the quotation is on p. 101 of *Fact and Fiction*. The full titles of works cited are given below:

code

AI   *Authority and the Individual.* New York: Simon & Schuster, 1949.

A1   *The Autobiography of Bertrand Russell,* vol. 1 (1872–1914). Boston: Little, Brown & Co., 1967.

A2   *The Autobiography of Bertrand Russell,* vol. 2 (1914–1944). Boston: Little, Brown & Co., 1968.

AP   *The Art of Philosophizing.* New York: Philosophical Library, Inc., 1968.

BW   *The Basic Writings of Bertrand Russell.* London: George Allen & Unwin, Ltd., 1961.

CBC   Canadian Broadcasting Corporation "Closeup" TV interview, 1959.

DMMM   *Bertrand Russell's Dictionary of Mind, Matter & Morals.* New York: Philosophical Library, 1952.

EGL　　*Education and the Good Life*. New York: Boni & Liveright, 1926.

EMW　　*Education and the Modern World*. New York: W. W. Norton & Co., 1932.

FF　　*Fact and Fiction*. New York: Simon & Schuster, 1961.

FVO　　*Freedom versus Organization*. New York: W. W. Norton & Co., 1934.

HSEP　　*Human Society in Ethics and Politics*. New York: Simon & Schuster, 1952.

HWP　　*A History of Western Philosophy*. New York: Simon & Schuster, 1945.

IPI　　*In Praise of Idleness*. New York: Unwin Books, 1935.

ITL　　*Invitation to Learning*. New York: Random House, 1941.

KEW　　*Our Knowledge of the External World*. New York: The New American Library, 1956.

MAO　　*Mortals and Others*. London: George Allen & Unwin, Ltd., 1975.

MPD　　*My Philosophical Development*. London: George Allen & Unwin, Ltd., 1959.

MM　　*Marriage and Morals*. New York: Bantam Books, 1959.

NHCW　　*New Hopes for a Changing World*. New York: Simon & Schuster, 1951.

P　　*Power*. London: George Allen & Unwin, Ltd., 1938.

PC　　*The Problem of China*. London: Allen & Unwin, Ltd., 1922.

PFM　　*Portraits from Memory*. London: George Allen & Unwin, Ltd., 1956.

PI　　*Political Ideals*. London: Unwin Books, 1963.

PSR　　*Principles of Social Reconstruction*. London: G. Allen and Unwin, 1916.

PTB   *The Practise and Theory of Bolshevism.* London: Unwin Books, 1920.

RGR   *Bertrand Russell on God and Religion.* Buffalo, N.Y.: Prometheus Books, 1986.

RSN7   *Russell Society News,* No. 7 (excerpt from Russell obituary in the *Los Angeles Times,* February 8, 1970).

RSN12   *Russell Society News,* No. 12 (excerpt from the *American Scholar* 36, no. 1).

RSN19   *Russell Society News,* No. 19 (excerpt from Edwards, *The New Dictionary of Thought*).

RSN27   *Russell Society News,* No. 27 (excerpt from *The Philosophy of Brand Blanshard,* 1980).

RSN34   *Russell Society News,* No. 34 (excerpt from *The Western Tradition.* Boston: Beacon Press, 1951).

RSN52   *Russell Society News,* No. 52 (excerpt from "My Philosophy of Life," an Australian radio program of July 9, 1950).

RSN66   *Russell Society News,* No. 66 (excerpt from *Invitation to Learning,* 1941).

RTF   *Roads to Freedom.* London: Unwin Books, 1966.

SE   *Sceptical Essays.* New York: W. W. Norton & Co., 1928.

SHM   *Bertrand Russell Speaks His Mind.* New York: Bard Books, 1969.

SO   *The Scientific Outlook.* New York: W. W. Norton & Co., 1931.

SP   *Speaking Personally.* Riverside RLP 7014/15.

SPBR   *Selected Papers of Bertrand Russell.* New York: Modern Library, 1927.

UE   *Unpopular Essays.* New York: Simon & Schuster, 1959.

UH   *Understanding History.* New York: Philosophical Library, 1957.

WIB   *What I Believe.* New York: E. P. Dutton & Co., 1925.

WW   *The Wit and Wisdom of Bertrand Russell.* Boston: Beacon
           Press, 1951.

Excerpts from BW, FF, IPI, MAO, P, PC, PFM, PI, PTB, RTF,
   and "Why I Am Not a Christian" (from DMMM) by permission
   of Routledge.
CBC from a talk given by Bertrand Russell on "Closeup," a 1959 TV
   program of the Canadian Broadcasting Corporation. Reproduced
   with permission.
DMMM: "Citizenship in a Great State." By permission of *Fortune*
   magazine.
RSN7 copyright © 1970, *Los Angeles Times.* Reprinted by permission.
RSN12 from a commencement address given at Colorado College, May
   30, 1966, reprinted in *The American Scholar,* vol. 36, no. 1, p. 40,
   Winter 1966–67. Used by permission of William Jovanovich.
RSN27 reprinted from the Library of Living Philosophers, vol. XV,
   The Philosophy of Brand Blanshard, edited by Arthur Schilpp, by
   permission of the publisher (La Salle, Ill.: Open Court Publishing
   Company, 1980), p. 88.
RSN52 reproduced by the kind permission of the Australian Broad-
   casting Corporation.
WIB: from *What I Believe* by Bertrand Russell. Copyright © 1925 by
   E. P. Dutton. Renewed 1953 by Bertrand Russell. Used by permission
   of the publisher, Dutton, and imprint of New American Library,
   a division of Penguin Books, USA, Inc.
Excerpts from *The Listener,* May 29, 1947, and RSN34 by permission
   of the British Broadcasting Corporation.
AI, A1, A2, AP, FVO, HSEP, HWP, NHCW, SE, SHM, SO, SPBR,
   and UE by permission of the Bertrand Russell Peace Foundation,
   Ltd.